LOVE IN SANSKRIT AND TAMIL LITERATURE

LOVE IN SANSKRIT AND TAMIL LITERATURE

A Study of Characters and Nature (200 B.C.-A.D. 500)

DEVAPOOPATHY NADARAJAH

MOTILAL BANARSIDASS PUBLISHERS
PRIVATE LIMITED • DELHI

First Edition: Delhi, 1994

ISBN: 81-208-1215-2

Also available at:

MOTILAL BANARSIDASS

41 U.A. Bungalow Road, Jawahar Nagar, Delhi 110 007
120 Royapettah High Road, Mylapore, Madras 600 004
16 St. Mark's Road, Bangalore 560 001
Ashok Rajpath, Patna 800 004
Chowk, Varanasi 221 001

Published with financial assistance from All Malaya Nattakkottai Chettiars' Endowment Fund, University of Malaya.

PRINTED IN INDIA

BY JAINENDRA PRAKASH JAIN AT SHRI JAINENDRA PRESS,
A-45 NARAINA, PHASE I, NEW DELHI 110028
AND PUBLISHED BY NARENDRA PRAKASH JAIN FOR
MOTILAL BANARSIDASS PUBLISHERS PVT. LTD.,
BUNGALOW ROAD, DELHI 110007

To

the memory of the late
Reverend Dr. Xavier S. Thaninayagam,
the first Professor of Indian Studies,
University of Malaya

Contents

Acknowledgements

I wish to express my gratitude to all those who made it possible to prepare the present work.

I am most grateful to Dr. D.H. Killingley, presently of the University of Newcastle-upon-Tyne, United Kingdom, who introduced me to Sanskrit Language and Literature while he was with the University of Malaya.

To my supervisor, Dr. R. Dhandayudham, I am thankful for the keen interest he took and the ready assistance provided throughout. I am also thankful to Associate Professor Dr. P. Arunachalam who supervised my thesis prior to his retirement. I am also appreciative of the valuable guidance of Dr. G. Sundaramoorthy of Madurai Kamaraj University, during his term in the University of Malaya and of the criticism provided by Professor C. S. Venkateswaran, former Professor and Head of the Department of Sanskrit, Annamalai University, Tamil Nadu.

My thanks are also due to Professor S. N. R. Kazmi for his valuable suggestions, to my colleagues in the Department, to Miss Viola D'Cruz who read through the thesis before and after it was typed, to Mrs. Gelda Adrian who typed this thesis and to the staff of the University of Malaya Library in helping me on many occasions to obtain the necessary books

D. NADARAJAH

Preface

The present work comprises eleven chapters. The first two discuss the various texts that have been useful to the study. The next six deal with the various characters used by the poets and dramatists in the treatment of love. While both Sanskrit and Tamil literature accept the hero and the heroine as the main characters in the drama of love, others like the harlots who contribute to the 'love-triangle', the friends of the hero and the heroine as well as their relatives, dependants and a number of other people have their own role. They provide the cultural and social restrictions or encouragement that develops the emotion fully. The last three chapters deal with nature. The division of land in Tamil Caṅkam poetry and the association of these divisions with aspects of love, the seasons in Tamil and Sanskrit literature and their influence on lovers and the use of imagery in both literatures to convey emotion in a manner culturally acceptable are considered in these chapters. The chapter on the personification of natural objects and imagery also deals with literary 'ornaments' (*alaṃkāras*) like *iṟaicci* and *dhvani* and with the genre introduced by Kālidāsa, the *dūtavākyam*. All chapters compare and contrast the use of the characters and nature in Sanskrit and Tamil literature.

All translations for Tamil texts are mine. For Sanskrit texts I have generally used the translations in the particular edition that has been used for reference. Except for the *Pratijñāyaugandharāyaṇam* the *Pratimānāṭakam* and the *Madhyamavyāyogam*, I have checked the translations against the text and made revisions where necessary.

Kata Pengantar

Tesis ini dikemukakan dalam sepuluh bab. Bab pertama dan kedua membincangkan teks-teks yang digunakan dalam kajian ini. Dari bab ketiga hingga bab kelapan ialah berkenaan dengan beberapa watak yang digunakan oleh para penyaer dan dramatis dalam perlakuan cinta. Sesungguhnya kesusasteraan Sansekerta dan Tamil menerima hero dan heroine sebagai watak-watak utama dalam drama cinta dan watak-watak lain pula, seperti penggoda yang menimbulkan 'cinta tiga segi', kawan-kawan hero dan heroine, saudara-mara mereka dan anak-anak buah mereka dan beberapa orang lagi memainkan peranan mereka yang tersendiri. Mereka mendukung kegiatan sosial dan budaya yang memantapkan perkembangan emosi. Tiga bab yang akhir ialah tentang alam semulajadi. Bahagian tanah dalam puisi Caṅkam Tamil dan perkaitan bahagian-bahagian itu dengan aspek cinta, pembahagian masa dalam kesusasteraan Tamil dan Sansekerta dan pengaruhnya terhadap kecintaan dalam kedua-dua kesusasteraan dibincangkan dalam bab yang kelapan dan yang kesembilan. Bab yang akhir tentang personifikasi benda-benda alam semulajadi dan imageri juga membincangkan 'keindaan' kesusasteraan *(alaṃkāra)* seperti *iṟaicci* dan *dhvani* dan satu genre kesusasteraan yang telah diperkenalkan oleh *Kālidāsa,* iaitu *dūtavākyam.*

Semua bab itu membandingkan penggunaan watak-watak dan alam semulajadi dalam kesusasteraan Sansekerta dan Tamil.

Note on Transliteration

SANSKRIT

Transcriptions of Sanskrit names and terms through English transliteration follow the transliteration system used in *A Sanskrit Grammar for Students* by Arthur A. Macdonell. The following is a key to the transliteration of Sanskrit letters.

Vowels

a	अ	ṛ	ऋ
ā	आ	ṛ	ॠ
i	इ	ḷ	ऌ
ī	ई	e	ए
u	उ	ai	ऐ
ū	ऊ	o	ओ
		au	औ

Consonants

k	क	ṭh	ठ
kh	ख	ḍ	ड
g	ग	ḍh	ढ
gh	घ	n	ण
ṅ	ङ	t	त
c	च	th	थ
ch	छ	d	द
j	ज	dh	ध
jh	झ	n	न
ñ	ञ	p	प
ṭ	ट	ph	फ

b	ब	ṣ	ष
bh	भ	s	स
m	म	h	ह
y	य	ḥ (visarga)	
r	र	ṃ (anusvāra)	
l	ल		
v	व		
ś	श		

TAMIL

Transcriptions of Tamil names and terms through English transliteration follow the transliteration system used in the *Dravidian Etymological Dictionary* by T. Burrow and M.B. Emeneau with the exception of ழ் = ḻ. The following is a key to the transliteration of Tamil letters.

Vowels

a	அ	e	எ
ā	ஆ	ē	ஏ
i	இ	ai	ஐ
ī	ஈ	o	ஒ
u	உ	ō	ஓ
ū	ஊ	au	ஔ

Consonants

k	க்	m	ம்
ṅ	ங்	y	ய்
c	ச்	r	ர்
ñ	ஞ்	l	ல்
ṭ	ட்	v	வ்
ṇ	ண்	ḻ	ழ்
t	த்	ḷ	ள்
n	ந்	ṟ	ற்
p	ப்	ṉ	ன்

However, for some terms which are in common use, their popular spelling is used, example, *Chera, Chola*.

List of Abbreviations

SANSKRIT

Abhi	*Abhijñānaśākuntalam*
Avim	*Avimārakam*
Budd	*Buddhacaritam*
Caru	*Cārudattam*
Kama	*Kāmasūtram*
Kuma	*Kumārasaṃbhavam*
Mady	*Madhyamavyāyogam*
Mala	*Mālavikāgnimitram*
Megh	*Meghadūtam (P. Pūrva; U. Uttara)*
Naty	*Nāṭyaśāstram*
Prat	*Pratijñāyaugandharāyaṇam*
Pratim	*Pratimānāṭakam*
Ragh	*Raghuvaṃśam*
Rtu	*Ṛtusaṃhāram*
Saun	*Saundaranandam*
Svap	*Svapnavāsavadattam*
TTP	*Thirteen Trivandrum Plays*
Vikr	*Vikramorvaśīyam*

TAMIL

Aink	*Aiṅkuṟunūṟu*
Akam	*Akanāṉūṟu*
Cilap	*Cilappatikāram*
Ciru	*Ciṟupāṇāṟṟuppaṭai*
Kali	*Kalittokai*
Kural	*Tirukkuṟaḷ*
Kurinji	*Kuṟiñcippāṭṭu*
Kurun	*Kuṟuntokai*
Malai	*Malaipaṭukaṭām*
Mani	*Maṇimēkalai*

Maturai	*Maturaikkāñci*
Mullaip	*Mullaippāṭṭu*
Nar	*Naṟṟiṇai*
Netu	*Neṭunalvāṭai*
Pari	*Paripāṭal*
Pat	*Paṭṭiṉapālai*
Patir	*Patiṟṟuppattu*
Perum	*Perumpāṇāṟṟuppaṭai*
Porun	*Porunarāṟṟuppaṭai*
Puram	*Puṟanāṉūṟu*
Tirum	*Tirumurukāṟṟuppaṭai*
Tol Porul	*Tolkāppiyam: Poruḷatikāram*

PART ONE

THE CHARACTERS

Chapter 1

Introduction

A GENERAL SURVEY

The history of Indian literature begins with the Vedic hymns, the content of which is religious. Since Vedic times Indian literature has been dealing with the teaching of norms and philosophy. The *Mahābhārata* and the *Rāmāyaṇa*, continued this tradition, though they made use of a story to do so. In the fourth century B.C. Pāṇini is believed to have written the *Pātālavijaya* and the *Jāmbavatī-Vijaya* which are not available. Patañjali is said to have composed some secular lyrics in the second century B.C. Between the second century B.C. and the second century A.D. which was also the time when the Tamil poets had been composing their anthologies, Prākṛt was cultivated and the *Sattasaī* of Hāla and the *Bṛhatkathā* of *Guṇādhya* (not the original version) are the fruits of the cultivation.[1]

Aśvaghoṣa

In the same period, (200 B.C.—A.D. 200) Aśvaghoṣa wrote numerous dramas, *kāvyas* and other works to propagate the Buddhist faith. His works were translated into Chinese between A.D. 414 and 421. This sets the lowest limit to his date.[2] He is also believed to be a contemporary of Kaniska of about A.D. 100.[3] Of his dramas, only fragments of *Śāriputraprakaraṇa* and two others are found.[4] Only one lyric of his is known because of a Chinese translation,[5] besides which Avadānas and Āryasūtra are attributed to him.[6] Only his two *kāvyas, Buddhacaritam* and *Saundaranandam* are available for detailed study. Both deal with Buddha and teach Buddhist *dharma*, though the latter is the story of his cousin who was forced to give up his love for his wife Sundarī to become a *bhikṣu*. To achieve his aim of propagating the Buddhist faith, Aśvaghoṣa uses the various *rasas* especially *śṛṅgāra* in his *kāvyas*.

Bhāsa

Bhāsa, the dramatist, is believed to have written after Aśvaghoṣa[7] but before Kālidāsa because he is mentioned in the play *Mālavikāgnimitram*. Winternitz is of the opinion that his plays originated in the fourth century A.D. and that the period from Pāṇini (fourth century B.C.) to that of Bhāsa (fourth century A.D.) may be called 'the classical or early classical period of Indian ornate poetry',[8] though by 'Indian' he seems to refer to Sanskrit poetry and drama. Thirteen plays are ascribed to him but some scholars are of the opinion that all of them are not his creations. However, Keith and many others hold the opinion that all of them are the works of Bhāsa.[9] These plays are: (1) *Pratijñāyaugandharāyaṇam*, (2) *Svapnavāsavadattam*, (3) *Avimārakam*, (4) *Cārudattam*, (5) *Pratimānāṭakam*, (6) *Abhiṣekam*, (7) *Bālacaritam*, (8) *Dūtavākyam*, (9) *Karṇabhāram*, (10) *Dūtaghaṭotkacam*, (11) *Ūru-bhaṅgam*, (12) *Madhyamavyāyogam* and (13) *Pañcarātram*.

Of these only the first four deal with love before marriage while the fifth, *Pratimānāṭakam*, deals with the love of Rāma and Sītā after their marriage. The *Madhyamavyāyogam* depicts to a certain extent the love and loyalty Hiḍimbī had towards Bhīma. All other plays deal with wars or messages regarding war, certainly not love. Only the plays that are relevant (i.e. *Pratijñāyaugandharāyaṇam, Svapnavāsavadattam, Avimārakam, Cārudattam, Pratimānāṭakam* and *Madhyamavyāyogam*) have been used for this study.

Kālidāsa

Though Saumilla and Kaviputra have been mentioned in Kālidāsa's *Mālavikāgnimitram* as famous dramatists, no works by these authors have come down to us. Kālidāsa, who is placed in the first century B.C. by writers like M.R. Kale and G.C. Jhala,[10] is generally accepted by others as having been a poet and dramatist of the Gupta age, perhaps during the reign of Kumāragupta (A.D. 413-455) and even Skandagupta (A.D. 455-480). This places him in the fifth century A.D.[11] Many works have been ascribed to Kālidāsa but those generally accepted are: (1) *Kumārasaṃbhavam*, Cantos 1-8., (2) *Raghuvaṃśam*, (3) *Ṛtusaṃhāram*, (4) *Meghadūtam*, (5) *Mālavikāgnimitram*, (6) *Vikramorvaśīyam* and (7) *Abhijñānaśākuntalam*.

Besides these, the *Nāṭyaśāstra* of Bharata and the *Kāmasūtra* have been used, especially in Chapter 1. The *Nāṭyaśāstra* is essentially a treatise on the various aspects of the Sanskrit drama and it is placed earlier than Bhāsa and Kālidāsa.[12] Its development of the doctrine of *rasa*, especially the *śṛṅgāra rasa* is useful for this study. The *Kāmasūtra* does not deal with literary situations but with 'all that is meant by love'. It treats the subject on the principle that 'all is fair in love and war'.[13] The Classical Sanskrit works seem to have known some version or other of the *Kāmasūtra*, for, in the *Buddhacaritam* some women are said to have been instructed in the art of love. Kālidāsa's description of the love-sports of Śiva and Pārvatī in the eighth canto of the *Kumārasaṃbhavam* and of the love-life of Agnivarṇa in the last canto of the *Raghuvaṃśam* show a detailed knowledge of such a treatise. While scholars like A.B. Keith argue that the modelling of the *Kāmasūtra* on the *Arthaśāstra* suggests that A.D. 500 is a reasonable date, many are of the opinion that it belongs to the fourth century A.D.[14] All of the texts deal, to some extent or other, with love and so have been used for this study.

Caṅkam Literature

Tamil literature dates back to the later centuries before Christ. The *Tolkāppiyam* is believed to be the earliest extant text in Tamil and the date has been moved up and down the centuries. It is usually accepted as a pre-Caṅkam work and is placed approximately at 300 B.C.,[15] though some modern scholars are of the opinion that it belongs to the fifth century A.D.[16] The Caṅkam works themselves, usually referred to as *Eṭṭuttokai* (The Eight Anthologies) and *Pattuppāṭṭu* (The Ten Idylls) have been composed by about 552 poets.[17] At an age when the world's population was still sparse and wars took their toll of human lives, the number of poets in each generation must have been very small, even during periods when many were educated and talented enough to understand and appreciate poetry. Hence these poets must have been spread over a number of generations, so that the Caṅkam period stretched over four or five centuries. The poems of this period do not deal with the city of Kāñci as they deal with the cities and ports like Pukār, Muciṟi, Toṇṭi, Maturai and Vañci, and this shows that they were written prior to the establishment of Pallava rule at Kāñci in A.D. 250. The detailed description of foreign trade, especially with Rome, found in these poems as well as the accounts and observations of Greek and Roman writers like the author of the *Periplus* (A.D. 70), *Pliny* (A.D. 77 or 78) and *Ptolemy* (A.D.140)[18] place these two collections in the period between second century B.C. and second century A.D. The *Eṭṭuttokai* consists of: (1) *Akanāṉūṟu,* (2) *Aiṅkuṟunūṟu,* (3) *Kuṟuntokai,* (4) *Naṟṟiṇai,* (5) *Kalittokai,* (6) *Paripāṭal,* (7) *Patiṟṟuppattu,* and (8) *Puṟanāṉūṟu,* of which the last two have been used only for cross-reference for they are not collections that deal with the theme of love.

In the *Pattuppāṭṭu*, which consists of: (1) *Tirumurukāṟṟuppaṭai*, (2) *Porunarāṟṟuppaṭai*, (3) *Ciṟupāṇāṟṟuppaṭai*, (4) *Perumpāṇāṟṟuppaṭai*, (5) *Mullaippāṭṭu*, (6) *Maturaikkāñci*, (7) *Neṭunalvāṭai*. (8) *Kuṟiñcippāṭṭu*, (9) *Paṭṭiṉappālai*, and (10) *Malaipaṭukaṭām*, the *Mullaippāṭṭu*, *Neṭunalvāṭai*, *Kuṟiñcippāṭṭu* and *Paṭṭiṉappālai* each deals with a different aspect of love. But the other poems too have been referred to whenever relevant themes or passages are found.

Tamil Epics

The *Cilappatikāram* and the *Maṇimēkalai* have been generally accepted as epics composed in the post-Caṅkam period. M. Varadarajan fixes this as the period A.D. 100-500,[19] T. P. Meenakshisundaram as fifth century A.D.,[20] Somasundaram Pillai calls it the 'age of Buddhism and Jainism' and places it between A.D. 250 and A.D. 600[21] and M. Rajamanikkam places both these epics in the second century A.D.[22] Whatever the actual year of composition may be, the *Maṇimēkalai*, on internal evidence, has been accepted as having been written at a later date than the *Cilappatikāram*[23] and both these works are usually placed prior to the fifth century A.D. Thus it is generally accepted that these works under study fall within the years 200 B.C. to A.D. 500.

CONVENTIONS REGARDING LOVE IN SANSKRIT AND TAMIL LITERATURE

Love

Indian love literature, unlike ancient Greek literature,[24] deals exclusively with the love or attraction between a man and a woman. Both Sanskrit and Tamil literatures use various words to denote this feeling. In the Sanskrit texts used for this study, terms like *anurāga*,[25] *sneha*,[26] *rasa*,[27] *kāma*,[28] *madana*,[29] and *abhilāṣā*[30] are used to denote love. But the chief concern of the *kāvya* or drama is to stimulate the sentiment of love or *śṛṅgāra* which is regarded as a means to pleasure (*kāma*).[31] Love is broadly divided into two aspects, *saṃbhoga* or union and *vipralambha* or separation. In Tamil literature we find the term *kāmam*[32] used very commonly though others like *kēṇmai*,[33] *toṭarpu*,[34] and *naṭpu*,[35] are also found in many poems. Usually the joy of union (*puṇartal*) is depicted in terms like *nakutal*[36] (laughter), while separation (*pirivu*) is referred to as causing disease or illness (*kāmanōy*).[37] The word *kātal*, though not very common, is not entirely missing.[38]

The *Nāṭyaśāstra*, however, describes it as *kāma*, the union of a man and a woman, which may end in joy or sorrow for all people but is mostly observed as leading to happiness even in unhappy situations. Though this is said to be love or passion which has an erotic element,[39] it has a psychological aspect which provides a sense of unity even in separation, so that, even the sorrow is beautiful and comforting in the knowledge of their love. *Śṛṅgāra,* on the other hand, has sexuality as its basis and brings joy only to the man and woman involved.[40] The *Tolkāppiyam* in Tamil deals chiefly with love that is mutual and based on the union of hearts. This has love or affection as an important element and is differentiated with the phrase *aṉpoṭu puṇarnta aintiṇai* and it excludes unrequitted love (*kaikkiḷai*) and excessive or lustful love (*peruntiṇai*).[41] Perhaps this is better expressed in the *Paripāṭal* by the phrase *kātaṟ kāmam*[42] meaning love that is not based on physical needs or attraction alone but has a romantic or psychological aspect as well. The *Kāmasūtra* emphasises the physical aspect of love. This basic difference in the attitude to love in these two literatures may be traced to their social needs and traditions. The Indo-Āryans had always stressed on the need for a son, not merely as a legal heir to the father's property but more as someone who would offer oblations to the dead forefathers. This need had to be fulfilled even if the son-less widow had to be united with her dead husband's brother or other relatives on her husband's side, as enjoined in the practice of *niyoga* which is also approved by the *Dharmaśāstras.*[43] The Tamils gave more importance to the family, especially the purity and good name of the family as guarded by the chaste and loyal wife, though a son or child is said to complete the family circle. The son in ancient Tamil society was important as a useful citizen and not as an offerer of oblations.

Conventions Regarding Nature

Ancient Tamil poetic convention divides the subject matter of poetry (*poruḷ*) into two broad divisions—*akam* or interior, dealing with love and aspects of family life and *puṟam* or exterior, dealing with all aspects of social life not included in *akam.* In *akam* poetry, love is treated as an emotion or *uripporuḷ* and it is the very basis of poetry. *Uripporuḷ* is the emotion, chiefly of the hero or heroine who fall in love, though other characters, like their friends, her mother, or foster mother also have a part to play. This emotion of love experienced by the hero and the heroine are again connected to external nature. External nature is divided into the *mutal poruḷ* consisting of space and time, though literally it is meant to be land (*nilam*) and time (*polutu*). These are further divided so that land consists of five geographical divisions—*kuriñci* or the montane region, *mullai* or the pastoral region, *marutam* or the riverine, agricultural districts, *neytal* or the maritime belt and *pālai* or the arid tracts. Though the Tamil country does not actually consist of arid tracts, certain parts of the mountain and pastoral districts are said to become dry and lose their vegetation in summer for want of rain.[44] Each of the five divisions, being a separate geographical unit is endowed with a specific environment, each with its own people, occupation and way of life, fauna and flora and is considered most suitable to depict a particular facet of love during a particular season and time of day. Thus the *kuriñci* region in the rainy season (*kūtir*) and at midnight (*yāmam*) is considered best to portray the clandestine love of young people (*puṇartal*). The pastoral region during July-August (the *kār* season) and evening (*mālai*) is most appropriate to depict the feelings of the heroine waiting for the return of her husband after completing his mission or of the returning hero (*iruttal*). The agricultural tracts (*marutam*) with its abundance and city life is the background for the infidelity of the husband and the sulkiness of the wife (*ūṭal*). Though there is no special season set apart for this aspect, dawn or early morning (*vaikarai, viṭiyal*) when the husband returns is considered the time of day most suited for it. The maritime region (*neytal*) with the melancholy lashing of waves, at sunset (*erpāṭu*) when the whole beach is quiet, provides the background for the *iraṅkal* or pining of the lady for her lord who is away. The desert tracts (*pālai*) in the heat of summer (*vēnil*) and midday sun (*naṇpakal*) is considered best to portray the heat of separation and anxiety experienced by both the lovers.[45] These divisions on the basis of land and nature are called *tiṇai* and the mention of the names *kuriñci, mullai, marutam, neytal* and *pālai* respectively is enough to give an experienced reader the whole background needed to understand a poem, however short it may be.

Though Sanskrit poetry has no such detailed conventions regarding the treatment of nature and love in literature, the *Nāṭyaśāstra* provides certain guidelines. Even in this treatise, the soul of poetry or *kāvya* has been *rasa* meaning sentiments or emotion and *śṛṅgāra*, variously translated as love, the erotic sentiment, etc., has been the queen of the *rasas*. The durable psychological state (*sthāyībhāva*) for this *rasa* is love[46] and it is stimulated in the hearts of the readers or audience by a mixture of various components like *vibhāva, anubhāva, vyabhicāribhāva* etc. Of these, *vibhāva* is considered the most basic component which consists of the cause or determinants of the emotion or *rasa*. *Vibhāva* consists of characters, especially the hero and the heroine, their good looks, the ornaments they wear to enhance their pleasant appearance etc. as well as the breeze, the moon, sea etc. In other words, this *vibhāva* means the determinants necessary to depict this emotion and external nature which acts as a stimulator of passion. This emotion of love is believed to owe its origin to men and women in their youth. It is dealt with in two different aspects—union (*saṃbhoga*) and separation (*vipralambha*). Determinants like the pleasures of the season, the enjoyment of garlands, unguents, ornaments, the company of beloved persons, objects that please the senses, splendid mansions, going to the gardens or parks and enjoying oneself there etc. are said to enhance the feeling of love.[47] Even the *Kāmasūtra* presupposes a life of leisure with garden, bower and flowers around the house for the enjoyment of love.[48] Since the *Nāṭyaśāstra* is a treatise on the rules and conventions of the Sanskrit drama, it does not deal with the use of nature in the composition of the drama. However, nature is accepted as influencing the feelings of the characters and it lays down rules as to how an aspect or object of nature is to be indicated to the audience. The six seasons of spring (*vasanta*), summer (*grīṣma*), rain (*prāvṛṣ*), autumn (*śarat*), early winter (*hemanta*) and winter (*śiśira*) are mentioned and so are the ways in which this environment is to be conveyed to the audience by means of representations on the stage.[49] For example, spring is to be indicated by the representation of acts of rejoicing, enjoyments, festivities and a display of various colours.[50]

Conventions—Characters

Convention in both literatures prefer the main characters, i.e. hero and heroine to be of a good social or family background. In Tamil literature they are to be equals and of families with a good standing for he is referred to as *kiḻavaṉ*[51] meaning a chiftain or a person with certain rights; the feminine term is *kiḻatti*. They are not to be referred to by individual names but names pertaining to the geographical division or *tiṇai* only.[52] In Sanskrit literature the hero or *nāyaka* is classified into *uttama* (superior), *madhyama* (moderate or middle) and *adhama* (inferior) and they are divided further[53] based on their characteristics which correspond to gods, kings, brahmins and merchants.[54] These four groups fall into the *uttama* or *madhyama* class. Similarly the *nāyikā* or heroine is a goddess, queen, woman of high family or a courtesan (*gaṇikā*). Though the *Nāṭyaśāstra* divides women into not less than 23 types depending on their physical and psychological attributes[55] and names them using various mythological beings (e.g. *yakṣa, ghandharva* etc.) and animals (e.g. tigers, elephants etc.), also divides them broadly into three classes based on their respectability. They are 'homely' (lit. inside, *ābhyantara*), 'public' (lit. outside, *bāhya*) and 'mixed' (lit. outside and inside, *bāhyābhyantara*). These denote a woman of respectable family, a courtesan and a woman of good family but who has not lived up to the respectability of her home, respectively.[56] The *Kāmasūtra*, however, divides the *nāyikās* in a more practical manner as a maiden (*kanyā*) a woman who is widowed or separated (*punarbhū*) and a courtesan (*veśyā* or *gaṇikā*).[57] But being a treatise dealing mainly with sexual enjoyment it also adds the wife of another and gives various reasons which a man may have for having relations with another's wife. In Tamil convention, the *gaṇikā* is not treated as an important character though the 'other woman', who may be a mistress, concubine or a harlot, is used as the cause for the sulkiness of the wife. There are also poems which are supposed to be what the harlot or concubine had said in a particular situation.[58] As in Tamil literary convention, the *adhama* or inferior class of men are not favoured for treatment as heroes in dramas or other generes of literature but are accepted.[59] The *Tolkāppiyam* also refers to conventions regarding other characters like the friends of the hero and heroine, the mother and foster-mother of the heroine, the dependants of the hero like the charioteer and the musician and others like wayfarers and monks.[60] The *Nāṭyaśāstra* too mentions in chapter 34 a number of other people besides the hero and heroine but their role in their love story is not spelt out though their role in the successful staging of the play is.

There is one group of characters in both Tamil and Sanskrit literature, who serve as messengers between the lovers. They are called *dūta* (male) and *dūtī* (female) in Sanskrit. In Tamil though the words *tūtu* and *tūtuvar* are used,[61] the term *tūtaṉ* or *tūti* is not used in ancient Tamil literature. There is, in the case of the married couples, a type of 'messengers' called *vāyil* mentioned by Tolkāppiyar. Though the function of these characters may be generalised as carrying messages or speaking on behalf of someone, there are some basic differences in the actual performance of their function in the two literatures.

The *Nāṭyaśāstra* treats messengers as people who carry the news of the heroine's love to the hero. If a heroine who is separated from her beloved suffered greatly from this separation, then she could send a *dūtī*, 'expert in love affairs' to speak to the man concerned, of her pitiable condition and the message 'should relate to passionate love'.[62] In the section on courtesans, the work enumerates the types of women who may be used as female messengers. They are, 'a wise woman, a female story-teller, a female ascetic, or a woman of the stage, an intelligent woman, a female neighbour, a female friend, a maid-servant, an unmarried girl, a craftswoman, a foster-mother, a nun or a female fortune-teller'.[63] While these people may be sent by the man or the woman in love, their function is to bring about a meeting between the two. The *Kāmasūtra* mentions a similar role though the lovers may not have met already and the various steps taken by the messenger to bring about this union may take a number of days. She not only talks to the reluctant lady about the man on whose behalf she is acting and the lady's good fortune that he should set his heart on winning her, but also brings her gifts and love-letters. The messenger acts as a secret go-between for the lovers. Typically the work divides the messengers into eight, based on what they do or are expected to do. Of these divisions, two need to be mentioned. They are the *svayamdūtī* (or *dūta*) and the *bhāryadūtī*. The former is a messenger who is treacherous and selfish. When a *dūtī* is sent to a man by a woman who is attracted to him or is in love with him, and the messenger, instead of speaking well of the woman who sent her, speaks ill of her, enumerating her faults, thereby hoping to win the man for herself, she is called *svayamdūtī*. A *dūta* who acts in the same manner is called a *svayamdūta*. The *bhāryadūtī* is a foolish wife, who in obedience to her husband, acts as a messenger between him and the woman he hopes to win for his extra-marital relationships.[64] The division of love-messengers in this manner, may be in keeping with the aim of the *Kāmasūtra,* which is pleasure, be it achieved within the confines of a marriage or in extra-marital relationships.

The messengers in ancient Tamil poetry do not include such unscrupulous or foolish persons. Their classification depends on the basic classification of love as *kaḷavu* i.e. love before marriage or *kaṟpu* i.e. love after marriage. In *kaḷavu* the most important person who acts as a messenger or go-between for the hero and heroine is her friend, the *tōḻi*. She speaks to both, chides them, advises them and arranges their secret meetings. The arrangement for their clandestine meetings is usually referred to as *tōḻiyiṟ kūṭṭam*. Sometimes though rarely, the hero's friend, the *pāṅkaṉ* may arrange such meetings and this is known as *pāṅkar nimittam* or *kūṭṭam*. But such meetings are so secretive that no one else besides the trusted friends of the two lovers take on the role of messengers. Sometimes the lovers arrange such meetings themselves without the third person and Tolkāppiyar thus mentions that they become their own messengers (*tūtuvar*),[65] though he uses the word *vāyil* to denote those who arrange meetings.[66] In *kaṟpu* or love after marriage, too, there are messengers but they do not have to arrange secret meetings. They are messengers in the literal sense of the term, carrying messages from the suffering wife to the husband in the war camp or vice versa.[67] There are instances of the girl who elopes with the youth of her choice sending messages to her friends and family.[68] But of more importance is the role of the messenger during their separation due to the hero's infatuation for a harlot. He is usually afraid of facing the wife's anger after his dalliances with the courtesans and in such situations he sends a messenger or *vāyil* to speak to her. Such a messenger will have to appease her anger by speaking of the good qualities of the hero as well as her own patience and the hero's love for her. The *Tolkāppiyam* mentions the people who may become such messengers. According to this text only twelve people may play the role of mediator in a marriage. They are the heroine's friend (*tōḻi*), her mother (i.e. the foster-mother, though the word *tāy* is used, for the real mother is never mentioned as having anything to do with the heroine's love-life), brahmins (*pārppār*), the hero's friend (*pāṅkaṉ*), the musician (*pāṇaṉ*), a woman from the musician class or family (*pāṭṭi*), youths in the service of the hero (*iḷaiyar*), guests (*viruntiṉar*), male and female dancers (*kūttar* and *viṟaliyar*), people with knowledge or education (*aṟivar*) and wayfarers (*kaṇṭōr*).[69] Their function is to abate the heroine's anger and persuade her to allow the hero into his marital home. They may also talk of the heroine's good qualities like her chastity, love for him, patience to carry out her domestic duties well etc. so that she relents. They may talk of these to him so that if he stays away from home too long, he would return home, feeling ashamed of his disloyalty.[70] The foster-mother normally speaks of family tradition and advises them, especially the heroine to do what is right and praiseworthy, while the *aṟivar* who may also do so, have also the right to chide them for their faults.[71] Whatever these mediators do, their main aim is the happy life of the hero and the heroine together,[72] so that the family and the social structure are saved.

Some messengers, like those mentioned in the *Kāmasūtra* are, however, found in Tamil literature; though not specifically mentioned in the *Tolkāppiyam*. But such messengers are usually associated with the harlots (*parattaiyar*). People like the *pāṇaṉ*, the *kūttaṉ* and the *viṟali*, whose livelihood depends on the promotion of the arts have a natural association with the harlots. The *pāṇaṉ* or bard, because of his talent at story-telling is persuasive in speech and therefore suitable for winning over rich men to patronise the harlots, who they claim are more beautiful, youthful and better versed in song and dance. The *viṟali* too is seen to be capable of acting as a go-between for in a *Naṟṟiṇai* poem, she is addressed as,

O woman
who has promised to win for our lord
new women for tomorrow.[73]

Even a washerwoman seems to perform this function, for a sulking wife tells her husband,

Your washerwoman,
who washes people's clothes,
does not go to the waterfront to wash.
She is busy searching (for new women)
and acting as a go-between.[74]

Thus these two women actually do what the *dūtī* described in the *Kāmasūtra* does, but because these people do not aim at uniting the hero and the heroine but attempt to unite the hero with another woman, their role as messengers is not given any prominence.

REFERENCES

1. M. Winternitz, *History of Indian Literature*, vol. 3, Delhi, 1963, p. 37. Also C. Kunhan Raja, *Survey of Sanskrit Literature*, Bombay 1962, p. 247 & others.
2. A.A. Macdonell, *A History of Sanskrit Literature*, Delhi, 1972, p. 320ff.
3. A.B. Keith, *A History of Sanskrit Literature*, London, 1966 edn., p. 56.
4. A.B. Keith, *Sanskrit Drama*, London, 1942, pp. 80-85.
5. *Ibid.*, p. 266.
6. Keith, *A History of Sanskrit Literature*, p. 56.
7. Keith, *Sanskrit Drama*, p. 201.
8. Winternitz, op. cit., vol. 3, p. 41.
9. Keith, *Sanskrit Drama*, pp. 91-92; *History of Sanskrit Literature*, pp. xii-xvi.
10. M.R. Kale, *The Meghadūta of Kālidāsa*, Delhi, 1969, p. 7; *The Kumārasaṃbhava of Kālidāsa*, Delhi, 1967, pp. xiii-xiv; G.C. Jhāla, *Kālidāsa—a Study*, Bombay, 1949. Chapter 1.
11. Keith, *A History of Sanskrit Literature*, pp. 81-82; Macdonell, *A History of Sanskrit Literature*, p. 321; Winternitz, op. cit., vol. 3, p. 44.
12. Keith, *A History of Sanskrit Literature*, p. 372.

13. *Ibid.*, p. 467.
14. *Ibid.*, p. 469; H.R. Aggarwal, *A Short History of Sanskrit Literature*, p. 59; Winternitz, *History of Indian Literature*, p. 623-24.
15. M. Rajamanikkam, *Tamil Moli-Ilakkiya Varalāru*, Madras, 1971, p. 84.
16. S. Vidyanathan, *Tamilar Cālpu*, Kandy, 1954, Chapter 2.
17. *Ibid.*, p. 309.
18. K.N. Sivaraja Pillai, *The Chronology of the Early Tamils*, Madras, 1932, pp. 162ff.
19. M. Varadarajan, *Tamil Ilakkiya Varalāru*, New Delhi, 1972, p. 24.
20. T.P. Meenakshisundaram, *A History of Tamil Literature*, Annamalainagar, 1965, p. 42.
21. J.M. Somasundaram Pillai, *A History of Tamil Literature*, Annamalainagar, 1968, p. 340.
22. Rajamanikkam, *Tamil-Moli-Ilakkiya Varalāru*, pp. 276, 297.
23. Meenakshisundaram, *A History of Tamil Literature*, p. 65.
24. C.M. Bowra, *The Greek Experience*, London, 1961, pp. 28-29.
25. M.R. Kale, *Svapnavāsavadatta*, Bombay, 1961, p. 90; *Abhi*, act 3. p. 70.
26. M.R. Kale, *Svapnavāsavadatta*, p. 102.
27. *Vikr*, act 2 vv. 3ff. l.2.
28. *Abhi*, act 3 v. 8.
29. *Ibid.*, act 3 vv. 8ff. l.14; *Rtu*, 4:6:11; *Vikr*, act 2 vv. 9ff. l.18.
30. *Abhi*, act 3 vv. 10ff. l.6; act 3 vv. 11ff. l.10.
31. Keith, *History of Sanskrit Literature*, p. 93; A.K. Warder, *Indian Kāvya Literature*, vol. 1, Delhi, 1972, p. 15.
32. *Kur*, 136, 204, 206.
33. *Ibid.*, 38, 91, 105, 244.
34. *Ibid.*, 373; *Nar*. 292:9.
35. *Kur*, 3.
36. *Ibid.*, 169, 320.
37. *Kur*, 5, 224, 400; *Kali*, 17:9, 27:22.
38. *Aink*, 400.
39. *Naty*, 24:94-95.
40. *Ibid*, 24:97.
41. *Tol. Porul*, 89.
42. *Pari*, 9:14.
43. Indra, *The Status of Women in Ancient India*, Banaras, 1955, p. 108. Also see *The Laws of Manu* Max-Müller, (Ed.) (*Sacred Books of the East*) vol. 25 IX:59.
44. *Cilap*, 11:64-66.
45. This is discussed in detail in the chapter on Landscape.
46. *Naty*, 6:17.
47. *Ibid.*, 6:44-45.
48. *Kama*, 4:15.
49. *Naty*, 26:27-36.
50. *Ibid.*, 26:32.
51. *Tol. Porul*, 90:153.
52. *Ibid.*, 57.
53. *Naty*, 34:3-9.

54. *Ibid.*, 34:19-21.
55. *Ibid.*, 24:99-143.
56. *Ibid.*, 24:151-152.
57. *Kama*, 5:4 and 5.
58. For example *Akam*, 276, 366.
59. *Tol. Porul*, 25.
60. *Ibid.*, 112, 113, 115, 147, 151, 166-68, 191.
61. *Kurun*, 106, 254; *Tol. Porul*, 117.
62. *Naty*, 24: 198, 199.
63. *Ibid.*, 25:9-10.
64. *Kama*, chapter 4, part 5.
65. *Tol. Porul*, 117.
66. *Ibid.*, 99:9.
67. *Aink*, 479; *Kur*, 106, 254; *Akam*, 333.
68. *Aink*, 489, 490.
69. *Tol. Porul*, 191.
70. *Ibid.*, 150.
71. *Ibid.*, 151, 152, 153.
72. *Ibid.*, 176.
73. *Nar*, 310:4-5.
74. *Kali*, 72:13-14.

Chapter 2

The Studies on Tamil and Sanskrit Literature of This Period: A Review

Comparative study of Sanskrit and Tamil literature is a relatively new field in Indology and certainly goes against the earlier view that everything Āryan is more cultured or everything Sanskrit is more pure and ancient than anything else in India. It is widely known and accepted that Indian literature does not mean just Sanskrit literature and other literatures of India are not necessarily imitative of or derived from Sanskrit literature. *A Dravidian Etymological Dictionary* by T. Burrow and M.B. Emeneau (1961) established and publicised the fact that Sanskrit has assimilated a number of Dravidian or indigenous words. It added greater momentum to comparative thought and works in these two great literatures of India for it stood to reason that if Sanskrit has assimilated phonetic sounds and vocabulary into its so-called 'pure' language fit for the god's *(devabhāṣā)*, then there may be the possibility of other non-Āryan features as well, in Sanskrit literature.

The late Rev. X. S. Thaninayagam, in the concluding chapter of his famous work *Nature in Ancient Tamil Poetry*, (1952), compares Tamil nature poetry to such poetry in Sanskrit, Greek and Latin and finally English. A scholar who had travelled widely and mastered a number of languages and through them had become exposed to the cultures and life of various regions and ethnic groups, he observes that a comparative study of nature poetry in any literature 'cannot but take into account as a fundamental consideration, geographical nature as obtaining in the country where the poetry originated.'[1] In the short section comparing Tamil and Sanskrit nature poetry which forms a part of his concluding chapter, he discusses chiefly, nature as treated by Kālidāsa. But his view of the relation between nature poetry in Tamil and Sanskrit is fair and his conclusion, valid.

> Certain common climatic features as well as common flora and fauna (the mango, the jasmine, the elephant, the deer) and mutual influences, originally not of great moment but gradually growing, are reasons for the resemblances which emerge between Tamil nature poetry and Sanskrit nature poetry . . . but the basic concept and interpretation of Nature in Caṅkam poetry differs considerably from nature poetry in Sanskrit.[2]

In this section, Rev. Thaninayagam does not fail to point out that Tamil nature poetry is more realistic and concrete.[3] He also points out the basic difference in both the literatures on the treatment of erotics.[4] Though his main concern is nature poetry, the idea of 'mutual influences, originally not of great moment but gradually growing', certainly brings out the relation between these two great literatures in the briefest and best possible way.

The first International Conference Seminar of Tamil Studies held in 1966, saw the presentation of some papers which are of significance to this field. P. Thirugnanasambandham in his paper, 'A Study of Rasa: Tolkāppiyar and Bharata' discusses in detail the *meyppāṭus* of the former and the *rasas* and the various *bhāvas* of the latter and among the points he makes are two that have a general bearing on the comparative study of Tamil and Sanskrit literature.

1. The contribution of Dravidians to the study of emotions in drama and poems is positive and sizeable.

2. Tolkāppiyar and Bharata have had before them a long tradition about the *meyppāṭus* or *rasas* which had several things in common like the non-inclusion of *śānta* and yet bear the stamp of individuality.[5]

He too accepts the fact that certain traditions though oral must have existed because both authors use terms like *eṉpa* (so they say) and *pūrvācāryāḥ* (former authors). V.I. Subramaniam in his paper, 'The Influence of Tamil in Mahābhārata'[6] discusses the two main recensions of the epic—the Northern and the Southern and points out that the Southern recension contains some differences which are necessitated by the culture of the people among whom it is current. He cites the legalisation of the marriage of Duṣyanta and Śakuntalā 'by introducing the royal Purohita who secretly performs the marriage'. From the Tamil point of view this is most important for an illegitimate child, unlike in the Northern recension and tradition, cannot be a hero. The marriage of Draupadī to the Pāṇḍava brothers is explained to be the result of her praying for a single husband five times. These variations in the Southern recension underline the differences in the two traditions regarding female chastity and marriage. This paper illustrates one of the many means of influence that one culture or literature may have on the other. Another, by K.K. Pillay, entitled 'Āryan Influence in Tamilaham during the Sangam Epoch',[7] discusses the migration of Āryans, though in small groups, to the south from about the fourth century B.C. for Kātyāyana 'specifies the Chola kingdom'. Their movement southwards was 'at different stages in different places'. He also mentions the use of the Āryan language in the training of elephants and that Āryans themselves were engaged in such work. The presence of Āryan dancers using bamboo as poles for rope-walking and other such evidences in Caṅkam literature is used to prove the presence of Āryans in the Tamil country of the Caṅkam period. Though these two papers discuss only one side each of the influence one culture had on the other, together they throw light on the possibility of mutual influence.

The Second Conference Seminar of Tamil Studies held at Madras in 1968 recognised this aspect of Indology or Tamil studies and there was a whole section, though relatively small, on comparative literature. In his two papers, 'The Monsoon in Ancient Tamil and Indo-Aryan Poetry' and 'Common Elements between Early Tamil and Indo-Aryan Literature',[8] George L. Hart III discusses the common conventions in both the literatures and rightfully observes that 'all conventions are far more systematised in Tamil than in Indo-Aryan'. The use of symbolism and the technique of suggestion which is more systematic and deeply entrenched in Tamil is also analysed. Both Tamil and Sanskrit literatures have so much in common especially in the 'classical literature', but the use of the monsoon season as the time of reunion, of summer as the time of travel etc. may have had the very climate and geography of the Indian subcontinent as its source. 'Tholkāppiyam and Akapporulh in Sanskrit Poetics' by N.V. Rajagopalan[9] points out the difference in the *rasas* of Bharata and the *meyppāṭu* of Tolkāppiyar. Under *meyppāṭu*, the *Tolkāppiyam* describes what are more like Bharata's *sthāyī bhāvas* and using the same term again lists thirty-two items which are very much like *vyabhichāri bhāvas* 'and many external circumstances of *akam* and *putam*'. He concludes that 'the Nāṭya Sāstra of Bharata indicates a well developed system of *rasa* which was not known to Tolkāppiyar' and that 'Tolkāppiyar was not aware of the Nāṭya Śāstra'. Further he argues that 'the *porulh* theory with its two divisions—*aham* and *putam* must be earlier than the *rasa* doctrine' and points out some of the possible areas of influence of the Tamil *poruḷ* theory on Sanskrit poetics, e.g., Bhoja calls the *śṛṅgāra rasa* by the name *Abhimāna* or *Ahaṃkāra*. He admits it is 'hazardous to come to any definite conclusions. But one cannot but conjecture. . .'

The Third Conference at Paris in 1970 also held a session (iv) entitled 'Tamil and Sanskrit', chaired by M.B. Emeneau and with papers presented by Jean Filliozat, Siegfried Lienhard and A. Muthuccumaru. Of particular importance and interest from the point of view of ancient Tamil literature is Siegfried Lienhard's paper entitled 'Akapporuḷ and Sanskrit Muktaka Poetry'. He brings out very clearly the striking similarities between the *akam* poems in Tamil and the single-stanza poems in Sanskrit. Apart from the fact that both types of poems he deals with in his paper have love as their main theme, and do not mention individual names and are characterised by brevity of form, they also share some other common traits which are more essential. All aspects of emotion or *uripporuḷ* found in the love poetry of the Caṅkam collections are found in the 'erotic *muktaka* poems in Sanskrit and Prakrit' and describe exactly the same phases of love and use the same 'time-frame' like the season and hours of day. 'The lovers unite happily in the cold winter-night; at the beginning of the monsoon the beloved longs for the return of the lover; the love-quarrel impends when the husband having spent the night in the company of public women, returns to his home by the hours of day-break; and when afflicted by the pangs of separation, the lover travels in summer across the country'.[10] Like the *akam*, the *muktaka* also reflects a situation or sentiment referring mainly to the lover or his beloved and a few other characters closely related to them. Even more interesting is the reference in *Sattasaī* to characters like the village-head, his beautiful daughter, the hunter, the hunter's wife, the peasant, the shepherdess[11] etc. which shows a background that is close to that found in the Caṅkam poems and the division of land that forms the basis of *akapporuḷ*.

Yet the authors on poetics quoted are necessarily post-Kālidāsan for we do not have earlier works other than Bharata's *Nāṭyaśāstra* and hence we have no conclusive proof that the *muktaka* poem in Sanskrit or Prākṛt is very old. Hāla's *Sattasaī* no doubt is usually ascribed to the 'early centuries of the Christian era'[12] and this is after the composition of at least some of the *akam* poems. The author himself observes that, 'it is to be noticed that the majority of Hāla's poems most probably were composed in South India, since Hāla, the compiler of the anthology belonged to the royal house of the Sātavāhanas.[13] Besides, as the paper itself points out, in the Sanskrit of Prākṛt poems the emotion or aspect of love treated, does not have a 'firm combination with a particular landscape.'[14] Nature and convention have not combined to produce the kind of symbolism that is essential to the actual understanding and appreciation of *akam* poetry in Tamil. Besides, the conventions regarding the characters, who may talk to whom, when etc. are rather fixed in *akam* poetry but are not found in Sanskrit or Prākṛt *muktaka* poetry. These show that the Sanskrit and Prākṛt *muktaka* poems have their origin, though indirectly, in a tradition that is more familiar with a geographical region which contains the various kinds of landscape like the mountains, rivers, pasture land, arable tracts etc. and the varying seasons which do not include *hemanta*; this points to South India.

In a subsequent paper entitled, 'Pālai poems in Sanskrit and Tamil,' Siegfried Lienhard discusses, what he terms, 'the field of poetic associations'. According to him it represents the sum total of all ideas and suggestions belonging to a certain type of poem, though only one or two or more of its elements will be realized in practice.[15] Choosing a few characteristic verses from Kālidāsa's *Ṛtusaṃhāram',* Hāla's *Sattasaī* and Vidyākara's *Subhāṣitaratnakośam,* he collects from them ideas and suggestions that indicate a definite field of poetic association. The desert (or the landscape parched by the heat of the sun), summer, noon-time and travellers, together with the separation of lovers, their pain of separation and the descriptions of parched districts with dry pools and whirls of dust form a definite field of poetic association between *muktaka* poetry in Sanskrit and Prākṛt and the Caṅkam *akam* stanzas. He also shows how the *mullai* type of poems correspond to those dealing with the onset of rain. But he does not fail to point out the main difference between the *muktaka* poetry in question and the

Caṅkam stanzas. The Tamil tradition treats *pālai* and *mullai* as two separate types of separation, namely *pirivu* and *iruttal* respectively, while Sanskrit and Prākṛt merely deal with both as *vipralaṃbhaśṛṅgāra*. Tamil, of course, has another kind of separation not found in the Northern tradition, that is, the *neytal* with *iraṅkal* as the aspect of love in separation. He concludes that though *muktaka* and *kāvya* poetry have had their own history and tradition in the north, the poetic practice of the *muktaka* writer sometimes most perfectly coincides with that of the *akam* poets of the Caṅkams, and therefore it is 'an incontrovertible fact, that at a certain period close relations must have been maintained between the Tamil grammar of poetry and Sanskrit poetics or between *akam* poets and the *muktaka* writers'. He also stresses that though what he has discussed are found in both great traditions—Dravidian as well as Old and Middle Indo-Āryan—they are 'less often and less consistently to be found in the latter. We have reason to assume that South Indian elements won their way into Prākṛt and Sanskrit *muktaka* writing'.[16]

The year 1975 saw the publication of two comparative works in Tamil. Both of these, *Oppilakkiya Nokkil Caṅka Kālam* by Kathir Mahadevan and *Caṅka Ilakkiya Oppīṭu* by R.M. Periyakaruppan compare Caṅkam literature with other ancient literatures like Greek, Latin and Sanskrit. Of the two the former studies Caṅkam poems from various angles. In his first chapter, Kathir Mahadevan compares nature poetry in Tamil with Greek, Latin and Sanskrit. Though this seems very much like Rev. X. S. Thaninayagam's last chapter, in his *Nature in Ancient Tamil Poetry*, he stresses one truth, that is, while the Greek, Latin and Sanskrit poems give a 'mythological colouring' to nature, Tamil poems present a more realistic treatment. He aptly concludes the chapter with a translation of a quotation from Rev. Thaninayagam's book that though there are 'common attitudes' the basic concepts and interpretation of nature in these literatures differ considerably. After a brief chapter on the need for and the benefits of comparative literature, he discusses heroic poetry in great detail, covering all aspects of *puram* poetry. He lists out the characteristic features of heroic poetry and deals with its genres in other literatures; e.g. *Iliad* and *Odessey*, Homeric hymns, oracles, lyrics odes, epitaphs and others. The fourth chapter on 'Suggestion in Poetry' is more pertinent to this study. It discusses the history of *dhvani* as an *alaṃkāra* in

Sanskrit poetry and the use of *uḷḷuṟai uvamam* and *iṟaicci* in classical Tamil poetry. He concludes the chapter with the observation that Tolkāppiyar had dealt with the technique of suggestion long before it was found in Sanskrit and that comparative studies help to establish and appreciate this fact. Then he compares the style in Sanskrit and Tamil poetry, discusses odes and lyrics, elegies and life in the *marutam* regions as found in the Tamil poems. He also has chapters on the poets and patrons, Caṅkam poetry as oral poetry and the oral compositions of the heroic age.[17] This work deals with Caṅkam poetry as a whole and treats, by choice, more of the heroic than of the erotic. Tamil literature is compared with other ancient literatures like Greek, Latin and other European literatures as well as with relevant sections of Sanskrit literature. As a pioneer work written in Tamil it is valuable and introduces the student of Tamil literature to the possibilities in more detailed comparisons.

The work of R. M. Periyakaruppan deals more with literary theories and contains four sections. Though the first is 'World Literature: An Introduction', he actually discusses Caṅkam, Sanskrit, Greek and Roman literatures in four separate chapters. In these chapters he deals with the writers of literature and literary theories as well as with the various genres of each of these literatures. The second section which deals only with Caṅkam literary theories, though not a comparative study in the strictest sense, is however a detailed discussion of the basic theories of ancient Tamil literature like *tiṇai* and serves as a good explanation of Tolkāppiyar's treatment of *muṉṉam, marapu uvamai* or *aṇi, uḷḷuṟai, iṟaicci, meyppāṭu, vaṇṇam, nōkku, vaṉappu* and *yāppu.* The third section deals in a similar manner with what he terms the general characteristics of Caṅkam literature and discusses the qualities of oral literature as found in the Caṅkam poems, their poetic forms, literary genres, psychology, imagery, symbols and myth. It is the fourth and final section that compares literary theories in Tamil and Sanskrit. In fact his chapter headings in this section show his reliance on Sanskrit literature though he actually compares the theories as put forward by Tolkāppiyar in Tamil and the various schools and theories in Sanskrit poetics. He discusses these under *alaṃkāra, rasa* which inevitably leads to a comparison of Bharata's *rasa* theory and Tolkāppiyar's *meyppāṭu, rīti* and *dhvani.*[18] In these chapters he has brought out the fact that though there seem to be so much in common in the literary theories in Tamil and Sanskrit, there are also basic differences especially in the division and classification of *alaṃkāra* or *aṇi*. Neither of the writers in Tamil have put forth any theories or views regarding the presence of such common features in Tamil and Sanskrit literature and literary theories.

The lack of any complete work that is devoted solely to a comparative study of classical literature in Tamil and Sanskrit is somewhat met with by George L. Hart's *The Poems of Ancient Tamil: Their Milieu and their Sanskrit Counterparts*, especially the second part of the book. He discusses the use of the technique of suggestion in Tamil and Indo-Āryan and is of the opinion that while in the *Mahābhārata*, the similes, metaphors and other figures are usually straightforward, they become more elaborate and 'occasionally contain more suggestion'[19] in the other epic, the *Rāmāyaṇa*. In the *Buddhacaritam*, 'the figures are even more elaborate than in the *Rāmāyaṇa* and the technique of suggestion appears occasionally', for like Vālmīki, Aśvaghoṣa too was concerned more with description rather than with 'suggestive figures'.[20] The 'suggestive technique' becomes more and more prominent in the *Sattasaī* though a large number of verses are still descriptive. He also observes, so rightly, that the poems in this anthology do not value chastity as much as the ancient Tamil poems do and therefore it shows a mixed Dravidian and Indo-Āryan origin. Kālidāsa uses this technique of suggestion more frequently and had elaborated it to reach its full development in the North. George L. Hart also offers an explanation as to why ancient Tamil poems used suggestion more than Prākṛt or Sanskrit. According to him the language of the Dravidians and their religion were responsible for their use of suggestion while the structure of Sanskrit (and Prākṛt which is quite similar to it) favour long descriptions and their highly developed mythology provided the story and need for description[21] for it often dealt with a realm that ordinary man was not familiar with. In his chapter on 'Prosody: Tamil and Indo-Āryan Parallels', he shows the similarities between the *āciriyappā* in Tamil and the *āryā* metre in Prākṛt, Pāli and Sanskrit and adds that, 'in the light of the diffusion into North Indian culture of many words from Dravidian languages, of elements concerning women and of literary conventions . . . it is not surprising that a metre closely related to Tamil metre should also appear in popular Indo-Āryan literature at this period.[22] In his chapter, 'Tamil Poetic Conventions and Indo-Āryan Parallels', he discusses both the *akam* and *puṟam* conventions in Tamil and shows how the similarities are more in love poetry than in those regarding kings or chieftains and their worthy traits or public life.

Concluding his discussion, the author puts forward the three possible explanations for such a relationship to exist between the Southern tradition (by which he must mean the tradition followed by ancient Tamil poems for there is nothing else that we have concrete proof of) and the pre-*Sattasaī* Sanskrit poetry: viz. Tamil could have borrowed these features from Sanskrit, Sanskrit could have assimilated them or they are a pan-Indian tradition that existed even before the epics. He gives excellent reasons as to why they cannot have been borrowed by Tamil from Sanskrit.[23] The frequency of their use in Tamil, the manner in which they are used and most of all their suitability to the poetry and the people, their way of life and their geographical background show that they belong to the south and not to the north. This itself makes it impossible for them to have been found in India as a whole; therefore they cannot have been pan-Indian. The only explanation possible is that they were found in the South and with more and more contact, found their way to the north and into Indo-Āryan or Sanskrit poetry.

He does, however, put forth another view that both Tamil and Indo-Āryan could have borrowed these or at least some of these from the 'Deccan culture'[24] or the 'megalithic civilisation which existed in South India primarily on the Deccan plateau in the first millennium B.C.'[25] He describes certain features and beliefs of the society which gave rise to the literature which we call Caṅkam poetry today and finds parallels in the 'Deccani civilisation'. He discusses the importance of the concept of *aṇaṅku*,[26] the places in which this power is inherent, the sacredness of this power and the need to control it so that it did not go out of control and bring destruction. He is 'virtually certain that oral bards similar to the *Pāṇaṉs* and *Kiṇaimakaṉs* existed all through the Deccani megalithic culture'. Pointing out the existence of a low caste of musicians called Panas in Orissa and the presence of low castes in South India whose functions include making music and magic, he theorizes that the poems of the Mahārāṣṭrī poets which occur in the *Sattasaī* are ultimately copies of the oral compositions of these bards who lived with them.[27]

The presence of a group in a particular place does not necessarily mean the existence of a common cultural or linguistic source for both areas. There is the possibility of migrations and any group from the non-Āryan south was bound to be relegated a low social or caste status in areas that were already influenced by the Āryan concept of caste. The use of some common themes is inevitable and a common source is possible. But the landscape described in the Tamil Caṅkam poems and the traditions followed by them and also found in the *Sattasaī* have more affinity to the Tamil landscape. Besides, though the *Sattasaī* and the Tamil anthologies are 'too close in time for the Prākṛt tradition to have borrowed from the Tamil one and then to have gradually reshaped the themes'[28] it cannot be denied that Tamil poems already had a concrete tradition. Even if we set aside the *Tolkāppiyam*, with its rules of tradition and convention, as a text of a later period, the fivefold division of love, (*akaṉaintiṇai)* and the two other aspects of love which are considered not ideal and their definite association with the fivefold division of land as well as with the division of year and day show that this tradition had been established in Tamil for a long time. For a certain idea to become a fixed convention to the extent of becoming a 'poetic language' to be understood alike by the poets or bards and their readers or audience, it takes decades if not centuries. This is just what had happened and we are not able to find poems in the *akam* section whose *tiṇai* is not identifiable. As George L. Hart himself explains, 'their conventions are quite complex. . . . By invoking any of the material associated with a *tiṇai*, the poet is able to evoke the mood and situation with which it is associated in the minds of the readers, at least in theory'.[29] The poems in *Sattasaī*, as pointed out by Siegfried Lienhard, have nearly all the elements of *poruḷ* considered essential for *akam*; possess a spirit of closeness to life and common realities; use ordinary people e.g. the village-head, his beautiful daughter, the hunter, his young wife, the peasant, shepherdess etc. 'but what is usually wanting is the firm combination with a particular landscape.'[30] He goes, even further to say that *Tolkāppiyam* may provide a new light on the study of Hāla's *Sattasaī*.[31]

The *Sattasaī* and Prākṛt, especially as spoken in districts along the borders of the Tamil country certainly have had an important function in the introduction of the Southern culture to the north and vice versa. This may not necessarily have been a conscious effort but something natural and inevitable. There are of course other factors like the coming of 'northern' religions like Jainism and Buddhism to Tamilnad and the use of Tamil by the exponents of these religions who are not native speakers of Tamil. Their use of literature, especially of the Jains, to spread their ideas must have certainly led to their trying out the existing forms of literature and introducing new ones as is clearly the case with the *Cilappatikāram* in Tamil. The presence of the long vowels *ē* and *ō* in some of the forms of Prākṛt, especially the Ardhamāgadhī, makes it easier for a speaker of that language to learn Tamil and to influence it and be influenced by its literature. Thus *Sattasaī* and Prākṛt are important in the relationship between Tamil and Sanskrit literature and the importance lies more in being the transmitter of culture and tradition than in being the common source for the northern and southern traditions.

While the texts discussed above deal with actual comparative studies of Tamil and Sanskrit and European literatures there are however, a number of other texts, especially on Tamil literature that suggest or mention in passing, such comparisons. In his work *The Treatment of Nature in Sangam Literature*, Dr. M. Varadarajan discusses in great detail the place of nature in the ancient Tamil poems, the nature poets of that period and objects of nature like the earth, the sky, and the flora and fauna as found in the Caṅkam poems. The most interesting and illuminating part of his book is the third one in which he explains the aptness of the similes used by the Caṅkam poets. In this section he not only explains the ability of the Caṅkam poets to observe keenly and express with brevity and clarity the similitudes in nature but also shows his own observation of things and ability to explain the similes so that their real aptness is understood after years of reading or listening without a proper grasp of their real meaning. According to him, in these poems 'there is a comprehensive portrayal of nature' but 'the Tamil poets do not express the loving delight or the tender awe awakened by nature in their own hearts' as the English poets like Wordsworth or Shelley.[32] On the other hand, 'like the Greeks they were in their thoughts and habits of life so much a part of nature itself'[33] so that man's moods and emotions are interpreted in relation to nature.

Prof. T.P. Meenakshisundaram too makes such comparative statements in his works. For example, in his paper entitled 'Tolkāppiyar's Literary Theory,' while discussing *meyppāṭu* he refers to them as 'poetic sentiments or *rasa*'. He mentions how Tolkāppiyar 'speaks of eight *rasas*; *nakai* or *hāsya; uvakai* or happiness which is something more extensive than *śṛṅgāra;* suffering or *śoka; vīra* or heroism; physical, moral, intellectual and spiritual; *iḷivaral* or *jugupsa* or a kind of shuddering at meanness; *krodha* or anger; *bhaya* or fear and *adbhuta* or wonder. Tolkāppiyar further elaborates the various emotions which play an important part in the various dramatic moments of *akam* poetry'.[34] Thus he compares the concept of sentiments but points out that ancient Tamil poetry had a more developed concept of the treatment of love in literature.

Another work of his, which does not deal with the texts under study but is nevertheless important and useful from the point of view of comparative studies in the treatment of love in Tamil and Sanskrit literature is *Vaḷḷuvar Kaṇṭa Nāṭum Kāmamum*. Here, while discussing the treatment of love or *kāmam* in the *Tirukkuṟaḷ*, he refutes the argument put forward by some that the *Tirukkuṟaḷ* follows the Northern tradition, especially in its treatment of love. He proves that the text follows the Tamil tradition by treating each couplet in the section *Kāmattuppāl* as a dramatic monologue as in the Caṅkam poems. It has nothing to do with Vātsyāyana's *Kāmasūtram* because the *Tirukkuṟaḷ* deals with ideal love and does not deal with heroines who are unchaste or disloyal. Though T.P. Meenakshisundaram discusses the *Tirukkuṟaḷ*, such observations throw light on the uniqueness of the treatment of love in the Tamil tradition.[35]

The *Tamil Concept of Love* by V. Sp. Manickam is a study of *akattiṇai* from various angles—research, division, source, aims, poems, poets and education. This certainly is no comparative study, but in his first chapter dealing with research, he upholds *akam* as a section of literature unique to the Tamil tradition. He explains that the colophon to the *Kuṟiñcippāṭṭu* which gives the context in which the poet composed the poem is proof of this. According to the colophon the poem was composed by Kapilar to teach Tamil to the Āryan king Pirakattaṉ (Prahasta?). Citing also from *Iṟaiyaṉār Akapporuḷ* and *Tirukkōvaiyār,* the author argues that *akam* literature was treated as being synonymous with Tamil and to do so, that literature must be the most important in that particular language than in any other, and more important than phonetics or prosody.[36] He also discusses *peruntiṇai* and *kaikkiḷai* and while doing so points out that the comparison of the seven aspects of love or *tiṇai* in Tamil and the eight forms of marriage found in the Āryan or northern tradition are not related. He admits, however, that it would be worthwhile trying to find out the similarities that exist between these two.[37] In his work it is *akam* that is studied and as such he is more concerned with the love between two 'equals' as in *akaṉaintiṇai*.

Kamil V. Zvelebil, though mainly a Tamil scholar, discusses in his works the nature of ancient or classical Tamil literature. In his earlier book, *The Smile of Murukan on Tamil Literature of South India,* he disputes the concept of a Dravidian literature but upholds the fact that Tamil literature is 'absolutely unique in the sense that, in subject-matter, thought-content, language and form it is entirely and fully indigenous, that is, Tamil'. He also observes that the obvious historical explanation for this is that 'the earliest vigorous bloom of Tamil culture', (by which he means the culture and literature of the Caṅkam classics) began before the Sanskritization of South India could have had any strong impact on Tamil society.[38] He also points out, rightly, that the literature of the Caṅkam period is 'the reflection of the life of an entire people, and not a particular class. The dramatis personae may be idealised but do not belong to a special group or groups of society as in Sanskrit literature where the Vedic literature is that of the 'Sacredotal class', the epics are the literature of the 'ruling barons' and the classical literature is the literature of the *nāgarika*. Ancient Tamil literature is truly 'literature about and of the people', but not 'popular' or 'folk' literature.[39] In chapter 1 of his later book, *Tamil Literature* which forms Vol. X, 1 of *A History of Indian Literature,* he discusses 'The Solitary Stanza' by which, of course, is meant the single stanzas of Tamil classical or Caṅkam poetry. While discussing the 'Beginning of Tamil poetry', he mentions that 'Aśoka's (272-232 B.C.) Southern Brāhmī script appears to have been adapted to the pre-literary Tamil phonological system' about 250 B.C. or later. It is also said that 'slightly earlier, a number of linguistic developments indicate that pre-Tamil evolved into Proto-Tamil and pre-literary Tamil. This stage of the language is reflected in its earliest inscriptions which show some peculiar features in phonology and morphology and a strong influence of Prākṛt on their vocabulary. In a somewhat but not much different language, and in a very different diction and style, the earliest bardic poetry transmitted orally during the pre-literary stage, now refined and transformed into a court poetry, began to crystallize around certain nuclei which became later, upon the application of lively criticism by a body of scholars, the core of the anthologies.'[40] This puts forward certain views which may need to be provided with proof or the source for reference. The influence of Prākṛt on Tamil is very possible and probable due to the nearness of the two languages. In fact, it is nearer to Tamil than Sanskrit in the geographical sense and the coming of Jains and Buddhists and their attempts to spread their faith through the vernaculars must have led to their speaking the Tamil language and naturally introducing their own vocabulary intentionally or unintentionally in their use of the local language. But unfortunately the text does not mention 'the earliest inscriptions' nor does it give any reference so that a first-hand knowledge or reference to such a vital source is not possible for the reader. Again, when calling the early Tamil poems 'Court poetry' we understand that it refers only to *puṟam* poetry that deals with a king's heroic exploits, justice and generosity and not *akam* poems which do not have anything to do with kings or their courts in particular. In the section on 'Language and Prosody' he stresses that 'the underlying principles of Tamil prosody are quite independent of Sanskrit metrics.'[41] But more relevant to this study is the observation on 'the place of nature and the conception of eros' in these poems. 'Nature has a prominent, but not a primary place in the poems. It is always an integral but subordinate component. It is never, not in a single poem, the goal of the poet's activity to praise or describe nature for its own sake'. This has also been pointed out by earlier writers like Dr. M. Varadarajan and it forms the essential difference in the treatment of nature in the Caṅkam poems of Tamil and Sanskrit literature. But there is a definite change in both the literatures especially after the composition of the epics in Tamil and the use of nature for suggestion or *dhvani* in Sanskrit.[42] The treatment of nature for suggestion is most useful in handling eros with a sense of decorum. 'As a rule, sex is handled in a delicate way, never vulgar or obscene, though the *akam* poems are sometimes very sensuous, charged with eroticism and containing sexual allusions; but always reserved and elegant'.[43]

A.K. Ramanujan too, discusses very briefly the characteristic features of Caṅkam poetry like the *akam* and *puṟam* divisions, the *Tolkāppiyam*, the role of nature in love poetry as the five landscapes, episodes, the 'two kinds of proprieties: those of the drama and those of the world'. Of more importance to students of Caṅkam literature is his section on poetic design in which he explains the use of nature as *uḷḷuṟai* or 'inscape' as he terms it. He concludes saying, 'In their antiquity and in their contemporaneity, there is not much else in any Indian literature equal to these quiet and dramatic Tamil poems.'[44]

For Sanskrit literature such comparative studies are relatively fewer and even the few authors who make an attempt at comparison seem to compare Kālidāsa to English poets like Wordsworth than to anyone nearer home. In some cases it is justifiable for they were foreigners and were therefore more familiar with their own literature than with another Indian literature. A.A. Macdonell, at the turn of the century, does not have anything to say of Aśvaghoṣa and Bhāsa, but discusses the works of Kālidāsa. Like all those who have studied Kālidāsa, he too realises that the *Meghadūtam* and the *Abhijñānaśākuntalam* are somewhat different from his other works in their treatment of man and nature. In the former are glowing descriptions of nature in which erotic scenes are interspersed and 'the poet adroitly interweaves the expression of human emotions. Perhaps no other work of Kālidāsa manifests so strikingly the poet's sympathy with nature'.[45] Macdonell is also of the opinion that 'in comparison with the Greek and the modern drama, Nature occupies a much more important place in Sanskrit plays'. No doubt, he has *Abhijñānaśākuntalam* in mind for he mentions the mango and other trees, creepers, lotuses, gazelles, flamingoes, parrots, cuckoos and others amidst which the characters of the play move and whom they address. This close proximity is close enough for nature to become 'an essential part of their lives'. Hence this influence of nature on the minds of the lovers is dwelt on in his works. Prominent everywhere in classical poetry, this element of nature luxuriates most of all in the dramas'.[46]

Kālidāsa's works elicit the same kind of appraisal from M. Winternitz. He is of the opinion that, 'Kālidāsa is always at the summit of his art in his sketches of sentiments in which descriptions of nature and human feelings are mingled inseparably together'[47] and mentions the *Meghadūtam* in connection with this statement. To him Kālidāsa is 'the unexcelled painter of nature to whom nature and man always appear as a single harmonious whole in such a way that each and every human feeling is reflected in nature. . .'[48] These two authors, though dealing respectively with Sanskrit and Indian literature as a whole, put forth in the briefest and clearest way possible, the treatment of nature in Kālidāsa's works and their significance in the portrayal of human emotions.

There are not many works dealing with the plays of Bhāsa and even these few are not usually comprehensive studies. *Bhāsa: A Study* by A. D. Pusalkar is a very important contribution to the students of Bhāsa. Pusalkar discusses each of the plays of Bhāsa and deals with the society and social conditions depicted in the plays, except in two chapters, both entitled 'Critical Study'. These contain many sections; one discusses the uniqueness of Bhāsa's characterisation. Bhāsa deals only with ordinary characters unlike Aśvaghoṣa, Kālidāsa and others and he is the only dramatist who has a play in which the hero and the heroine do not appear on the stage,[49] (*Pratijñāyaugandharāyaṇam*). Even Rāma and Sītā in the *Pratimānāṭakam* are treated as ordinary royal characters with no superhuman powers. Bhāsa's descriptions of nature are real, pure and simple with hardly any flights of imagination. 'His sense of fact is much stronger than his imagination. This peculiarity of Bhāsa will be more evident when we compare Bhāsa's descriptions with similar ones from Kālidāsa, Harṣa, etc.'[50]

Both T.G. Mainkar and S. Sabnis compare Kālidāsa to Wordsworth. The former rightly points out that neither the Yakṣa of the *Meghadūtam* nor Śakuntalā of the *Abhijñānaśākuntalam* can be separated from their background of nature and Kālidāsa's settings are rarely urban. 'Nature and human beings are so one in his poetry that the Wordsworthian ideal seems to have been accomplished here'.[51] But Sabnis seems to compare Kālidāsa to Wordsworth for the realistic details of plant life as well as for the beautiful allusions to various plants in their relation to human life and sentiments.[52]

G.C. Jhala does not have a separate chapter on the treatment of nature or characters in Kālidāsa. But while evaluating each work, he deals with this and naturally, the *Abhijñānaśākuntalam* receives the most attention from this point of view. According to him, 'Nature in the *Śakuntalā* is not mere background—it has entered into the warp and woof of the drama. Indeed no other writer, not even Kālidāsa in any of his other works, has shown or succeeded in showing that deep, intimate understanding of relation between man and nature . . . without nature *Śakuntalā* would be impossible'.[53]

While the works discussed above throw some interesting light on the study of classical literature in Tamil and Sanskrit, works like those of George L. Hart III and S. Lienhard certainly provide most useful guidelines and suggestions for such a comparative study of these literatures. In this study, however, only the characters and the use of nature in the classical literature of Sanskrit and Tamil are examined.

REFERENCES

1. X.S. Thaninayagam, *Nature Poetry in Tamil*, p. 121.
2. *Ibid.*, p. 123.
3. *Ibid.*, p. 124.
4. *Ibid.*, p. 128.
5. *Proceedings of the First International Conference Seminar of Tamil Studies*, K.L. 1969., vol. II.
6. *Ibid.*, vol. II, pp. 132-37.
7. *Ibid.*, vol. I, pp. 271-79.
8. *Proceedings of the Second International Conference Seminar of Tamil Studies*, Madras—India 1968. Published in 1971, pp. 162-70.
9. *Ibid.*, pp. 171-78.
10. *Proceedings of the Third International Conference Seminar: (Paris 1970)* Pondicherry, 1973, p. 113.
11. *Ibid.*, p. 115.
12. H.R. Aggarwal, *A Short History of Sanskrit Literature*, Delhi 1963, p. 112.
13. *Proceedings of the Third International Conference Seminar: (Paris 1970)*, p. 114.
14. *Ibid.*, p. 113.
15. *Professor Nilakanta Sastri Felicitation Volume*, Madras, 1971, p. 416.
16. *Ibid.*, p. 422.
17. K. Mahadevan, *Oppilakkiya Nōkkil Caṅka Kālam*, (T), Madurai, 1975.
18. R.M. Periyakaruppan, *Caṅka Ilakkiya Oppīṭu: Ilakkiyak Koḷkaikaḷ*, Madurai, 1975.
19. George L. Hart, *The Poems of Ancient Tamil*, Berkeley, 1975, pp. 170-71.
20. *Ibid.*, p. 172.
21. *Ibid.*, pp. 182-96.
22. i.e. 3rd or 2nd century B.C. *Ibid.*, p. 207.
23. *Ibid.*, pp. 277ff.
24. *Ibid.*, pp. 252ff.
25. George, L. Hart, *The Relation between Tamil and Classical Sanskrit Literature*, Wiesbaden, 1976, p. 320.
26. *Ibid.*, p. 321.
27. *Ibid.*, p. 327.
28. George L. Hart, *The Poems of Ancient Tamil*, p. 252.
29. George L. Hart, *Poets of the Tamil Anthologies*, Princeton, 1979, p. 5.

30. Siegfried Lienhard, *Akapporuḷ and Muktaka Poetry*, p. 113.
31. *Ibid.*, pp. 113-17.
32. M. Varadarajan, *The Treatment of Nature in Sangam Literature*, Madras, 1957, p. 400.
33. *Ibid.*, p. 405.
34. T. P. Meenakshisundaram, Tolkāppiyar's Literary Theory, *Proceedings of the First International Conference Seminar of Tamil Studies*, vol. II, Kuala Lumpur, p. 6.
35. T.P. Meenakshisundaram, *Vaḷḷuvar Kaṇṭa Nāṭum Kāmamum*, Madras, 1957, pp. 159-214.
36. V. Sp. Manickam, *Tamil Concept of Love*, Madras, 1962, pp. 2-3.
37. *Ibid.*, pp. 139ff.
38. Kamil V. Zvelebil, *The Smile of Murugan*, p. 4.
39. *Ibid.*, p. 12.
40. Kamil V. Zvelebil, *Tamil Literature*, p. 11.
41. *Ibid.*, p. 32.
42. This is discussed in detail in Chapter 11, 'Personification'.
43. Kamil V. Zvelebil, *Tamil Literature*, p. 42.
44. A.K. Ramanujan, *The Interior Landscape*, Bloomington, 1967, p. 115.
45. A.A. Macdonell, *A History of Sanskrit Literature*, Delhi, 1971, (2nd edn.), p. 284.
46. *Ibid.*, pp. 298-99.
47. M. Winternitz, *A History of Indian Literature*, vol. 3, Pt. 1, p. 133.
48. *Ibid.*, p. 278.
49. A.D. Pusalkar, *Bhāsa: A Study*, Delhi, 1940, pp. 92-94.
50. *Ibid.*, p. 99.
51. T.G. Mainkar, *Kālidāsa: His Art and Thought*, Poona, 1962, pp. 207-209.
52. S.A. Sabnis, *Kālidāsa: His Style and His Times*, Bombay, 1966, p. 339.
53. G.C. Jhala, *Kālidāsa: A Study*, Bombay, 1940, p. 170.

Chapter 3

The Hero

The study of the various characters in Tamil and Sanskrit love poetry must necessarily take into account the literary form and some conventions that govern them. The Caṅkam poems are lyrics or short literary pieces which deal with a particular aspect of love and do not give as much importance to the person as to the universality of the emotion concerned. When a Caṅkam poet sings of a youth and a maiden falling in love, he does not pay attention to their names. Only their background and qualities are considered important for they affect the nature and quality of the emotion, which though universal, is considered most personal to the two people concerned. The two Tamil epics, the *Cilappatikāram* and the *Maṇimēkalai* and the works of Aśvaghoṣa, Bhāsa and Kālidāsa, are on the other hand long narrative poems or dramas which deal with the love of particular individuals and the length as well as the conventions of these literary works require detailed accounts of their background and character as well as their names. Besides, the social stratification and divisions as seen in the Caṅkam poems are different from those found in the other Tamil or Sanskrit works under study, which deal with the divisions of society based on caste or *varṇa* while the Caṅkam poems deal with the division of society based on the geographical division of land.

Family and Social Background

The hero in classical literature, be it Tamil or Sanskrit, comes from a good, noble family with at least a reasonable amount of wealth. The Tamil poems of the Caṅkam period, with the fivefold divisions of land, speak of chieftains or sons of chieftains from the various geographical divisions. The hero of the *kuṟiñci* section of the poems is referred to as *malaikeḻunāṭaṉ,*[1] *naṉmalaināṭaṉ,*[2] *malaināṭaṉ,*[3] *kuṉṟukeḻunāṭaṉ,*[4] *kuṉṟanāṭaṉ*[5] or *varaināṭaṉ,*[6] all these names meaning that he is the chief of the hilly tracts. The slopes covered with jungle give him the name *kāṉakanāṭaṉ*[7] meaning the chieftain of the forest or jungle country. The hero from the agricultural tracts being the chief who owns such land is usually referred to as *ūraṉ*[8] or *makiḻnaṉ*.[9] The chieftain who owns the *mullai* region, the natural home of shrubs, and suitable for the cultivation of drier crops, is named the *puṟavaṇināṭaṉ*,[10] the lord of the beautiful shrubs and *vaṉpulanāṭaṉ*,[11] the lord of the drier fields. Since these fields yield in plenty he is *naṉvayalūraṉ*[12] (the lord of good fields). He is also called *potuvaṉ*[13] and *āyarmakaṉ*[14] in the *Kalittokai*. These two terms refer to his occupational community and need not necessarily refer to a high social position. But we have to bear in mind that the *Kalittokai* does not always deal with characters of the higher social order but also sings of the love affairs of the lower community like the midgets and the deformed people. The hero of the maritime tracts is the chieftain of that district and is called *cēṟppaṉ*,[15] *koṇkaṉ*[16] or *tuṟaivaṉ*.[17] There is no permanent *pālai* region in the Tamil country. During the very hot season certain mountainous and pastoral regions turn arid for lack of rain[18] and hence there is no special name given to the hero of the *pālai* poems. A poem in the *Aiṅkuṟunūṟu*, however, uses the name *mai-varaināṭaṉ*,[19] the chief of the dark hills, while in another he is addressed as *iṟu-varai-nāṭa*[20] probably referring to the mountain slopes cracking because of the scorching heat of summer. Of all these names, those with the term *kiḻavōṉ* are the names that show his social position best.

This term means that he is the owner or possessor of the type of land mentioned and therefore has all the rights and respect due to him as such. The hero of the poems of the hilly region is called *malai-kiḻavōṉ*[21] or *kāṉaṉ-kiḻavōṉ*,[22] the possessor of the hills or forest slopes; the hero of the agricultural tracts is named *ūr-kiḻavōṉ*,[23] the chief of the towns or villages; the hero of the pastoral poems is called *nāṭu-kiḻavōṉ*,[24] the chief of the rural tracts and the hero of the maritime districts is called *tuṟai-kiḻavōṉ*[25] or the chief of the ports. These names suggest that the main male characters chosen by the poets for the drama of love depict men from a higher strata of society. At the same time these names keep to the tradition of not mentioning the personal names of the heroes, for Tolkāppiyar specifies that:

In the five divisions of love of human beings, the name of a

person is not mentioned specifically.
It (the mention of names) may be found in *puram* poetry but is never found in *akam* poetry.[26]

This means that the names for the characters have to be general class, occupational or geographical names only. Since the poems are to deal with the love of human beings (*makkaḷ*), it is not surprising that divine, semi-divine or superhuman heroes are not dealt with in Tamil classical literature.

Even in the literary works that deal with specific characters mentioning their names, like in the epics *Cilappatikāram* and the *Maṇimēkalai* in Tamil and the Sanskrit *kāvyas* of Aśvaghoṣa and Kālidāsa and the dramas of Bhāsa and Kālidāsa, the heroes are always from the higher social castes, the division being based on *varṇa*. Though we have no specific mention of heroes from the Brāhmaṇa caste, we have none from the Śūdra caste either. Utayakumaraṉ from the *Maṇimēkalai* is a Chola prince[27] and therefore of the Kṣatriya caste. Sarvārthasiddha or Buddha,[28] Nanda, his half-brother,[29] Udayana,[30] Duṣyanta,[31] Purūravas[32] and all the kings and princes mentioned in the *Raghuvaṃśam* belong to the Kṣatriya caste. Agnimitra though a Brāhmaṇa by birth, is described like any other king without any indication to his caste.[33] We have only one each in the Tamil and Sanskrit works from the Vaiśya caste—Kōvalaṉ in the *Cilappatikāram* and Cārudatta from the *Cārudattam*. Kōvalaṉ is the son of the rich and generous merchant Mācāttuvaṉ[34] while Cārudatta is a rich trader who has lost his wealth.[35] Though their financial circumstances seem so diametrically opposed, the terms used to denote their fathers seem so alike. Kōvalaṉ is the son of Mācāttuvāṉ while Cārudatta is the son of a Sārthavāha and in both names *cāttu* (T) and *sārtha* (S) mean merchants.

Unlike in Tamil literature, in Sanskrit literature we also find some semi-divine and superhuman heroes. The only instance of the semi-divine hero is Viṣṇusena also known throughout the play as Avimāraka in the *Avimārakam*. He is depicted as the son of Agni, the god of Fire and Queen Sudarśanā of Benares before her marriage and adopted by her sister Sucetanā, the Queen of the Sauvīras.[36] The most prominent of the superhuman heroes is Śiva who is simply treated as God. He had not come down in human form but is the Eternal[37] and Unknowable[38] principle who is loved and revered as the Father of the Universe.[39] This may be contrasted with Kālidāsa's treatment of Rāma who is openly admitted as the Supreme Being[40] or Viṣṇu but incarnate in human form as Rāma.[41] Sarvārthasiddha too in spite of his Kṣatriya lineage, is according to Aśvaghoṣa, the 'most excellent of Bodhisattvas'.[42] Thus both Rāma and Sarvārthasiddha are superhuman though born as human beings in Kṣatriya families. Another superhuman character is the Yakṣa in the *Meghadūtam*. Here we have no name given to him and he is merely known by his class name, very much like the heroes of the Tamil *akam* poems. He is a subject of Kubera, the god of Wealth and his home is in Alakā,[43] the legendary city, but due to a curse resides in Rāmagiri.[44] The only character in Tamil who could be compared to these heroes is Cāttaṉ in the *Cilappatikāram*. He is a deity known by the same name. He comes to the rescue of Mālati whose step-son had choked on her milk while she had nursed him, and being afraid of the consequences, she begs for the child's life at Cāttaṉ's temple. He asks her to go to a particular park and pick up the child but he himself appears as the child. He grows up in the family and goes through life in the normal way till he marries Tēvanti. Later he shows her his true form and asking her to go to his temple, disappears.[45] Cāttaṉ is by no means the hero of the epic but he may be compared to the superhuman characters found in the Sanskrit works.

Age

The age of the heroes is not stated clearly except for Kōvalaṉ who is said to have been sixteen years old at the time of his marriage to Kaṇṇaki.[46] However, even in his case we do not know the age at which he falls in love with Mātavi. Most of the heroes are young or still in their youth. The term *viṭalai*[47] is used quite often in the Caṅkam poems, especially in those dealing with the elopement of the hero and the heroine. It refers to a young man between the age of eighteen and thirty.[48] There is also the term used even to this day, *kāḷai*,[49] meaning literally the bull but used to denote a strong, young man of about the same age group as *viṭalai*. A foster-mother (*cevili*) in an *Akanāṉūṟu* poem describes the man who has taken her girl along with him as follows:

The youth with
a shield embedded with gems,

a spear with a good handle,
a brave heart
and abounding strength,
For whom my excellent daughter
with great modesty
is suitable.[50]

In the *Maṇimēkalai* too, the age of Utayakumaraṉ is not mentioned but we know he is young because it is stated that he could have been mistaken for Murukaṉ, the god of Youth and Beauty, had it not been for his garland of *ātti* flowers which identified him as the Chola prince.[51] Sarvārthasiddha is clearly described as being young.[52] Viṣṇusena's modesty and lack of conceit in spite of his youth seem to be the marvel of the court of the king of Kuntibhoja.[53] Aja is depicted as having reached the proper age for marriage at the time of Indumatī's *svayamvara*.[54] Most heroes of the *Raghuvaṃśam* are young and even kings like Dilīpa, Raghu, Daśaratha, Kuśa, Atithi and Agnivarṇa are depicted as young and of a suitable age for love and marriage, though very few of these heroes are specifically mentioned as being young. Dilīpa, for instance, is depicted as one who is married and childless for a sufficient number of years to become concerned with his childless state and yet, Kālidāsa describes him as young (*navaṃ vayaḥ*).[55] Similarly, Udayana is also said to be young in both the plays even though he is already married to Vāsavadattā[56] in the second play. Though nothing specific is mentioned for Purūravas, the Yakṣa and Cārudatta except that they are already married even when introduced in the respective texts, we may assume that they are still in their youth.

The two exceptions are Duṣyanta and Agnimitra. Duṣyanta has married many times[57] perhaps in the hope of obtaining a son and heir to continue his race. From Haṃsapadikā's song at the beginning of Act V we may infer that his Chief Queen Vasumatī is too old for the pleasures of love and this certainly does not leave him young by the time he meets Śakuntalā. In the case of Agnimitra, he must already be quite old when he sees Mālavikā in a portrait for he has a son old enough to lead the band of soldiers to follow the horse prepared for the Aśvamedha sacrifice, defeat the *Yavana* cavalry that tried to take the horse and return victorious to make the horse sacrifice possible.[58]

Of all these heroes, Śiva alone stands out as the Eternal Being[59] who is beyond birth, death or the process of aging and is the Father of the Universe.[60]

Good Looks

Apart from the general stress on the youth of the heroes, there is another characteristic usually mentioned together with youth and that is the good looks of the hero. In the Caṅkam works, his ornaments and well-groomed hair are said to enhance his handsome appearance but his broad shoulders or chest (*akalam, mārpu*) are said to cause lovesickness to the heroine.[61] Since in the Caṅkam love poems the description of places and people is not made directly by the poet himself, such descriptions or references are made by the various characters to suit the context. For example, in a *Kalittokai* poem, a travelling hermit answering the foster-mother of a heroine who had eloped with the youth of her choice, says:

We did not miss them.
We saw them on the arid path.
You seem to be the mother
of the bejewelled modest maid
who chose (to traverse) the shadeless desert
with the youth
of masculine beauty and greatness.[62]

Here we find the hermit mentioning not merely his good looks but his masculinity and greatness as well, thus pointing out that the youth is worthy of the girl and her love. Even in the *Cilappatikāram*, Kōvalaṉ who is much-talked-of among the young female circles because he is young and handsome, is introduced thus:

He too was named Kōvalaṉ.
His spreading fame made the earth
too small to contain it.
Moon-faced maidens,
whose sweet words surpassed music,
revealed their love for him
while praising him fondly
in their own groups, saying,
'He is the Red God incarnate.'[63]

The fact that he is considered the 'Red God' himself shows that he is as young and handsome as Murukaṉ. Utayakumaraṉ too is not specifically described as good-looking but again the idea is implied in his being compared to Murukaṉ, who wears a garland of *kaṭampa* flowers.[64]

The Sanskrit works, however, mention this characteristic quite regularly, either explicitly or with the help of comparisons or similes. When Sarvārthasiddha wishes to go out of doors, his father orders that a pleasure-party be organised, befitting not only his own affection for his son but also the son's youth and beauty thus implying that he is very handsome.[65] When Sarvārthasiddha sets out from his palace the citizens admire their prince. Some praise his appearance while others eulogise the beauty of his face.[66] Other women who see him ride past think that he is like Puṣpaketu, the flower-arrowed god of Love.[67] His eyes and his hands resemble the lotus[68] and he is broad-chested (*viśāla-vakṣāḥ*)[69] befitting a hero of the royal line he is born into. Dilīpa is described as being invested with an indescribable beauty and therefore looking like a god or Buddha.[70] His son Raghu who was handsome in all his limbs during his childhood[71] excels even his father when he grows up, with long arms, strong shoulders, broad chest and long neck,[72] thereby fulfilling the then accepted standards of masculine beauty. Aja's youth enhances his good looks[73] and he too is faultless in all his limbs.[74] Kālidāsa does not take the trouble of mentioning that each of the princes of the line of Raghu is handsome. Apart from Raghu himself, his father Dilīpa and his son Aja, Kālidāsa describes only Kuśa's good looks[75] probably to single him out as the only prince of the line who is sought after by the Nāga king to give his sister in marriage.[76]

In the plays of Bhāsa, we find that even Śakāra, who is jealous of Vasantasenā's love for Cārudatta concedes that Cārudatta is 'merely good-looking' (*nayana-mātra-saṃsthulyam*).[77] Udayana's beauty is attested to not only by Vāsavadattā,[78] but also by the nurse and the maid who declare that Darṣaka, the king of Magadha, gives his sister to him in marriage of his own accord because of Udayana's youth and beauty besides his other qualities[79] and that he is the god of Love himself without his bow and arrows.[80] Viṣṇusena is a handsome youth with a 'divine form'[81] that Magadhikā exclaims, 'I feel he must be the god of Love himself'[82] and a Vidyādhara who sees him just when he is about to kill himself thinks that he must be another Vidyādhara who perhaps has lost his superhuman qualities; 'No one else could have such beauty'.[83] Kālidāsa has depicted all the three kings in his plays as being endowed with the dignity and good looks that befit kings. In the *Mālavikāgnimitram*, the two dance masters wonder at Agnimitra's majesty and splendour[84] while in the *Vikramorvaśīyam*, Purūravas is likened to the moon, due to his splendour[85] and Urvaśī finds him more pleasing to the sight than when she first set her eyes on him, (*prathama-darśanāt saviśeṣaṃ priyadarśano mahārājaḥ pratibhāti*).[86] Duṣyanta is described as having a dignity of mien and majesty.[87] The treatment of Śiva as the Supreme Being does not allow for much description regarding his appearance but still the marriage procession through the city of Oṣadhiprastha gives the citizens, especially the women, the opportunity of seeing Śiva dressed as a bridegroom. They are glad that he is united to Pārvatī whose beauty is equal to his. They wonder if Kāma was really burnt by the wrath of Śiva, or had Kāma given up his body out of shame, for Śiva is more handsome than the god of Love himself.[88] The *Meghadūtam* being a monologue of the Yakṣa himself, does not rightly, contain such references to his own good looks.

Dress, Ornaments and Cosmetics

In Caṅkam literature masculine beauty endowed by nature is considered further enhanced by the use of suitable dress, ornaments and cosmetics or toiletries. The Tamil poems dealing with a life very close to nature, mention fresh flowers as being used in abundance by both the sexes. Men sometimes tuck them in their hair,[89] but more often the flowers are stringed into garlands and worn either in their hair or round the necks. The garlands or chaplets worn in the hair are called *kaṇṇi*[90] and seem to have been quite popular. They are made of various flowers depending, of course, on the geographical division. A hero from the mountainous region is depicted as wearing a chaplet of *vēṅkai* flowers,[91] another as wearing one of ixora flowers[92] and yet another hero from the same region as wearing a chaplet of *kuvaḷai* blooms gathered from the mountain pool.[93] While the youths who arrive to participate in the *ēṟu-kōḷ-viḻā* wear chaplets of various flowers like the *koṉṟai, kāyā, veṭci, piṭavu, taḷavu, kullai, kuruntu, kōṭal* and *pāṅkar*, the hero wears a chaplet of *kāyā* flowers.[94] Even more popular than these chaplets are the garlands worn round the necks. The general name for these is *mālai* but the special name for those worn by men is *tār* and this term is found often in Tamil literature. The heroes in Caṅkam literature as well as Kōvalaṉ and Utayakumaraṉ are shown as wearing garlands,[95] which not only serve to reduce the feeling of heat, but also give a gay, festive look to the wearer. Besides these, ornaments of gems and pearls are also worn by the men, for the word *pūṇ* is also mentioned[96] and the terms *cuṭarp-pūṇ*[97] and *maṇi-kiḷar āram*[98] must refer to chains and necklaces with bright gems. Another important ornament worn by men during the Caṅkam period is the *kaḻal*[99] which is worn on the ankles and symbolises the heroism of the wearer. The Tamil works do not mention their heroes as wearing any garment like the modern shirt. The upper part of the body is usually uncovered and during the warm season the cool sandal paste is smeared on the body to keep it cool and fragrant. The common term for this paste is *cāntu*[100] meaning paste, but quite often the word *āram*[101] is also used. *Āram* could also mean pearls and in poems where the hero is described as wearing *cāntu* we may safely infer that the additional word *āram*[102] refers to necklaces or chains of pearls. All these garlands, pastes and ornaments make the hero look like a king or prince and according to a heroine, his humility and suppliance in love seem rather incongruous with his regal appearance.[103] A complete picture of the handsome, well groomed youth of Caṅkam standards is found in the *Kuṟiñcippāṭṭu* in which the heroine's friend relates to the foster-mother the circumstances that led to the girls meeting the hero.

A youth appeared;
His curly hair was well oiled
and smeared with the cool, scented paste
of the hard sandalwood.
He drew his fingers through his hair
to help it dry sooner.
In his hair, made fragrant
with the smoke of the black aloewood,
dark and glossy like sapphires
and attracting beautiful, striped bees,
he wore
a cool, fragrant chaplet of various hues

strung from choice blossoms
of the hill and valley, trees and tanks of the slopes
and another of the white screw pine flowers,
together with a lovely, single braid
of the green-stemmed,
pretty-petalled *pittikam*
thus making his noble head
awe-inspiring.
Behind one ear he tucked
the pretty shoots of the *acōku*
that blooms bright red like fire,
so that they rubbed against his sinewy shoulders.
On his high and broad chest
smeared with sandal paste
and where strength resides,
he wore a fragrant garland
with traditional ornaments.
In his long arms with well-built wrists
he held a painted, well-strung bow
with chosen arrows.
He wore an ornate belt
securely (round his waist).
When he moved,
his bright golden anklets,
. . .best among ornaments. . .
tinkled round his faultless legs.[104]

The Sanskrit works do not mention the dress of the hero in detail except for King Atithi in the *Raghuvaṃśam* and Śiva as a bridegroom in the *Kumārasaṃbhavam.* Atithi on the day of his consecration is bathed ceremoniously and valets help him with his dress. They dry the ends of his hair with the smoke of incense (*dhūpa*). They adorn his hair and fasten strings of pearls and rubies. Garlands too are interwoven in his hair. Cosmetics including sandal paste further perfumed with musk are applied to his body and figures of leaves are painted on his body with a yellow pigment.[105] This shows that even the heroes in the Sanskrit works do not wear a shirt, at least on ceremonious occasions. The dress of Śiva also seems to be very much like that of Atithi but Śiva does not need the aid of valets. He merely transforms his old dress to suit the new occasion. Finally he appears with white fragrant paste on his body, a bright crest jewel, white silk garment with a yellow border of the figure of swans, *tilaka* mark on his forehead and ornaments round his hair, neck and arms.[106]

As in the Tamil works here too we find the use of fragrant cosmetic pastes and ornaments, but fresh flowers and garlands do not seem to play an important part. This could be due to the environment, for the Tamil society depicted in its classical literature, especially the Caṅkam poems, is much closer to nature. Even cities like Pukār and Maturai as described in the *Cilappatikāram* have suburbs where people live a life in which nature has a great role. But in the Sanskrit dramas and *kāvyas* this closeness to nature is not felt to the same degree as in the Tamil poems and hence the abundant use of flowers is not found in them.

Heroism

The trait most admired in the heroes of both Tamil and Sanskrit works is heroism which includes courage and bravery. The Caṅkam poems bring out this quality of the classical Tamil hero with many true-to-life situations. Most of the *kuṟiñci* poems depict him as a fearless hunter looking for animals or tracking them down on the mountain slopes.[107] Quite often he is accompanied by dogs which aid in the hunting.[108] He carries his bows and arrows[109] or his spear in readiness to brave the foes or fierce animals and hence he is pictured as carrying the spear that is bright and sharpened, ready for use whenever necessary.[110] This heroism is found both in relation to his love when he braves dangerous mountain paths to meet his lady-love,[111] and to his duty, when he sets out for distant lands across the arid tracts infested with highway robbers.[112] In either case it is the determination in his mind that adds to his courage.

Mountain chief!
Are there others besides us
who are anxious for you?
You traverse the narrow, rocky path,
unmindful of the dense darkness of midnight,
when roaring thunder strikes,
severing the striped, hooded heads
of snakes.

> You have only your unobstructible heart
> and the spear for company,[113]

says a maid, thereby bringing out the dangers of the hero's nightly journey for the sake of love and at the same time letting him know of his beloved's anxiety for his safety.

> To acquire the fruit of his effort,
> with an indomitable heart
> and his spear for company
> . . . . . .he has traversed
> the hot, waterless, arid tracts,[114]

complains a heroine, whose lord has gone in search of wealth in faraway lands. Thus in separation as well as in union, the heroic traits of the hero are mentioned as something that is natural to him. In the *Cilappatikāram* and the *Maṇimēkalai*, the social situation is different. The heroes of both the epics belong to wealthy homes and live in cities. Hence the need for physical prowess or to go in search of wealth is not present, though Utayakumaraṉ being the Crown Prince who would one day inherit the Choḷa kingdom would also inherit the duty to protect his realm. He is, therefore expected to be heroic and perhaps trained to be so, for Sutamati addresses him as:

> the Courageous Prince
> with broad shoulders
> that shine in action (i.e. battle).[115]

When an elephant, large as a mountain, becomes uncontrollable, he is able to control it within minutes.[116] But this traditional quality of heroism is attributed even to Kōvalaṉ from the merchant class, and like Utayakumaraṉ, he too is talked of as having controlled a raging elephant and saved an old brāhmaṇa from being killed.[117] This incident is also found in the Sanskrit works. Udayana who is well versed in elephant lore is set free by King Pradyota to tame the elephant Nālagiri which has gone wild[118] and this gives him the long awaited opportunity to escape. Viṣṇusena who goes about in disguise, cannot disguise his valour when he sees the elephant, 'rushing to the Princess's palanquin.'[119] His easy way with elephants and his ability to make them do as he pleases is described to the king by Bhūtikā.[120] Kālidāsa too uses this incident to illustrate the heroic nature of Aja. While camping on the banks of the Narmadā, a huge elephant, also 'comparable to a mountain' (*śailopamaḥ*), with ichor flowing from its temples, throws the whole camp into confusion putting the horses and warriors to flight. But Aja aims at the elephant's forehead, trying not to kill him but to make him turn back. Once it is hurt, the animal takes the form of a *ghandharva* and relates how he is cursed to be an elephant until such time when Aja's arrow will pierce his forehead.[121] We find reference to this kind of valour in the *Abhijñānaśākuntalam* when the king hears of an elephant that became alarmed at the sight of a chariot and had thus become uncontrollable. Duṣyanta hastens to make sure that such incidents do not recur, but we are not told clearly if he himself controls the raging elephant.[122] An even more popular form of depicting the hero's valour in the Sanskrit works is to depict him as being helpful to Indra himself in overcoming his enemies. Daśaratha, the great chariot-warrior who holds sway over the people of Uttarakosalā, conquers the earth all by himself and has the other kings bowing before him as the gods bow to Indra.[123] Hence he becomes a helper (*sahāya*) of Indra.[124] Purūravas and Duṣyanta too are of such service to Indra and this helps them in their love life. Indra is willing to allow Urvaśī to remain on earth with Purūravas as long as he lives, in return for the king's alliance with the god in the event of hostilities between the gods and the demons.[125] Duṣyanta is able to meet Śakuntalā and he is reunited with her during his return journey from Indra's heaven after helping Indra to overcome his enemies.[126] Raghu, however, is depicted as one who encounters Indra himself in battle, while guarding his father's sacrificial horse[127] after having defeated Kubera and other kings.[128] Rāma's valour is depicted in Canto Eleven of the *Raghuvaṃśam* where his killing of Tāḍakā and her son[129] and the breaking of Śivadhanuṣ to win Sītā are related.[130] The greatest test of his valour is of course his final victory over Rāvaṇa. Even heroes for whom no specific incidents are mentioned to illustrate their heroic qualities, some little reference or simile may be found which help to conform to this tradition of depicting brave heroes.

Compared to Murukaṉ or Skanda

The youth and beauty of the heroes are usually brought out by comparing them to Murukaṉ (Tamil) or Skanda (Sanskrit), also known variously as Guha, Kumāra or Kārtikeya. In the Caṅkam works the hero is referred to as one who moves about the village or the slopes, like *Murukaṉ*.[131] In an *Akam* poem, a maid fearing that the couple's clandestine affair might soon be detected by her mother, asks the heroine what would then happen to her relationship with the hero. She asks,

On the tall mountain
where deities dwell and streams flow
enabling the long-trunked elephant
that had killed the big tiger
to wash its spotted forehead
smelling of flesh,
our hero came bearing the spear
that shines like lightning,
lighting his nocturnal path
by removing the dense darkness
of the fearful mountain caves.
Unmindful of the harassing rain
he came alone.
The blowing wind indicates
the lasting fragrance of his chaplet
of ipomea (*kūtaḷam*) blooms
interspersed with the fragrant wild jasmines
that grow by the streams.
His body thrilled with joy,
he entered our short-eaved house
with the backyard
where pepper creepers spread on rocks.
Mother seeing this
and mistaking him for Murukaṉ
praised him and sprinkling
red millet and water,
worshipped him.
What would happen to our relationship
with the lord of the lovely mountain
where the peacock of sapphire hue

calls, beautifying the moving branches
of the *vēṅkai* that blooms like gold?[132]

In the *Cilappatikāram,* Kōvalaṉ is introduced as being much-talked-of among the maidens as the Red Lord or Murukaṉ[133] while the incident of Utayakumaraṉ controlling the elephant is described thus:

He rode fast on a speedy horse,
checked the fury of the strong elephant
and rode back in his chariot
followed by escorts.
Holding the lotus-shaped staff of the chariot,
he made it known
only by his garlands and chaplets
that he was not
the God who wears the *kaṭampu*
which blooms with the rains.[134]

Here the 'God who wears the *kaṭampu'* is Murukaṉ or Skanda, the god of Youth, Beauty and Heroism. He is also described as being young and handsome like the god who destroyed the Krauñca hill,[135] another reference to Skanda and his valour.

Sarvārthasiddha sitting beside his nurse is said to look like the son of Agni (i.e. Skanda)[136] and his father's joy at his birth is likened to that of Bhava or Śiva at the birth of Kārtikeya.[137] Even in the *Raghuvaṃśam,* heroes like Aja, Daśaratha, Atithi and Rāma are compared to Skanda. Aja sitting on the throne of jewels spread with costly carpets looks like Guha on the peacock[138] and after his marriage to Indumatī he is the visible form of Skanda with Devasenā.[139] The prowess of Daśaratha equals that of Kumāra, the destroyer of the Krauñca mountain.[140] Rāma facing Paraśurāma in battle resembles the son of Hara (Skanda) and is overcome with compassion[141] that is born of true heroism. Atithi's valour is like that of Kārtikeya and he is well-versed in military strategy.[142]

Strength and Generosity

This valour and also physical and moral strength makes it possible for them to achieve their aim, be it wealth or fame. A heroine of the *Kuṟuntokai* tells her maid that the hero is 'firmer than the rocks'[143] and another from the *Kalittokai* is of the opinion that her lover will not return without obtaining whatever he had set his heart on.[144] Dilīpa is compared to the Mount Meru for his all-surpassing strength and firmness.[145] The ideal hero is one whose strength and heroism are tempered with love and compassion. This quality is mentioned often and it is important if they are to be portrayed as loving and lovable. This gentle quality is generally brought out by their kindness to man and beast as well as by their generosity. In the *Kalittokai*, a maid consents to the hero's request for help in obtaining the favours of the heroine, saying,

> Being kind and gentle,
> you offer
> chariots as fast as the wind
> and elephants
> to poets who come to you.
> Your hands know no rest
> because of your generosity.
> There is no harshness in you,
> not even to use the goad-stick
> on the running horses.
> Knowing all these,
> I shall unite her with you.[146]

This quality of gentleness in man or woman is likened to water, for a hero declares,

> The *kuṟava* maid's water-like gentleness
> has overcome my fire-like strength,[147]

while a friend of the heroine in the *Kalittokai* is confident that

> he is gentler than
> the waters of his hill.
> His generous hands
> give away chariots
> to those who approach him
> (for such favours).[148]

This gentle compassion to other beings and kindness to men is found in the Sanskrit heroes as well. Dilīpa's compassion is so visible in his body that the female deer is not frightened in spite of the bow he carries and he is described as one who is accustomed to relieving those in distress.[149] Gentle nature is considered further enhanced by education. Hence Dilīpa makes his son Raghu, the *yuvarāja*, on 'seeing that he was gentle by nature and by education'.[150] Thus we may infer that all good kings depicted in the Sanskrit works are at least expected to possess this quality in spite of, or rather because of, the heroism and valour that are essential to protect their kingdoms. Viṣṇusena possesses 'a warrior's radiance. He is both gentle and strong'. These traits make Bhūtikā doubt if he could really be of ignoble birth as he claims.[151] Cārudatta's kindness is seen in his great generosity which leads to his poverty so that the *vidūṣaka* feels that even his poverty is charming on account of the cause (*ramaṇīyoyaṃ daridrabhāvaḥ*).[152]

This generosity is so much a part of their pride and honour that the heroes consider it rather disgraceful to turn away those who ask of them help or wealth. To the Tamil hero *ītal* (generosity or charity) is important and dear, dearer than the dark-haired beloved adorned with flowers,[153] and he can never be hard-hearted enough to turn away those who come to him seeking aid.[154] Since it is so shameful not to give to those who need help,[155] he would rather give his own body if he has nothing else.[156] We see this ideal in Kōvalaṉ too. He gives away riches during the naming ceremony of his daughter Maṇimēkalai and is kind and generous to particular people in need. The epic relates various incidents in which he helps people to start life anew. Once he is so moved by the tears of a mother that he begs the demon which kills wrongdoers to set free her son and take his life instead. When the demon refuses saying that he cannot exchange the life of a sinner for that of a good man, he consoles the relatives concerned and protects them for many years.[157]

The same attitude is seen in the Sanskrit heroes regarding generosity. Raghu has spent his great wealth performing the *viśvajit* sacrifice. Yet when a student comes to ask of him the gifts necessary to satisfy the teacher who has demanded the exorbitant sum of 'four and ten crores of money in accordance with the number of *several* lores', Raghu feels that it would bring him reproach if he were to send him away to seek the gifts elsewhere. So he asks the disciple to stay in the fire-sanctuary and wages a war against Kubera to obtain the necessary wealth to satisfy the disciple's need.[158]

Desire for Fame

The main reason for this obsession with generosity is, besides kindness to others, their desire for fame or good name and fear of blame or reproach. The Caṅkam heroes are usually referred to as being 'distinguished by the praises of many',[159] and as having a good heart that desires good fame (*nallicai*).[160] Perhaps more important than their desire for fame is their fear of blame and a maid tries to console the heroine using this aspect of the hero's character:

> He was not content
> with the wealth he had.
> He feared the slander
> of his enemies with scornful hearts.[161]

Among the Sanskrit heroes, the only hero who seems to be so preoccupied with slander and reproach, apart from Raghu[162] is Rāma, who though convinced of the purity of his wife, sends her away to the forest to save himself from the scorn of his subjects.[163] Perhaps this is part of their *aṟam* (Tamil) or *dharma* (Sanskrit), a concept that is most difficult to translate into another language. It consists of their conduct and code of morality and the heroes are always shown as being anxious not to break it. Hence one who does not fear what should be feared is considered one who follows no *aṟam* (*aṟaṉili*).[164] A good man is also impartial like the balance rod of the weighing scales.[165] In the Sanskrit epics Dilīpa is pictured as one who has *dharma* as the basis of his life so that *artha* and *kāma* are tempered by it.[166] In the case of Rāma the very reason for his birth is the establishment and protection of *dharma* (*dharma-saṃrakṣaṇārtha*).[167] Nala is said to have followed *dharma* and Sudarśana learns the three aims of life, viz., *dharma, artha* and *kāma*.[168] This is perhaps expected of all the kings and we find Duṣyanta trying to ascertain first the caste of Śakuntalā before deciding to give in to the dictates of his heart. Later when repudiating her it is *dharma* that he is concerned about, for, it would not be right to accept the wife of another.[169]

Respect for Religion

The hero's respect for religion, worship and the hermits or sages who are normally preoccupied with religious activities do not seem to be apparent in the *akam* section of the Caṅkam poems for these poems deal only with love and all other qualities that have a direct bearing on his love life. There are however, references to men and their relationship with the sages. A wife, angry because her husband had been disloyal to her, refuses to let him enter the house. When questioned by her friend, she says,

My lord is not in a distant country
with mountains between us.
Neither is he in a town
whose tree-tops are not discernible (i.e. far).
He is near enough to be seen
and approached.
Yet, like those who live with the sages,
He has renounced me in his heart.
Long ago I did care for him.[170]

Though the hero of this poem has not actually renounced his wife or home, the wife is using the renunciation of other men as an example to illustrate the uncaring attitude of the husband while in the company of the courtesan. She also tries to show by contrast his sensuous life. It is the *puṟam* section of the Caṅkam poems that deals with this aspect in detail. Even hermits are pictured as having loved and lived a normal life as the head of the family. One poem from the *Puṟanāṉūṟu* says:

Now his hair has thinned and is discoloured
like the shoots of the blinding tree (*tillai*).
He plucks the leaves of the hedgebind wood (*tāḻi*).
Earlier he was the hunter
who fettered with his eloquence
the modest peacock that graced his home,[171]

meaning that in his youth he had wooed his wife with loving words. Kings and chieftains are religious enough to perform various sacrifices and to respect and protect those who perform such rituals. The poet Kapilar, praises the chieftain Malaiyamāṉ Tirumuṭikkāri for his religiosity and generosity saying:

O Kāri, with good feet
adorned with the *kaḻal*!
Your land cannot be overrun
by the sea or by the enemies.
It belongs to the brahmins
who guard the sacrificial fires.
It has lasting wealth and a victorious army.
The wealth offered by embassies
from the three great kings
who also shower praises to secure your alliance
belongs to the bards who sing your lineage.
So you have nothing for yourself
except the shoulders of your modest, soft-spoken wife
whose chastity matches that of the northern star.
You are truly great.[172]

Even ordinary people seem to have been respectful to the ascetics who are pictured as being wandering mendicants,[173] or hermits in the forest.[174] Hospitality or *viruntōmpal,* which includes hospitality to sages, students far away from home or travellers, is treated as a very important aspect of the duties of a householder. It is so important that even the quarrels between a husband and wife over his infidelity, must be forgotten in showing this hospitality. This makes it possible for the hermits to obtain food and water for their meals and even extra water to carry in their pots.[175] In the *Cilappatikāram* too, this respect and duty towards the sages is cherished. Kōvalaṉ is not only respectful to the Jaina nun Kavunti, but is very pleased to have her company during his journey to Maturai with his wife.[176] This deep reverence for the hermits is found in Dilīpa and nearly all his descendants who have the constant help of their Rājaguru Vasiṣṭha. When he sets out for the hermitage he is anxious that the peace of the penance grove is not disturbed and hence takes with him the least number of attendants possible.[177] Even Duṣyanta who practically changes the penance grove into a pleasure garden is a pious man by nature and is most helpful to the hermits.[178] Being kings who follow tradition, they also believe in expiatory rites and sacrifices or *yajñas.* Dilīpa goes to the hermitage for the purpose of performing the proper ceremony after consulting his *guru* and serves Surabhī devotedly till he achieves his aim.[179] Raghu performs the *viśvajit* sacrifice[180] while Agnimitra attends the *aśvamedha* sacrifice performed by his father.[181] Cārudatta too is portrayed as one who has faith in worship and piety.[182] The *varṇāśrama dharma* of the north makes it obligatory for these heroes to repair to the forest or hermitages with their wives once their duties towards their family, and in the case of kings, to their kingdoms, are fulfilled. Hence Raghu having established his son on the throne as the king of his realm, goes away to the forest to live the life of an ascetic. Kālidāsa explains that

> The descendants of Dilīpa, having transferred their
> royal fortunes to their qualified sons,
> and themselves becoming self-subdued,
> betook themselves in their old age
> to the life of ascetics,
> whose garments are the bark of trees.[183]

'The qualified sons' or *guṇavatsuta* also have to be married before they can take over the responsibilities of king and householder. Kaṇva in the *Abhijñānaśākuntalam*, refers to this when advising Śakuntalā on her duties in her husband's home:

> When thou shalt long have been a co-wife of the earth
> bounded by the four cardinal points,
> and settled in marriage Duṣyanta's son by thee,
> a matchless warrior,
> then with thy husband who shall have transferred
> the burden of family-cares to him (*tadarpita-kuṭumbabhāreṇa*)
> thou shalt set foot again on this peaceful hermitage.[184]

But we know that this ideal is not always followed, for Agnimitra whose son is a great warrior, does not seem anxious to get his son married so as to hand over his family and state burden. Instead, he is busy wooing Mālavikā and finding ways of marrying her without displeasing Queen Dhāriṇī.

The Arts

The heroes of both Tamil and Sanskrit literature, being men of leisure and wealth, are not actively involved in the daily routine of earning a living and this makes it possible for them to patronise and sometimes even practise some form of fine art or other. The Caṅkam heroes are always described as being charitable and one community that seems to be in constant need of financial aid is that of poets and bards. Poems from the *Puṟanāṉūṟu* and the *Pattuppāṭṭu* contain abundant evidence to this. Even in the works taken for this study we find that the heroes are usually accompanied by bards or musicians called *pāṇaṉ* and they often help in the affairs of love as well, especially in the role of a messenger to appease the angered and wronged wife.[185] Since he patronises musicians the hero is also known as 'the lord of the musicians' (*pāṇar perumakaṉ*).[186] Kōvalaṉ's attraction for Mātavi is due, not to her beauty alone but also to her skill in music and dance. But Kōvalaṉ can play the lute so well that Mātavi herself who has learnt these arts since she was five, recognises his ability to sing and play on the lute.[187] He enjoys music so much that he can enjoy playing on the lute, in spite of having heard recently of Mātavi's sorrow at his departure and his own realization that she is faultless and that he himself is to be blamed.[188] Utayakumaraṉ's knowledge of music or any other form of art is not mentioned but he is certainly a *rasika* who could be deeply moved by music.

> The city youths
> in the company of bangled maids
> played on the stringed lute.
> Their *iḷi* tune and their rhythm
> tore at his heart as a spear.[189]

The heroes in Sanskrit literature are also well versed in the arts and are happy patrons but their skill is not limited to music alone. Sarvārthasiddha is shown to have enjoyed music played by the beautiful singing women of the palace and as having been susceptible to it despite his calmness.[190] Of the princes of the line of Raghu, only Agnivarṇa, the licentious king, is depicted as enjoying song and dance. He is versed in playing the *vīṇā* well enough to thrill his own heart as well as that of his lady-love.[191] He is also proficient in dancing and is capable of instructing the girls in whose company he enjoys song, dance and love.[192] Cārudatta in his appreciation of the sound of the *vīṇā* compares it to a gem, a confidante, a wife and co-wife for it is refreshing, and augments the pleasures of love.[193] Udayana too is proficient in music. His lute, Goṣvatī, is used to catch elephants[194] for he could tame the hearts of elephants,[195] even the hearts of wild ones,[196] with his expertise in music. Knowing this Vāsavadattā's parents engage him as her music teacher hoping they would fall in love.[197] Duṣyanta is the only hero in Kālidāsa's works to be shown as an accomplished painter. His portrait of Śakuntalā is so life-like that the *vidūṣaka* not realizing that it is a mere painting of her in the same setting in which the king had first seen her, tries to drive away the bee that hovers over her face.[198]

One more fact is to be observed regarding the heroes of the Sanskrit dramas. They always speak pure Sanskrit to maintain their dignity and status. In the world of Sanskrit drama, the highest ranking characters always speak Sanskrit while the other characters speak different Prākṛts. It is indeed strange to note that the heroines even if they are queens or princesses, speak a variety of Prākṛts. This aspect of the heroines will be dealt with in chapter 4. The hero speaking a different dialect is not found in Tamil literature. A comparative study of this aspect would have been possible if ancient Tamil dramas were available. However, in the *Kalittokai* poems, which unlike the other Caṅkam poems include dialogues between the hero and the heroine[199] and the heroine and her friend,[200] a different dialect is not used for the hero, or any other character.

Exceptions to These Conventions

We find that there is a general tendency in both the classical literatures to sing only of heroes from the higher social classes, and Tolkāppiyar has reflected this in his book of conventions. According to him the love of servants (*aṭiyōr*), attendants (*viṉaivalar*) and other such people who do the biddings of their masters and mistresses *(ēval marapiṉ ēṉaiyōr)* may be sung in poems but they cannot be included in the fivefold divisions of love poetry[201] for the quality of the emotion would be inferior. The *Kalittokai* collection somehow makes an exception to this rule. It not only contains poems depicting the love of the working class but also contains a love dialogue between a male midget and a hunchbacked woman.

Midget: O woman of gentle form,
bent like a shadow in the water
and moving about here with shrunken shape!

What austerities have you performed
that I would converse with you?
Wait a while.

Hunchback: Mother!
You midget born prematurely
and unbearable to see!
Son of an *āṇṭalai* bird!
You stop me saying, 'I desire you'.
Do you think I am to be touched by the like of you?

Midget: You cause me unbearable affliction
with your form
like the worthy, bent ploughshare
that has been broken off.
I cannot bear myself.
I shall live only if you show favour.

Hunchback: (To herself: Look at his intentions!)
You uneducated dwarf!
Like a gambling board made to stand!
You touch me in broad daylight saying,
'Come to my house'.
Tell me.
Do you have (other) women?

Midget: Listen good woman,
bent like a skinned crane
that has its body higher than its head
and a sword-like beak!
If I embrace you to my bosom
your bent body would hurt (me).
If I embraced from the back
I would feel ticklish.
Yet I can't help wanting to embrace you.
Show me favour.
I shall embrace from the side.

Hunchback: Get away, O Base Man!
You half man! Give up your intentions.
Many are those who would protect me

embracing this imperfect form
like the creeper that has wound itself
around the bent portion of a tree.
This adulterous man says
he would embrace from the side.
You dwarf!
Is the hunchback who is desired more
than the sweetmeat of blackgrams
baser than you?

Midget: (As if to himself)
I have said, 'I love you'
and have followed her.
Yet she has moved away.
See the way she bends!

Hunchback: My heart!
I have refused him.
Yet he approaches, swaying his arms
like a tortoise standing on its hind legs.
Look at him walking like Cupid!

Midget: Yes see the walk of Cupid
Who brings people together. (He demonstrates)

Hunchback: O see!

Midget: We shall look for a place to embrace and be happy.
I swear by the king's feet
that I shall not make fun of you.

Hunchback: Let it be so.
Sweet One! I give in.
I would rather people in the temple do not laugh
saying, 'Hey! a goblin is hopping about
with another'.
O man with the form of an incomplete gold plate!
We shall go away to the park.
There we shall embrace to our satisfaction
like the seal on the palm-leaf roll
of those with faultless knowledge.[202]

Though this poem has been included in *aintiṇai* poetry which deals with the heroes and heroines from the upper strata of society, the reason for Tolkāppiyar setting such poems apart from the others is rather obvious from the dialogue above. The mutual respect and admiration that forms the very basis of love is lacking, for they ridicule each other's deformity. Their feelings border on lust, for the hero, even after giving reasons as to why it is not possible for him to embrace her normally, still wishes to do so. His unveiled invitation to love-making sounds rather coarse and is certainly very different from the emotions and speech of the hero in the usual love poems that deal with the finer aspects of love called *aṉpoṭu puṇarnta aintiṇai.*[203]

REFERENCES

1. *Kurun,* 201; *Nar,* 116:6.
2. *Kurun,* 115.
3. *Ibid.,* 83, 96, 134, 143, 150; *Aink,* 202:4, 205:3, 262:3, 273:3, 286:3.
4. *Aink,* 295:6.
5. *Ibid.,* 246:6.
6. *Ibid.,* 289:4.
7. *Ibid.,* 253:3; *Kurinji,* 197-99.
8. *Kurun,* 8,10, 85, 91, 127, 181; *Nar,* 40:11, 180:3; *Aink,* 36:1, 83:3; *Kali,* 66:8, 71:8, 74:5, 75:9, 77:7.
9. *Aink,* 24:3, 37:1, 38:1, 45:5, 52:4, 66:2; *Kali,* 73:32; *Nar,* 70:8.
10. *Aink,* 405:4.
11. *Ibid.,* 469:2.
12. *Ibid.,* 459:5.
13. *Kali,* 101:44, 104:14, 74, 105:51, 64, 111:7.
14. *Ibid.,* 105:58.
15. *Ibid.,* 108:2, 117:4.
16. *Ibid.,* 104:4, 121:1.
17. *Ibid.,* 103:2, 109:2, 111:3.
18. *Cilap,* 11:62-66.
19. *Aink,* 301:4.
20. *Ibid.,* 309:5.
21. *Ibid.,* 204:5; *Kali,* 40:34, 41:44.
22. *Aink,* 250:3.
23. *Ibid.,* 41:4.
24. *Ibid.,* 404:4, 406:4, 407:4.
25. *Nar,* 54:11.
26. *Tol. Porul,* 57, 58.
27. *Mani,* 4:27-28.

28. *Budd*, 2:17.
29. *Saun*, 2:57.
30. *Svap*, TTP. p. 44.
31. *Abhi*, p. 9.
32. *Vikr*, p. 17.
33. *Mala*, pp. 13-14. Also Nilakanta Sastri (Ed.) *Age of the Nandas and the Mauryas*, Delhi, 1952, p. 246.
34. *Cilap*, 1:33-34.
35. *Caru*, p. 79. Act I, vv. 17 ff.
36. *Avim*, IV: p. 90.
37. *Kuma*, 3:17.
38. *Ibid.*, 5:7.
39. *Ibid.*, 6:80, 83.
40. *Ragh*, 10:72.
41. *Ibid.*, 10:44.
42. *Budd*, 1:19.
43. *Megh*, U: 15 and p. 66.
44. *Ibid.*, p. 1.
45. *Cilap*, 9:5-36.
46. *Ibid.*, 1:34.
47. *Aink*, 303:4, 305:4, 310:4, 364:4, 393:5; *Akam*, 7:12, 315:4.
48. *Tamil Lexicon*.
49. *Aink*, 372:2, 382:2, 385:1, 391:5, 400:5.
50. *Akam*, 369:18-21.
51. *Mani*, 4:47-50.
52. *Budd*, 2:24.
53. *Avim*, I : p. 36.
54. *Ragh*, 5:40.
55. *Ibid.*, 2: 47.
56. *TTP*, p. 49.
57. *Abhi*, II: vv. 8ff.
58. *Mala*, V: p. 151.
59. *Kuma*, 5:7.
60. *Ibid.*, 6:80.
61. *Kurun*, 362: 5-7, 73:3; *Akam*, 22: 2-3; *Nar*, 104: 7-8; *Aink*, 46:2, 51: 3-4, 205:4-5.
62. *Kali*, 9: 9-11.
63. *Cilap*, 1: 35-39.
64. *Mani*, 4: 47-50.
65. *Budd*, 3:3.
66. *Ibid.*, 3:11.
67. *Ibid.*, 3:24.
68. *Ibid.*, 5: 74, 84.
69. *Ibid.*, 5:74.
70. *Ragh*, 1:46, 47.
71. *Ibid.*, 3:22.
72. *Ibid.*, 3:34.
73. *Ibid.*, 5:38.

74. *Ibid.*, 6:69.
75. *Ibid.*, 15: 65.
76. *Ibid.*, 16: 82-87.
77. *Caru*, I: p. 75.
78. *TTP*, pp. 48, 49.
79. *Ibid.*, p. 49.
80. *Ibid.*, p. 50.
81. *Avim*, I: v. 7.
82. *Ibid.*, IV: p. 82.
83. *Ibid.*, IV: p. 90.
84. *Mala*, I: p. 19.
85. *Vikr*, I: p. 15.
86. *Ibid.*, II: p . 43.
87. *Abhi*, I: p. 27.
88. *Kuma*, 7:66, 67.
89. *Aink*, 201:2; *Akam*, 102: 9-10.
90. *Nar*, 121:7, *Kali*, 101:39, 102: 35-37.
91. *Akam*, 38:1, 288: 3-4.
92. *Ibid.*, 48: 8-9.
93. *Kurun*, 321: 2.
94. *Kali*, 103: 1-9, 52.
95. *Akam*, 38:2, 82:14, 102: 11; *Aink*, 33:4, 182: 1-2, 362: 3; *Kurun*, 258: 1., *Cilap*, 2: 82-83; *Mani*, 4:50.
96. *Akam*, 32:2.
97. *Aink*, 353:2.
98. *Kali*, 135:18.
99. *Kurun*, 7:1, 15:14-15, 356:2.
100. *Akam*, 48:11, 388:16; *Kurun*, 150:3.
101. *Akam*, 102:10, 288:2; *Kurun*, 161:6, 198:7.
102. *Kali*, 52:7, 11, 15.
103. *Akam*, 32:2-4.
104. *Kurinji*, 107-27.
105. *Ragh*, 17: 21-27.
106. *Kuma*, 7: 32-34.
107. *Kali*, 37:2; *Akam*, 82:11.
108. *Kurun*, 179: 1-2; *Akam*, 118:5, 388:14-15; *Kurinji*, 130-31.
109. *Akam*, 48:12, 38:4, 82:10; *Kali*, 7:5, 50: 6-7.
110. *Kurun*, 15:5; *Akam*, 221: 5-6.
111. *Akam*, 72:16-18, 202:9-14, 212:9-13, 258:10-11; *Kurinji*, 251-61.
112. *Kurun*, 12:3-4, 16:1-3, 77:2-3, 274:3-4, 390:3-5; *Nar*, 164:6-7, 352:1-3; *Akam*, 109:10-12, 375:3-5; *Kali*, 4:3-5.
113. *Akam*, 202:8-15.
114. *Ibid.*, 217:3-4, 7.
115. *Mani*, 4:112.
116. *Ibid.*, 4:44-45.
117. *Cilap*, 15:42-53.
118. *Prat*, IV: p. 33 vv. 19ff.
119. *Avim*, I: p. 36.

120. *Ibid.*, I: p. 38.
121. *Ragh*, 5:42-55.
122. *Abhi*, I: vv. 33ff.
123. *Ragh*, 9:1, 10, 13.
124. *Ibid.*, 9:20.
125. *Vikr*, I: p. 154, vv. 19ff.
126. *Abhi*, VII: pp. 201-30.
127. *Ragh*, 3:59-62.
128. *Ibid.*, 4 &5:26.
129. *Ibid.*, 11:14-21.
130. *Ibid.*, 11:44-46.
131. *Akam*, 118:5.
132. *Ibid.*, 272.
133. *Cilap*, 1:35-38.
134. *Mani*, 4:44-50.
135. *Ibid.*, 5:13-14.
136. *Budd*, 1:66.
137. *Ibid.*, 1:93.
138. *Ragh*, 6:4.
139. *Ibid.*, 7:1.
140. *Ibid.*, 9:2.
141. *Ibid.*, 11:83.
142. *Ibid.*, 17:67.
143. *Kurun*, 187:4 (*Kalliṉum valiyaṉ*).
144. *Kali*, 61:15-16.
145. *Ragh*, 1:14 (*atirikta sāreṇa*).
146. *Kali*, 50:15-20
147. *Kurun*, 95:4-5.
148. *Kali*, 42:19-21.
149. *Ragh*, 2:11, 25.
150. *Ibid.*, 3:35.
151. *Avim*, I: v. 7.
152. *Caru*, TTP. p. 76.
153. *Akam*, 131:1-5.
154. *Ibid.*, 53:13-15.
155. *Kali*, 2:11, 15, 19.
156. *Ibid.*, 42:25-27.
157. *Cilap*, 15:54-75.
158. *Ragh*, 5:18-30.
159. *Aink*, 473:1.
160. *Kurun*, 143:4.
161. *Akam*, 111:1-3.
162. See fn 158 above.
163. *Ragh*, 14:35ff.
164. *Kali*, 42:26.
165. *Ibid.*, 42:13-15.
166. *Ragh*, 1:21, 23, 25.
167. *Ibid.*, 14:4.

168. *Ibid.*, 18:7, 50.
169. *Abhi*, I. v. 28, V. v. 28.
170. *Kurun*, 203.
171. *Puram*, 252.
172. *Ibid.*, 122.
173. *Kali*, 9:1-4.
174. *Puram*, 251, 252.
175. *Kurun*, 277.
176. *Cilap*, 10:63-64.
177. *Ragh*, 1:37.
178. *Abhi*, I. vv. 11, 13, V. vv. 9, 11.
179. *Ragh*, 1:33, 81, 2:63-65.
180. *Ibid.*, 4:86.
181. *Mala*, V. p. 150.
182. *Caru* (*TTP*), p. 82.
183. *Ragh*, 8:10.
184. *Abhi*, IV. v. 19.
185. *Kali*, 70:21-23.
186. *Aink*, 458:3.
187. *Cilap*, 7 v. 1:17-20.
188. *Ibid.*, 13:104-13.
189. *Mani*, 19:24-27.
190. *Budd*, 2:29-31, 4:37.
191. *Ragh*, 19:13.
192. *Ibid.*, 19:35, 36.
193. *Caru*, III, v. 1.
194. *TTP*, p. 10.
195. *Ibid.*, II: v. 12, p. 21.
196. *Ibid.*, IV: v. 17, p. 33.
197. *TTP*. p. 67.
198. *Abhi*, IV: vv. 8ff.
199. *Kali*, 96, 97.
200. *Ibid.*, 104, 107.
201. *Tol. Porul*, 25, 26.
202. *Kali*, 94.
203. *Tol. Porul*, 89.

Chapter 4

The Heroine

As in the case of the Caṅkam hero, the heroine too is not mentioned by name. Since the Tamil society during the time of the Caṅkam poems was not classified according to *varṇa* or caste, we only find reference to her social class based on the geographical division of land, family, occupation or wealth. But the heroines in the two Tamil epics and the Sanskrit *kāvyas* and dramas are divided on the basis of their birth in a particular *varṇa*. The nature of the Caṅkam poems also makes it impossible for them to depict any character as fully as an epic, a *kāvya* or a drama can.

In Tamil and Sanskrit classical literature, all the heroines cannot be said to come from noble families, though nearly all are from well-to-do families. Caṅkam poems that deal with the mountainous districts refer to the heroine or the *talaivi* as *koṭicci*. This term, according to the old commentary of the *Aiṅkuṟunūṟu*, means the 'heroine of the *kuṟiñci* district'.[1] But V. Swaminathaiyar himself in the introduction to his edition of the *Kuṟuntokai* mentions that the term *koṭicci* refers to women of the hilly tracts,[2] and this view is supported by many poems from the various Caṅkam anthologies, in which the term *koṭicci* is used to denote a *kuṟava* maiden in general and not the heroine.[3] But when a *kuṟava* maid is treated as the heroine, and the term *koṭicci* is used to denote her, then there is usually enough evidence to show that she is from a family of good standing and not one from the working class.

(i) Very close to the mountain
is the town, where dwells
the *koṭicci* with plump upper arms.
(She is) the sister
of the forester with long arrows,
and skilled in archery.[4]

(ii) The *koṭicci* with a gentle, swaying walk

is the younger sister of the forester
with the arrow that had gored
the ichor-lined cheeks of the elephant
and wealthy with rich, fatty foods.[5]

Thus quite often the heroine is referred to as the sister of a forester and this would mean that she is from a family well-known for the heroism and valour of its men. She is also 'the modest daughter of the owner of the forest tracts'[6] and 'the beloved daughter of the lord of the hilly tracts'.[7] Some *Kalittokai* poems describe her as the only daughter of a well-to-do family:

She is the pet daughter
of the family inhabiting the cottage,
rich in jack-fruits
that fall from the many-branched trees
on to the resin-covered rocks,
and with an abundance of rice,
but hankering for children,[8]

thereby showing that she is treated as a rare gift of God to be loved and cherished.

In the *mullai* region she is depicted as the wife and mother waiting for the return of the husband, away on account of his duty.[9] But even here, her social position as the wife of a chieftain or a man of wealth and social standing is clear. The hero returns in a chariot driven by the charioteer and he is followed by *iḷaiyōr* or attendants.[10] The *Aiṅkuṟunūṟu* poems depict her as the happy wife and mother who enjoys music played by the musician or *pāṇaṉ* in her own home.

The musicians sang
the *mullai* tune.
The wife with the bright forehead
and adorned with glittering jewels
wore *mullai* flowers.[11]

Even before marriage, she seems to have been the daughter of a family that possessed rich and beautiful tracts of *mullai* land. She is described as 'the modest daughter of the owner of land fit for dry cultivation',[12] 'the beloved daughter of the owner of lovely bushland'[13] and 'the daughter of the owner of the land filled with bushes'.[14] The *Mullaikkali* also mentions a heroine who is the daughter of the village chief.[15] But true to its character, the *Kalittokai*, deals with heroines from the ordinary or working class people as well. When a hero complains that his beloved is a thief, who residing in his heart, has taken full possession of it, she asks:

> Your heart,
> How can it be possible for me
> to reside in it and possess it?
> Will it take food for my brother
> in the fields of dry cultivation?
> Will it take the milking vessel
> to my father
> guarding the herds?
> Will it take care of the calf,
> my mother allowed to graze
> in the harvested millet fields?[16]

This clearly shows that she is not from a home where they had servants or subordinates to attend to the daily work but had to share out the chores among the members of the family.

The *marutam* poems too depict her as the wife and mistress of the household (*maṉaiyōḷ, maṉaimaṭantai*).[17] Again the house of which she is the mistress is rich in grains[18] and able to support or employ such people as musicians (*pāṇar*)[19] and charioteers (*pākaṉ, valavaṉ*).[20] The heroine of the coastal regions is said to be 'the beloved daughter of a maritime chief'.[21] Though the *pālai* poems do not usually have specific names for the hero or heroine, we do come across the term *eyiṉar taṅkai*[22] meaning the sister of the hunter who inhabits the dry tracts.

The epics, both Tamil and Sanskrit, deal with women of the higher castes. There are no heroines from the Brāhmaṇa caste and though Cārudatta's wife's name Brahmaṇī sounds as if she might be from the Brāhmaṇa caste, there is no clear indication to that. In fact, since the husband is portrayed in the play as a trader,[23] she too must have belonged to the Vaiśya caste. The Tamil epics do not have heroines from the Kṣatriya caste either. But most of the *kāvyas* of Aśvaghoṣa, Bhāsa and Kālidāsa deal with royalty and therefore with Kṣatriya heroines. Sundarī's parentage or family background is not mentioned in the *Saundaranandam*. Neither is Yaśodharā's mentioned in the *Buddhacaritam*. But Sundarī being the queen of Nanda and Yaśodharā, the wife of the Crown Prince means that they are of the same caste as their husbands. Similarly, Vasumatī, the chief queen of Duṣyanta and Dhāriṇī, the chief queen of Agnimitra have to be accepted as heroines of Kṣatriya lineage. Vāsavadattā the princess of Ujjain,[24] Padmāvatī the princess of Magadha,[25] Kuraṅgī the princess of Vairantya and the daughter of King Kuntibhoja,[26] Sītā in the *Pratimānāṭakam* as Maithilī, the princess of Mithilā,[27] Auśīnarī the princess of Kāśi and the chief queen of Purūravas,[28] Mālavikā the princess of Vidarbha,[29] Sudakṣiṇā the princess of Magadha and the wife of Dilīpa[30] and Indumatī the sister of the king of Vidarbha later married to Aja[31] are all of Kṣatriya origin. Śakuntalā, strictly speaking, will have to be considered as a heroine of the Kṣatriya caste because she is the daughter of Viśvāmitra, a former king though her mother is Menakā, an *apsarā* from the court of Indra.[32] In fact it is on this basis that Duṣyanta who is so concerned about following *dharma*, decides that she is suitable for marriage to a Kṣatriya. Kaṇṇaki, the heroine of the *Cilappatikāram* is the daughter of the rich and famous Mānāykaṉ, a maritime trader of Pukār and therefore of the Vaiśya caste.[33] Maṇimēkalai, the daughter of Kōvalaṉ and Mātavi is also of the same caste if we are to accept the argument of Duṣyanta regarding Śakuntalā. But usually, the daughter of a courtesan is treated as one herself. There are no heroines of the Śūdra caste mentioned in either the Tamil or Sanskrit texts taken for this study. Both, however, mention heroines of the *gaṇikā* (Sanskrit) or *kaṇikai* (Tamil) class. Mātavi who bears Kōvalaṉ his only child Maṇimēkalai, is a leading danseuse in the Chola capital of Pukār.[34] Vasantasenā of Bhāsa's *Cārudattam* also belongs to the *gaṇikā* class.[35] While the Tamil works under study do not deal with heroines from any other class, the Sanskrit works deal with 'supernatural' heroines. Hiḍimbī in the *Madhyamavyāyokam* is a demoness or *rākṣasī*,[36] Urvaśī is an *apsarā* or nymph of Indra's heaven,[37] and Kumudavatī is a Nāga princess with her abode below the waters of the river Sarayu.[38] The heroine of the *Meghadūtam* is merely referred to as the wife of the *yakṣa* living in Alakā.[39] We have two instances of incarnations of the great goddesses. Pārvatī is depicted as the incarnation of Satī or Śakti herself[40] while Sītā in the *Raghuvaṃśam* is treated as Lakṣmī and therefore not born of the womb.[41] Apart from these important female characters, we also have Haṃsapadikā and Irāvatī whose family backgrounds are not mentioned in the plays concerned.

Her Youth

A very important characteristic of the heroine that is almost always emphasised is her youth. The Caṅkam poems that deal with courtship, whatever the geographical region, refer to the heroine as being young. A hero who has fallen in love with a maiden from the hilly tracts describes her and his own malady thus:

The beautifully-lined baby
of the small, white snake
tortures the elephant of the wilds.
So does she torture me—
She, young in years
with new teeth and hands
adorned with bangles.[42]

Many poems refer to the heroine as a *maṭantai* or a woman between nineteen and twenty-four years of age.[43] A *Naṟṟiṇai* hero says:

'You do not play
with your bright-jewelled friends.
You do not weave garlands
from the broad-petalled *neytal*.
You stand alone in the maritime park
where flowers bloom.
Who are you?'
I asked humbly,
'Are you a goddess
of the large ocean
containing clean waters,
with beauty that cannot be impaired
by the eyes of those who behold?
Are you a maiden who lives near the dark backwaters?
Tell me, O *Maṭantai*,' said I.
In reply,

her sharp teeth were disclosed in a smile
and her dark eyes
filled with tears.[44]

Even some poems that deal with the married life of the couple or of their separation after their marriage use the term *maṭantai* for the heroine.[45] It is also used for a bride.[46] There is, however, a poem that gives the foster-mother's impression of a heroine who has eloped, thus:

'Your breasts begin to show;
The thorn-like (sharp) teeth are bright;
The hair is long enough to be knotted;
You wear the cool, leafy garment.
Do not go anywhere
with your roaming group of friends.
In this ancient habitat
are spirits that might harm.
So accept protection and
do not go even to the entrance.
You are not a *pētai*,
My clever little girl.
You have passed the *petumpai* age,'
said I.
Fearing that I knew her fault,
my daughter left the protection
of our bright, good home.
(She left) like a doe that flees
a (hunter's) net when detected,
and has traversed this desert
with a youth
who carries the white spear
which knows no defeat.[47]

This poem refers to the heroine as one who has just passed the *petumpai* age, i.e., reached the *mankai* age or turned thirteen. But we cannot forget the fact that mothers or foster-mothers whose daughters have eloped usually keep talking of the girls as being very young and gentle and find it difficult to accept the fact that their daughters have grown enough both physically and emotionally to know of love. The foster-mother in this poem must have merely emphasised the fact that the girl has just reached maturity. Again, the age of thirteen cannot be taken to be too young, for the *Cilappatikāram* refers to Kaṇṇaki as being twelve years old when she is married.[48] Mātavi too is twelve when she gives her maiden performance and is considered old enough to become the mistress of the man wealthy enough to buy her emerald necklace from her maid.[49] Though Maṇimēkalai is introduced as a nun even in the first Canto of the epic, her youth is never forgotten. She is repeatedly referred to as a young woman with the grace, beauty and tenderness of a creeper (*ilaṅkoṭi*).[50] Her youth is further emphasised when a member of the Buddhist Saṅgha reporting the death of Utayakumaraṉ describes her saying:

> Her breasts have not grown,
> Her words are not mature.[51]

The Chola Queen tells the king:

> Sceptered King,
> The prison is not suitable
> for the wise maiden
> who wasting her youth
> which is hard to come by,
> makes Cupid
> with the sugarcane bow in his hand,
> powerless,[52]

though the Queen's intentions do not match these words.

In the Sanskrit works, too, we find the stress on youth. Aśvaghoṣa, however, does not pay attention to the youth of the heroine in either of his epics. But Yaśodharā, having been chosen as one who can keep Sarvārthasiddha bound to the pleasures of the senses must certainly have been young to match the youth of the prince. Sundarī too must have been young enough for the pleasures of youth and even when she suspects that Nanda has perhaps stayed away because of another woman, she is only worried that her rival might be more beautiful and not younger.[53] Vāsavadattā is still a little girl to her mother while the *vidūṣaka* describes her as 'a young girl whom all might see in innocence,' but she is old enough to rouse the passion of love in Udayana's heart.[54] Very aptly her youth is not mentioned in the *Svapnavāsavadattam*. Instead, Padmāvatī's youth is given prominence. The maid thinks that she should enjoy the 'charming days of girlhood' while she may[55] and the *vidūṣaka* praises her youth along with her other qualities.[56] Even Vasantasenā, though already a famous courtesan desperately desired by Śakāra, is depicted as young. The *viṭa* is of the opinion that she spurns Śakāra in spite of his royal connections because of the 'pride of her youth'.[57] Sītā in the *Pratimānāṭakam* is also referred to as a child though mature and traditional in her conduct.[58] Kuraṅginī's youth is said to be in keeping with her beauty which attracted Avimāraka the moment he saw her.[59] Of Bhāsa's heroines, Brāhmaṇī is not mentioned as young and is not important for the love theme of the play, but we know that being the wife of Cārudatta she too must have been young like him, but having been married for some years, must have lost the fresh appeal of youth.

Kālidāsa has portrayed heroines of various ages, but those chosen for the treatment of love are always young. Dhāriṇī is quite old, with a grown-up son who can lead an army to victory.[60] Vasumatī is also old, judging from the song of Haṃsapadikā[61] whose age is not clear. Similarly, Auśīnarī and Sudakṣiṇā are not very young, having been married for some time. There are others like Indumatī and Sītā whose ages or youth is not mentioned but we know clearly that they are young for they are considered suitable for marriage and a *svayamvara* is held for each of these princesses.[62] Kumudavatī, the Nāga princess, is referred to as a young girl or *bālā*.[63] Among the heroines in Kālidāsa's dramas, Śakuntalā alone is clearly mentioned as being in the prime of her youth, with swelling bosoms that make her old bark garment a little tight for her and Duṣyanta cannot help himself praising the youthfulness of her body and limbs.[64] Mālavikā who is betrothed by her brother to be married to Agnimitra is considered a young woman, new to love.[65] Urvaśī, being an *apsarā*, is ageless and therefore eternally young. Pārvatī, though Śakti herself, is born as the daughter of Himavān and goes through the normal process of growth and reaches her youth before she begins to wait on Śiva during his *tapas*. In fact her youth is such that it is an ornament or *alaṃkāra* on its own and is as effective as a flower-arrow of Kāma, for youth causes her body to be unfolded like a new blossom.[66]

Beauty

Another important characteristic of the heroine is her beauty. The Caṅkam poems usually depict her as being the fairest among her group of friends or *āyam*. A *Kuṟuntokai* poem mentions a heroine of the hilly district who is the prettiest among all the maidens on the hill-slope [67] and a heroine of the maritime tracts complains:

> The chief of the maritime region,
> where the fragrant screw-pine
> with its sword-edged leaf
> serves as a well of spears,
> is indeed cruel.
> But if news of his cruelty spreads
> for others to know,
> it would be worse
> than losing my beauty
> praised as the best among the group
> in the lovely coastal parks.[68]

On the whole, Caṅkam poems deal with the beauty of a particular limb or part of the face, for example, upper arms, forearms, eyes, forehead, teeth, or even the smile, to suit the context of the poem and this is taken to be indicative of the heroine's beauty.

> Long may you live,
> My friend!
> If I could only embrace
> even for a single day
> the small, gentle body
> of the young maiden
> who has bound my heart forever
> with her large upper arms
> and lovely hair,
> I would not desire to live
> even for half a day
> after that.[69]

In this poem, the plump upper arms and her hair are enough indication of her great beauty that has bound his heart to her. But other Tamil works, especially the *Cilappatikāram*, deal with the beauty of the heroine in a more detailed fashion. But as in the Sanskrit dramas, unlike in the *kāvyas,* the beauty is not described by the author but by other characters. Kaṇṇaki's beauty is such that in spite of the sensuous satisfaction that her husband derives from her, is pure, gentle and natural. So Kōvalaṉ uses gods and the gentle birds to describe her beauty.

> The sapphire tinted peacocks
> with thick dark plumes
> shamed by your grace
> take refuge in the cool forest.
> O maiden with a pretty forehead!
> The *aṉṉam,* having lost
> to your gentle walk
> hides itself in shame
> behind flowers in the field-pond.
> Poor little parrots,
> overcome with shame
> because of your prattling words—
> a mixture of music
> from the lute and the flute
> with nectar—
> do not leave your flower-soft hands
> (in the hope of imitating you).[70]

Mātavi is beautiful and glamorous so as to be described as 'a flowering creeper of gold'[71] and even while condemning her in the presence of the maid, we find that Kōvalaṉ is still conscious of her beauty.[72] Her education in the art of make-up enables her to accentuate this beauty with elaborate baths, dress and jewellery.[73] Maṇimēkalai, in spite of the nun's garb she is introduced in, is constantly described as a young woman of great beauty. Apart from the impassioned picture of her as portrayed by Utayakumaraṉ,[74] we have the descriptions of the other characters in the epic. Sutamati, her friend, seeing her shed tears while listening to the tragic story of her father and his lawful wife Kaṇṇaki, says:

> If Kāmaṉ were to see the tears fall
> from the corners of the eyes
> which put to shame

the choicest of blue lotuses
in the moon-like face of Maṇimēkalai
he would tremble,
discarding his weapons.
Will men leave, were they to see her?
Surely they are hermaphrodites
if they are unmoved.[75]

Eṭṭikumāraṉ describes her beauty which has been uncared for and not attended to in a nunnery as:

Like flowers
kept within a well-made casket
her great beauty faded,
Maṇimēkalai, born of Mātavi,
enters the park.[76]

Even the king Puṇṇiyarācaṉ who sees her for the first time, asks a monk,

She has great beauty unequalled among women.
The movements of her eyes
don't agree with Kāmaṉ.
She listens to instructions on *Dharma*
with the vessel in her lovely hands.
Who is this peerless woman?[77]

But she seems to have been unaware of her charms and is committed to the life of a Buddhist nun, in spite of her attraction for Utayakumaraṉ.

Of Aśvaghoṣa's heroines, Sundarī's beauty receives more attention than Yaśodharā's. The latter is merely mentioned as being equal or a match (*tulyābhidhānam*) to Sarvārthasiddha and comparable to Śrī,[78] while Sundarī bears that name because of her majesty and beauty which shines all the more because of her association with Nanda. There is no human being whose entrancing beauty could match that of Sundarī.[79] Though the *Pratijñāyaugandharāyaṇam* does not mention anything regarding Vāsavadattā's physical charms, we know that she must have been beautiful enough to attract the attention of the young Udayana in prison. The *Svapnavāsavadattam* does not give as much prominence to her beauty as to her love and sacrifice. Yet the king is reminded of her 'charming loveliness' and the 'sweetness of this face' at the sight of her portrait.[80] But Padmāvatī's beauty is clearly praised in the play. Vāsavadatta finds her beautiful and the king, though his heart is bound to Vāsavadattā, finds his new queen beautiful, charming and virtuous.[81] Vasantaka himself mentions more or less the same qualities while giving his own opinion of the new queen.[82] Vasantasenā's charms are very clear from the way the enamoured Śakāra chases her with the help of the *viṭa*, though his sentiments are far from being praiseworthy. The *viṭa*, trying to persuade her to stop fleeing them, asks her why she should give up her gazelle-like gentleness, the delicate grace and sidelong glances and flee in terror.[83] Cārudatta finds that 'she shines like a digit of the moon'.[84] Sītā of the *Pratimānāṭakam* is endowed with such natural beauty that she not only looks lovely in a bark garment but turns the bark into gold.[85] Rāvaṇa refers to her as the 'large-eyed lady'[86] and this obviously is an indication of her physical attractions. Kuraṅginī has natural beauty which is enhanced when she is dressed up.[87] Even Santuṣṭa who is the closest friend of Avimāraka is of the opinion that though the prince is very handsome, his looks are paled next to the natural beauty of the princess.[88] Sudakṣiṇā, like her husband, is invested with indescribable beauty.[89] Indumatī is 'the creator's masterpiece of creation of a maiden princess for she is full of charming loveliness in manner and speech.'[90] Sītā is perfect in every limb (*bhasamāṅgarāgā tanuḥ*) and is therefore endowed with a beautiful form.[91] The divine loveliness of Pārvatī is described in detail in the *Kumārasaṃbhavam* and finally Kālidāsa says:

> In short, she was created by the Creator of the Universe
> with great effort, as if with a desire to see
> all beauty combined in one form,
> by gathering together all the standards of comparison,
> and placing them, each in its place.[92]

Her natural beauty is such that even the severe penance and the carelessness regarding personal appearance and toiletries during that period cannot impair it. Even while performing the *pañcāgnisthāna tapas* her face is as lovely as a lotus (*kamala-śrīyam*).[93] The *yakṣī* is so beautiful that she could have been the first woman to be created and therefore serves as a model for other women to be created subsequently.[94] The beauty of Śakuntalā is artless and natural and this makes her an ornament of the hermitage of Kaṇva.[95] To Duṣyanta, she is a worthy object to be seen (*darśaṇīyam*).[96] The loveliness of Mālavikā cannot be contained even by the clothes of a maid-servant that she is wearing. She looks so extraordinary in the painting with the Queen and her retinue, that the king cannot help himself enquiring about such an extraordinary (*abhūrva*) person.[97] But seeing her in person the king feels that the painter has not done justice to her form and beauty which would satisfy the fancy of a teacher of dance.[98] Urvaśī is of course a paradigm of beauty like the other *apsarās*, Menakā and Rambhā, and to Purūravas, she is so beautiful that even the peacock renowned for its beauty deserves to take a look at her, for she is worthy of being seen.[99]

It is noticeable that Tamil classical poetry does sing the beauty of the heroine, which after all is important in love poetry, for without beauty, the youth would not have been attracted to her. But in these poems, beauty is usually denoted by the mention of one or two limbs or parts of the body, for example the eyes, hair, arms or complexion while the rest is left to be inferred. Even such references are found only in the poems which are supposed to be the words of the hero who is in love with her, her friend, her mother or her foster-mother. Others like the hermits do not describe her physical beauty but her virtue as in the *Kalittokai* poem where a hermit tells the foster-mother:

> You seem to be the mother
> of the bejewelled modest maid
> who crossed the difficult tracts
> with the youth of masculine beauty and greatness.[100]

He sees only her modesty and the jewels which must have glittered in the midday sun, but the hero's external appearance is praised because his build, broad shoulders and faultless limbs would also imply physical strength and valour.

Chastity

A quality that is almost universally expected in Indian heroines is their purity or chastity, which sometimes is conveniently forgotten, while dealing with heroines who are courtesans. The Caṅkam poems do not have any heroine from this class, and hence chastity is an important quality that is praised. The Tamil concept of chastity expects not merely the physical purity of the heroine throughout her life, but her loyalty to the hero of her choice as well. It is this quality that prompts her to hide her husband's faults from others, sometimes even her closest friend, however much he might hurt her. A friend praises this quality in the heroine saying:

> The maiden who made possible his festivities
> has become a true mother.
> She has concealed the cruelty
> of the chief of the district,
> where the farmers bend
> the tender branches of the river portia (*kāñci*)
> with fragrant flowers,
> till the pollen from the clusters
> that resemble bunches of green gram
> smear their bodies.
> She comes to receive him
> so that he is embarrassed (at his own infidelity).[101]

This acceptedly is not an easy quality to acquire for it combines her love for him as well as the good name and welfare of their home and her large-heartedness to forgive him as she would her own child. This great quality exalts her to a divine plane and it was then believed that a chaste woman had certain divine powers. Chastity, according to the Caṅkam poets, makes a woman calm and self-controlled (*aṭaṅkiya kaṟpu*[102] and *āṟiya kaṟpu*[103]) and therefore divine (*kaṭavuṭ kaṟpu*[104]). Such women brightened their homes and brought fame. The *Akanāṉūṟu* sings of a 'good maiden who was the light of her family with her divine chastity'.[105] The ancient Tamils also believed that the failure to observe propriety and decorum by their women would bring about disaster to their families and even the villages concerned. The friend of a heroine in the *Kalittokai*, expresses this while trying to persuade her family to give her in marriage to the youth of her choice.

> She sported with us
> in the swift, desirous stream.
> Growing weary, she was carried away by its currents
> and she closed her lotus-eyes in terror.
> He jumped in,
> with his fragrant, swaying garland

of mastwood blossoms, and,
clasping her jewelled body to his,
he brought her to the bank.
There is the gossip that his broad chest
and her lovely breasts are united.
The greatness of my friend is such,
that she could bring down the rare rain
if necessary.
He too,
is the son of the chieftain
of the vast forest region, where
if the moon, eclipsed by the smoke of aloewood
from the tree-house,
were sighted above the mountain,
they would prepare ladders,
thinking it were a honeycomb on their mountain.
Oh residents of the little village!
the four-leaved yam will not yield its roots,
the hilltops will not have any honey,
the garden millet will not yield ears of grain,
for the mountain dwellers have not observed
what is right.
On the mountain slopes that attract the eye
and where the gloriosa suffuses its fragrance,
the arrows of the archers fail not,
only because their modest wives
with soft, bamboo-like arms
never wrong their husbands
but are devoted single-mindedly to them.[106]

These ideas of chastity are given greater importance by the *Tirukkuṟaḷ* which attributes divine powers to a chaste woman. Her penance and greatness lie merely in her self-control and contentment, while her ideal or 'object of meditation' is her lord and the home that centres round him. A woman who is able to guard herself, her husband and her home morally is indeed endowed with extraordinary powers. Hence the *Kūraḷ*,

The woman who worships not God, but her husband,
when such a one says, 'Let there be rain',
it descends.[107]

This makes her seem as powerful as the sages who could curse or command the elements. The paragon of chastity, even in the Cańkam poems is *Aruntati* (Tamil) or *Arundhatī* (Sanskrit), the chaste wife of the sage Vasiṣṭha. She is transformed into a star (Alcor of the Great or Northern Bear) because of her purity. She is usually referred to as *vaṭamīṉ* or northern star and is used as a comparison for women of purity. A *Kalittokai* poem praises a woman thus:

> She is resplendent with chastity,
> fit to be revered and extolled,
> like the northern star.[108]

The *Paripāṭal* also uses the name Cāliṉi for this divine star that shines in the north.[109]

Such concepts of chastity pave the way for the great Kaṇṇaki. In the epic, she is introduced as a young maiden about to be married. Even at the outset the author seems to be conscious of her greatness as a chaste woman, for apart from mentioning her beauty, he sings her chastity as an important trait.

> She too,
> adored and praised by women saying,
> 'Her's is the praiseworthy form of Lakṣmī
> seated on a lotus;
> The greatness of the faultless Northern Star
> is like her chastity,'
> was desired by pure and lofty qualities.
> Kaṇṇaki is her name.[110]

The author has reversed the comparison, especially for chastity, in order to emphasise this quality in the heroine who is to become the Goddess of Chastity (*Pattiṉit-teyvam*). Her chastity is such that even Kavunti, the Jaina nun who would bow to no other than *Arhat*, is convinced that she is a goddess. Kavunti while asking a shepherdess to take care of Kaṇṇaki tells her,

> In the scorching heat of the sun,
> though trembling with pain,
> and faint with thirst,
> this great, creeper-like lady
> was oblivious to her own suffering

but thought only of her beloved's.
Apart from this excellent goddess
who has taken the vow of chastity
indispensable for women who are pleasant wives,
we have not seen a greater deity.
Don't you know that rains never fail,
prosperity does not decline
and victory of the great monarch does not diminish
in a country where virtuous women live?[111]

The priestess of Durgā too, in her trance, points to her and says:

She is the daughter of the Koṅku country,
the lady of the Kuṭaku hill,
the idol of the South.
She is the quintessence of *Tapas*.
She is like a great gem to the world,
—a great, divine gem.[112]

The divine power of her chastity is shown later in the epic when she confirms the tragic news of her husband's death and his innocence, with the Sun.

'The Lord of the scorching rays !
You know all that happens on this earth
girt with bouncing waves.
Is my husband a thief?'
'He is no thief,
Lady with black, carp-like eyes!
Blazing flames will consume this city.'[113]

In the court of the Pandya king she vows 'If I am a chaste woman (*pattiṉi*) I shall destroy Maturai with its king'[114] and later calls upon fire to consume the city which it does, showing thereby that not only the rain clouds but all the elements obey a chaste woman.

Mātavi does not command the elements but she is a chaste and loyal woman in spite of her birth in the *gaṇikā* class. Even after she realises that she has no right to share the joys and sorrows of Kōvalaṉ's life, her love for him, the only man in her life, does not diminish. This steadfast love raises her from the normal practices of courtesans and makes her virtuous and chaste. She renounces her life of leisure, wealth and art to become a Buddhist nun,[115] accepting till death a life of more deprivations and restrictions than that of a widow. She takes with her their daughter Maṇimēkalai who is also initiated as a nun in the Buddhist Saṅgha.[116] As such, Maṇimēkalai's relationship with the world is of an entirely different nature except for her attraction for Utayakumaraṉ who dies an untimely death.

The Sanskrit works examined do not seem to give much importance to this particular quality of their women. Aśvaghoṣa does mention that Yaśodharā is chosen to be the wife of Sarvārthasiddha, among other things, for the moral excellence of the family and her own chastity. She is called a *sādhvī* (chaste woman),[117] a *pativratā* (a woman loyal to her husband), and *guṇavatī*[118] (a woman endowed with virtues). But no such qualities are mentioned for Sundarī. Even in Bhāsa's plays, the *Svapnavāsavadattam* mentions that both the wives of Udayana are virtuous, but the term virtue is used in a general manner, for, in the same breath the *vidūṣaka* adds that Vāsavadattā has an additional virtue, that of giving him sweetmeats.[119] But in the depiction of Sītā, both Bhāsa and Kālidāsa have conformed to the Tamil concept of chastity. When Rāma in the *Pratimānāṭakam* asks Lakṣmaṇa to dissuade Sītā from following him to the forest, Lakṣmaṇa says that he would not dare to do so for it is 'an opportunity so laudable'.

> Moonlight follows the moon even in eclipse.
> When the forest tree falls, the creeper lies on the ground.
> The lord of elephants is not deserted by his mate
> though bogged in the mire.
> Let her make her pilgrimage practising virtue,
> for husbands are as gods to women.[120]

King Daśaratha in his lament after their departure to the forest refers to her as a devoted wife.[121] This is the only text among those under study in which the chaste woman is compared to Arundhatī. Rāvaṇa while disguised as an ascetic, tells Rāma:

> She alone is an Arundhatī among the women of the world,
> for they name thee with respect as her spouse.[122]

Later, Bharata while enquiring from Sumantara of Rāma, Lakṣmaṇa and Sītā, asks 'Have you seen the double of Arundhatī's good character?'[123] An ascetic at Janasthāna praises her as being, 'pure and chaste as the gods, as seers divine and perfected saints'.[124]

Sumitrā, asking of them from Sumantara, says, 'child as she is . . . she is no child in conduct.'[125] The idea and sentiment in this remark is very much like those expressed by a foster-mother in a *Naṟṟiṇai* poem.

> In childhood,
> the nurse holding in one hand
> a vessel full of milk and honey,
> and in the other, a little flower-soft stick,
> bade her drink.
> But she refusing,
> toddled around the shed with her tinkling anklets
> to be chased around
> by the aging nurse.
> How did such a playful girl come to possess
> such knowledge and decorum
> in family matters?
> Now she refuses the luxuriant rice
> from her father's house.
> She is happy to take irregular meals
> as scarce as trickling water.[126]

In both, the Indian woman's ability to share the lot of her husband happily, even in times of hardship is expressed clearly.

Kālidāsa refers to Sītā as *sādhvī*[127] (a chaste woman), *śuddha*[128] (pure, chaste), *patidevatā*[129] (one to whom her husband is god) and *satī*[130] (virtuous or chaste woman). After returning from the forest, when Sītā falls at the feet of her mothers-in-law saying that she has been the cause of her husband's sufferings in the forests, they contradict her with the words,

> Rise, O Daughter,
> Why? Was it not on the contrary
> by your own virtuous conduct
> that your husband got safe
> through the great calamity
> with his brother?[131]

This is comparable to the *Kalittokai* poem mentioned earlier.[132] Even Sītā's request to Mother Earth,

> If there is no transgression (in my conduct)

towards my husband
in thought, word or deed,
O Goddess who sustains all !
Please contain me within you [133]

seems to be merely a negative and meeker expression of the sentiment found in Kaṇṇaki's vow at the Pandyan court.

The love and loyalty of Vasantasenā, ever since she first saw Cārudatta, is not to be doubted. But her life before she meets him has been that of a *gaṇikā*, for her maid (*ceṭī*) who has served her for at least sometime before she meets Cārudatta, seeing her dressed up asks, 'Since the livelihood of a *gaṇikā* is unnecessary (*aprayojana*) you must be in love with someone.' This suggests that dressing up to please others and earning a living[134] through her charms and good looks had been her normal way of life till she met him. But now that she loves him, such a life is not necessary or desirable any more. Urvaśī, the dancer at Indra's court is loyal to Purūravas, though she would have known other men (or *devas*) in Indraloka besides the men whose excellent *tapas* made Indra jealous enough to send her, like other *apsarās*, to seduce and thereby make them lose all their religious merits.[135] She is wont to continue her position and function as an important danseuse when she returns to the court of Indra after the death of Purūravas. Though she is loyal to her husband and loves him intensely, she cannot be compared to the wives who are also depicted as loving mothers, for in order that she may stay longer with her husband she hides the news of her son's birth (an heir to his line) from her husband and allows the child to grow up in a hermitage.[136] Her only excuse is that she cannot bear to be separated from Purūravas.

All other heroines, though not described in specific terms, are certainly chaste women with great love and loyalty towards their husbands. But we must bear in mind that the word *chastity* did not mean exactly the same thing to the Ancient Tamils and the Indo-Āryans. To the Tamils chastity was so important that *mullai*, the pastoral region and the aspect of love ascribed to it, viz., *iruttal* or patient waiting of the wife are identified with this virtue. The *mullai* blooms themselves became symbolic of conjugal felicity and chastity so that wives are said to wear the jasmine or *mullai* flowers as a sign of chastity. In poetry, they became meaningful similes, like: 'Chastity as perfect as the *mullai*' (flowers).[137]

These white and fragrant flowers are symbolic of the purity and fame virtuous women possessed. The Indo-Āryans did not stress perfect purity in their women. To them sons were important for various reasons, most of all to perform religious rites for the dead parents. So a woman who could not have a son by her husband was allowed to have one by his brother or a male relative of his family. This, they felt, would make the son a true descendant of her husband's line (*sagotra*). This practice called levirate or *niyoga* was also allowed in the case of young widows who were childless or had no sons.[138] Besides, to them loyalty seems to have been restricted to the period beginning with marriage and ending with the death of the husband. The *Śatapatha Brāhmaṇa* relates that during the marriage ceremony the bride is asked for the names or at least the number of lovers she had. After she indicates by holding the appropriate number of stalks of grass, certain ceremonies are again performed and these are believed to expiate her of her sins.[139] Sukanyā given in marriage to a 'descrepit and ghostlike man' turns away the handsome Aśvins who desire to win her love, saying, 'I shall not forsake my husband while he is alive, to whom my father gave me,'[140] implying of course that such loyalty is commendable and that it is not necessary to continue being loyal to him after his death. Even in the *Mahābhārata* we have the practice of *niyoga* as seen in the lineage of the Kauravas and the birth of the Pāṇḍavas. Damayantī herself who had been reluctant to leave Nala in the forest in spite of his request to do so, prepares for a second *svayamvara*. Whatever her own reasons are for holding it, the kings and the princes are not deterred by the fact that she was previously married and had children.[141] But we also notice that Damayantī, Sāvitrī and Sītā are treated in some ways as being powerful because of their chastity. The slow but steady intermixture of cultural ideas must have already begun and the stories in the *Mahābhārata* and the *purāṇas* which extol chaste women must have been the result of this. By the time the texts under study were written some concepts had become accepted as norms but had not become as important as they were in the Tamil texts. So Sītā alone is extolled in these texts because of such respectful treatment accorded to her in the *Rāmāyaṇa*.

Modesty

In love poetry, another characteristic of the heroine which is treated as being important is modesty or shyness (*nāṇam* in Tamil and *lajjā* or *vinaya* in Sanskrit). The concept of maidenly reserve in Tamil poetry is explained by Tolkāppiyar:

> Since modesty and shyness are found in the woman in love,
> her desires are seen only in her gestures
> and not spoken explicitly.[142]

This means that she is shy to discuss her love with anyone except perhaps her friend and feels shy in the presence of her lover. A youth who is attracted to a maiden, finding her shy and reserved, asks her:

> You do not respond to my words
> but bend your lovely face in modesty.
> If love wells up all of a sudden
> is it easy (for me) to bear it?[143]

This modesty is a quality that is inborn in girls and comes to light when they come of age. A *tōḻi*, trying to point to her friend's lover that their lengthened period of clandestine courtship is becoming the topic of gossip (*alar*) of the village, also makes clear that they are therefore made to abandon their maidenly reserve which had been with them for a long time.[144] She also tries to point out to the hero that forsaking modesty is like a good, chaste woman giving away her child.[145] Even after marriage this forms an important quality that tempers the love life of the chaste wife and she is not happy to lose it on any account. A wife, explaining to her friend why she refuses to allow her philandering husband to enter the house, says:

> Though living in the same town
> He does not come to this section.
> Even when he does,
> He doesn't embrace me properly.
> He moves away uncaringly
> Like one seeing a stranger's grave,
> so that love, that has destroyed modesty
> and caused (me) to lose good sense

has gone far away
like an arrow discharged from a bow.[146]

Because it acts as a check on love and in the case of clandestine lovers, on their meetings, there is often a tension between love and modesty. It does not mean that in such cases the women are actually devoid of this quality, but merely that they are reduced to such straits that it is the hero's duty to protect them and to prevent any action that might cause them to lose their decorum and decency.

Even when love triumphs over modesty, it only means that she would meet her lover in secret. One maiden pities her modesty which has kept her company for so long but is being destroyed by love.

Modesty is to be pitied
for it has suffered long with me.
Like the small, high sandbank
of the white-flowered sugar-cane
that erodes and falls due to the lashing of water,
it endured as long as it could,
but pressed by love, it will abandon me.[147]

A youth who has been fortunate enough to meet his beloved is aware of this tension and the final triumph of love.

The dark beauty with soft beautiful tresses
fragrant with the flowers that bloom with rain
on the profit-yielding hill of Ōri
covered with jack trees abundant in fruits,
came and showed me favour.
For, like the floods after rain
that cannot be contained by a dam of salt
her love was not contained by the bounds of modesty.
May she live long![148]

Yet this modesty prevents the maiden from talking about her love to her mother or disclosing it to the others. One heroine relates to her friend how, seeing her pale and ill, her mother lovingly asked her what was wrong and she nearly told the truth, forgetting her maidenly reserve which is dearer than life itself.[149] This was in keeping with Tolkāppiyar's evaluation of modesty and chastity, for, he was of the opinion that maidenly reserve (*nāṇam*) is more valued than life itself but chastity is valued more than maidenly reserve itself.[150] This concept of modesty is sometimes used by the friend of the heroine to persuade the hero to ask for the lady's hand in marriage without delay. One such friend asks the heroine, knowing very well that the hero is within hearing distance,

> Transgressing mother's strict watch
> and going beyond the large gateway
> into the village square,
> during the daytime for many to see,
> shall we ask openly,
> 'Where is his village
> adjoining large fields?'[151]

She uses the term *vāyviṭṭu* meaning 'to speak clearly without any reservation' so that the hero would know the dire state that prompts them to even think of such an action.

Often the friend who is also a constant companion would know of the affair and this would make it easier for the heroine. Sometimes the heroine herself might relate it subtly to the friend. The companion would then inform her own mother or the heroine's mother and make arrangements for the wedding. But there are instances when out of fear and their maidenly reserve they cannot discuss this with their mothers and they decide that the heroine elopes with the hero. This aspect of love known as *uṭaṉpōkku* is dealt with by many Caṅkaṃ poems, for the *Akanāṉūṟu* collection alone contains 36 poems on this aspect. From these poems we are able to gather the reason for the elopement. The main reason is fear of the mother who is strict about such matters,[152] or the fear of marriage to someone else.[153] This elopement is also considered an act that transgresses maidenly reserve but is thought necessary by the girls to safeguard their chastity. Quite often their fear is unfounded for usually the mothers later bewail the fact that they had been ignorant about their daughters' choice. One mother, however, hears many times of her daughter's connection with a particular youth but keeps quiet fearing that she might feel ill at ease due to her modesty (*nāṇuvaḷ*) and when the daughter goes away without the parents' knowledge, the mother blames herself for having kept quiet.[154]

The Sanskrit works do not seem to give much importance to this quality though it is mentioned as a praiseworthy trait found in the heroines. Of the two heroines in Aśvaghoṣa's works, only Yaśodharā's qualities, suitable for a loving spouse and mother are mentioned. So among other commendable qualities we also find modesty or a sense of decorum (*vinaya*) mentioned in one single word.[155] Among Bhāsa's heroines, we have no opportunity to know of Vāsavadattā's behaviour before marriage, and even after marriage, we only know her in separation and disguise. In the case of Padmāvatī, though she is attracted to Udayana because of his fame, she does not meet him before marriage. However when he is discussed by the maids and Vāsavadattā is dragged into the conversation, Padmāvatī keeps a decorous silence and only makes a noncommital remark:

> He is not, of course, inaccessible to the people
> and beauty fascinates the hearts of all.

She falls silent when her betrothal to Udayana is announced by the nurse.[156] The nurse in the *Avimārakam*, who is anxious over Kuraṅginī's malady, finds that the Princess is 'particularly unusual' for she has not disclosed to anyone what is really wrong with her, and wonders if she is ashamed of her behaviour or even afraid. But her friend and daughter of the nurse, Nalinikā asserts that the Princess told her everything[157] though how and when she confided in her friend is not known. This might have helped us in assessing this trait in her. Later in the company of her maids she is afraid that she might give herself away[158] and when her friend whispers something in her ear (obviously that Avimāraka would come to her apartment that night) she exclaims, 'I am afraid my virtue is lost' (*hīnaṃ cāritram*).[159] There are no stage directions to show if she is shy or bashful about it.

Among Kālidāsa's heroines, Pārvatī is seen to observe this decorum when questioned by Śiva in the guise of an ascetic as to the actual purpose of her severe penance. She is unable to speak of her love for Śiva, so she looks at her friend who explains to him that Pārvatī's love for Śiva is the cause of her austerities. But she herself confirms these words though with difficulty (*kathaṃ cit*), after rehearsing the speech in her mind for a long time.[160] This *lajjā* again manifests itself in her when the Śaptarṣis come to ask for her hand in marriage to Śiva.[161] In the *Raghuvaṃśam*, Indumatī is portrayed as being modest and bashful during her *svayamvara* but when her companion Sunandā completes her run-down on each of the suitors present, she has to subdue her feeling of *lajjā* and choose Prince Aja as her husband.[162] During the wedding ceremony she is the typical bashful bride (*lajjāvatī*).[163] Śakuntalā however, seems to be more akin to the Tamil heroines in this matter. While the king and her friends discuss her parentage, she keeps quiet but the stage direction clearly states that she showed 'amorous bashfulness' (*śṛṅgāra-lajjā*).[164] The description of her state by Duṣyanta:

> Although she mingles not her speech with mine
> Yet when I speak, she turns her ear directly opposite to me.
> Granted that she does not stand with her face turned towards mine,
> nevertheless, her eyes for the most part
> are not turned towards any other object,[165]

or

> She averted her eyes when I stood facing her
> And she smiled (as it were) from some other cause.
> Hence love whose course was checked by modesty
> was neither fully displayed (by her) nor yet wholly concealed,[166]

is comparable to that of a heroine in the *Tirukkuṟaḷ*.

> When I look at her she looks at the ground;
> When I don't, she looks (on me) and smiles gently.[167]

He uses the words *vinaya* (modesty) and *apragalbha* (reserved). Mālavikā feels shy (*lajjā*) because she is in love with the king whose feelings are not known to her and it is made worse because she has not the courage to speak about it to her friend.[168] Urvaśī states very clearly that she had cast aside her *lajjā* when she came to meet the king,[169] who could not have gone in search of her anyway. But her position as an *apsarā* also makes it impossible for her to observe such codes of decorum. It is noteworthy that this quality is not mentioned for Vasantasenā.

Like chastity, this quality of modesty seems to have been more important in Tamil poetry, for it is considered the basis for chastity. This is clearly stated in the *Puṟanāṉūṟu* poem: 'Chastity which does not exist without modesty.'[170] There are no synonyms for the word chastity (*kaṟpu*) in Tamil. Besides a number of situations are made possible by this quality as are some aspects of love poetry itself. In Sanskrit literature it is merely an additional trait that makes the heroine seem innocent in matters relating to love and helps to intensify the love and longing of the hero. As a result, though this characteristic is important to both Tamil and Sanskrit love literatures, its role is somewhat different in each case.

Education

Though these heroines are from well-to-do families, it is difficult to ascertain the exact amount of formal education or accomplishments in the various arts that they may have acquired. The Caṅkam poems show that the arts like music and dance are usually indulged in, in groups, though occasional references to wives of respectable families or heroines singing are also found. An *Akanāṉūṟu* poem mentions that a *kuṟava* maid sings the *kuṟiñci* tune so sweetly that the elephant which is eating the crops in the field is overcome by the melody and it dozes off as it stands. Her knowledge of music helps her guard the crops without having to wake her husband who happens to be asleep at that time.[171] Usually the songs and dances were religious, social or occupational in nature. For instance, the young heroine guarding the millet field with her friends sings while keeping watch, for the song is useful in keeping the birds away. The tune perhaps is such as to frighten away the parrots and it is known as the *kiḷi kaṭi pāṭal*.[172] A warrior's wife seems to have sung the *kāñcī* tune to the accompaniment of the flute and the lute in order to keep away the evil spirits which were believed to harm wounded people.[173] Since the sad *viḷari* tune was believed to keep the kites away from the corpses, another warrior's widow entreats the musicians to play the appropriate music so that she can sing the tune and protect the body of her late husband.[174] But we find that sometimes, when young maidens indulge in such songs, they sing the praises of the hill or country belonging to the hero who has won the heart of their friend, the heroine. The usual song is the *vaḷḷai* which is sung when they husk or pound grain.[175] This song is usually about the deities they worship, the king or chieftain (who is normally the father or brother of the heroine) or her lover and his country or hill. This song is not considered an artistic accomplishment for its own sake but is something common and had its special purpose in love poetry. The mention of the hero's name or his place of residence may give rise to gossip which can be made use of by the companion (*tōḻi)* to persuade the hero to expedite the marriage.[176] Sometimes the hero overhearing them sing of him and his cruelty because of his delay in marrying her, would ask for her hand without further delay.[177] There is also a *Kalittokai* poem that describes how the heroine feels so much relief and happiness because they had sung of the hero.

> When we sang his praises (together),
> my friend's emaciated, gentle upper arms
> filled out,
> just as if the chieftain
> of the bamboo-swaying slopes
> had shown his favour.[178]

The two types of dance common among the Caṅkam Tamils seem to be the *tuṇaṅkai* and the *kuravai* and both are in the nature of folk dances in which both sexes participate. Often a youth who is interested in a particular girl would dance beside her and this is one way of making the others know of his interest in her. But apart from this ability to create situations useful in love poetry, the knowledge of song and dance is of no particular importance in the relationship of the hero and the heroine.[179] In the urban areas or the *marutam* or agricultural districts, decorum also prevented the wives or heroines from participating in such dances and we find that a separate group of women cultivated this art so that they filled the need for diversion among wealthy men. This situation is well depicted in the epic *Cilappatikāram* where Kaṇṇaki is portrayed as the good, chaste wife. But Kōvalaṉ attracted by the dance and music of Mātavi buys the emerald necklace and along with it her services. The arts are considered necessary for her so that she learns song, dance and the art of make-up for seven years and also receives training in the sixty-four arts.[180] Yet, when she discards her life as a courtesan she makes sure that her daughter Maṇimēkalai has no opportunity to have any connection with the arts.

The heroines of the Sanskrit texts under study also are knowledgeable in these arts though the *kāvyas* of Aśvaghoṣa do not depict Yaśodharā or Sundarī as having any practice or knowledge of the arts. In Bhāsa's plays, some heroines seem to have known music. Vāsavadattā is interested in learning to play the lute and in spite of her father's opinion:

> What does she want a teacher for, just when about to be married? Her husband will teach her,[181]

she seems to have gone to Uttarā, a lady musician for lessons on the Nārada lute, and later learns from Udayana. This intensifies the grief of Udayana when he sees his lute Goṣavatī which was lost at the same time as the reported death of his queen. Besides music, Vāsavadattā is also accomplished in other ways. She is able to string flowers together into lovely garlands and this is made use of in the play to heighten her sorrow and sacrifice by making her weave the wedding garland for Padmāvatī and Udayana.[182] Padmāvatī and other heroines of Bhāsa, other than Vasantasenā are not shown as being proficient or keen in the arts. Even among Kālidāsa's heroines, Mālavikā may be said to be the only human heroine proficient in song and dance. This again could have been due to her position as a maid in the palace with the function of pleasing and entertaining the queen. Irāvatī too learns dancing under a different teacher but her ability is not shown on the stage. We are however informed that her skill does not measure up to that of Mālavikā.[183] The *yakṣī* is depicted as trying to divert herself by playing on the *vīṇā* and singing a song that she herself had composed with the words so arranged to signify her husband's name. This shows her musical talent though at the time of her separation from her husband it is not of much use to her.[184] Vasantasenā is a *gaṇikā* and hence proficient in various arts. The *viṭa* chasing her through the streets of the capital refers specifically to her skill in dancing.[185] He is also convinced that because she had learnt the arts, and acted on many stages (*raṅgapraveśena kalā*) she could change her voice to suit the character depicted.[186] Later in the play, she is clearly called an actress or *nāṭakastrī*.[187] Urvaśī's knowledge of the fine arts does not receive much treatment in the *Vikramorvaśīyam*. Only her acting in the play *Lakṣmīsvayamvaram* is mentioned, for her preoccupation with her thoughts of Purūravas makes her mention his name in the course of the drama instead of the name Puruṣottama. For this she is cursed by the sage Bharata in Indra's court to lose her divine power. Though Indra later grants her the boon of returning to his realm, this curse enables her to leave Indraloka and live with Purūravas.[188] The arts do not seem to have been very necessary for the heroines though many are skilled in at least one of them, the favourite being music.

As discussed in chapter 1, the *Kalittokai* poems deal with heroines who do not conform to the characteristics mentioned above. For example the hunchbacked woman in the *Kalittokai* poem is by no means beautiful. Her youth and chastity seem doubtful. She is compared to a skinned stork. This suggests that she is lean besides being bent and probably past the prime of youth. Her boast that she is 'desired more than sweetmeats made of blackgram' and that there were many men who were prepared to protect her and to embrace her crooked form shows her lack of modesty if not chastity.[189] Yet such women are elevated to the position of heroines in love poems and this is something peculiar to the *Kalittokai* collection.

On the other hand, the Sanskrit dramas which deal with heroines from royal households (except for Vasantasenā who is a *gaṇikā,* Śakuntalā who is Kṣatriya by virtue of being Viśvāmitra's daughter and Urvaśī who is an *apsarā*) classify them with the children, the afflicted, the illiterates, the low-born characters, the servants and those who are intoxicated,[190] from the point of view of the language to be used in their conversation. A *gaṇikā* or an *apsarā* (or *devagaṇikā*) must have been educated enough to converse intelligently and with authority on various subjects. Even Śakuntalā, who grew up in a hermitage which is usually considered an equivalent to a residential school in its own way, could not have lacked the necessary education to speak the Sanskrit language. But convention made it necessary and we find that all heroines are made to speak the Prākṛt dialect. Such conventions regarding the use of different languages or dialects are not found in Tamil literature.

REFERENCES

1. V. Swaminathaiyar's 5th edn., 1957, p. 133.
2. V. Swaminathaiyar, *Kuṟuntokai,* 1962, p. 22.
3. *Kurun,* 360:6; *Akam,* 58:5, *Kali,* 48:11; *Aink,* 282:2, 296:1, 300:1.
4. *Kurun,* 335:5-7.

5. *Akam*, 132:4-8.
6. *Nar*, 102:8.
7. *Ibid.*, 44:12.
8. *Kali*, 50:11-14; also see *Kali*, 56; *Aink*, 255-60.
9. *Aink*, 401-10, 442:4-5; *Akam*, 24:17-18, 44:1-4, 54:1-3.
10. *Nar*, 42:6.
11. *Aink*, 408, also 410.
12. *Ibid.*, 421:3.
13. *Ibid.*, 424:1.
14. *Ibid.*, 430:3.
15. *Kali*, 117:6.
16. *Ibid.*, 108:30-33.
17. *Aink*, 81:5, 87:3, 86:4; *Nar*, 100:7.
18. *Akam*, 176:20; *Aink*, 66:4.
19. *Kali*, 71:14.
20. *Ibid.*, 71:10; *Akam*, 56:13.
21. *Nar*, 101:8.
22. *Aink*, 363:2, 364:1.
23. *TTP*, p. 79.
24. *TTP*, p. 35.
25. *Svap*, *TTP*, p. 42.
26. *Avim*, p. 30.
27. *TTP*, p. 157.
28. *Vikr*, p. 57.
29. *Mala*, p. 141.
30. *Ragh*, 1:31-33.
31. *Ibid.*, 5:39, 40.
32. *Abhi*, p. 28, 29.
33. *Cilap*, 1:23.
34. *Mani*, 3:1-6, 4:67-68.
35. *TTP*, pp. 78, 86.
36. *Ibid.*, p. 151.
37. *Vikr*, pp. 5, 7.
38. *Ragh*, 16:79-85.
39. *Megh*, p. 7.
40. *Kuma*, 1:21, 53.
41. *Ragh*, 11:14, 15, 13:26.
42. *Kurun*, 119.
43. Women were divided into 7 age groups: (1) *Pētai*, 7 years and less, (2) *Petumpai*, 11-12 years, (3) *Maṅkai*, 12-17 years, (4) *Maṭantai*, 19-24 years, (5) *Arivai*, 25-30 years, (6) *Terivai*, 31-39 years, (7) *Pēriḷampeṇ*, 40 years and above. *Tamil Lexicon*, also D. Nadarajah, *Women in Tamil Society*, p. 46.
44. *Nar*, 155.
45. *Kurun*, 242:4; *Aink*, 415:1, 427:1, 462:3, 491:3.
46. *Mulai*, 30-31.
47. *Akam*, 7:1-13.
48. *Cilap*, 1:21-29.
49. *Ibid.*, 3:10-11, 164-69.

50. *Mani*, 4:125, 5:1, 11:53, 57, 146, 19:15, 21:12.
51. *Ibid.*, 22:181.
52. *Ibid.*, 23:27-30.
53. *Saun*, 6:16.
54. *TTP*, p. 18, 26-27.
55. *Ibid.*, p. 47.
56. *Ibid.*, p. 56.
57. *Ibid.*, p. 81.
58. *Ibid.*, p. 170.
59. *Avim*, pp. 48-49.
60. *Mala*, p. 150. act 5 v. 16.
61. *Abhi*, p. 128. act 5 v. 1.
62. *Ragh*, 5:39, 11:38-40.
63. *Ibid.*, 16:83.
64. *Abhi*, pp. 17-19.
65. *Mala*, p. 115, v. 15.
66. *Kuma*, 1:31, 32.
67. *Kurun*, 125.
68. *Ibid.*, 245:2-4.
69. *Ibid.*, 280.
70. *Cilap*, 2:53-61.
71. *Ibid.*, 3:157.
72. *Ibid.*, 8:74-108.
73. *Ibid.*, 6:76-108.
74. *Mani*, 4:97-104.
75. *Ibid.*, 3:20-25.
76. *Ibid.*, 4:65-67.
77. *Ibid.*, 25:7-10.
78. *Budd*, 2:26.
79. *Saun*, 4:3-5.
80. *TTP*, p. 68. act 6 v. 13.
81. *Ibid.*, pp. 44, 45. act 4 v. 4.
82. *Ibid.*, p. 56.
83. *Ibid.*, p. 77. act 1 v. 9.
84. *Ibid.*, p. 83. act 1 v. 27.
85. *Ibid.*, 160
86. *Ibid.*, p. 189. act 5 v. 16.
87. *Avim.*, p. 82.
88. *Ibid.*, p. 103.
89. *Ragh*, 1:46.
90. *Ibid.*, 6:11, 29.
91. *Ibid.*, 13:57, 13:24.
92. *Kuma*, 1:31ff and 49.
93. *Ibid.*, 5:20, 21.
94. *Megh*, U. 22.
95. *Abhi*, act 1 v. 18-21.
96. *Ibid.*, p. 51.
97. *Mala*, p. 7.

98. *Ibid.*, p. 37.
99. *Vikr*, p. 109 v. 9.
100. *Kali*, 94.
101. *Kurun*, 10.
102. *Ibid.*, 338:7.
103. *Patir*, 16:10.
104. *Kurun*, 252:4.
105. *Akam*, 184:1.
106. *Kali*, 39:1-18.
107. *Kural*, 55.
108. *Kali*, 2:21.
109. *Pari*, 5:43-44.
110. *Cliap*, 1:25-29.
111. *Ibid.*, 15:139-48.
112. *Ibid.*, 12:47-50.
113. *Ibid.*, 18:50-53.
114. *Ibid.*, 21:36-37.
115. *Ibid.*, 27:103-108.
116. *Mani*, 2:55-57.
117. *Budd*, 2:26.
118. *Ibid.*, 6:33.
119. *TTP*, pp. 55, 56.
120. *Ibid.*, act 1 v. 25. p. 165.
121. *Ibid.*, p. 168.
122. *Ibid.*, p. 187.
123. *Ibid*, p. 193.
124. *Ibid*, p. 197.
125. *Ibid.*, p. 170.
126. *Nar*, 110.
127. *Ragh*, 14:51, 86.
128. *Ibid.*, 14:14.
129. *Ibid.*, 14:17.
130. *Ibid.*, 14:58.
131. *Ibid.*, 14:6.
132. See above fn. 107.
133. *Ragh*, 15:81.
134. *TTP*, pp. 84-85.
135. *Vikr*, act 1. p. 4.
136. *Ibid.*, act 5. pp.142ff.
137. *Ciru*, 30: *Akam*, 274:13-14; *Nar*, 42:10-11.
138. Max-Müller, *The Sacred Books of the East*, vol. 2, Oxford, 1896, pp. 165-66, 270-71.
139. *Ibid.*, vol. 26 OUP Rep. 1963. p. 275.
140. *Ibid.*, vol. 12. OUP Rep. 1963. pp. 396-97.
141. D.P. Malaviya, *Nalopakhyana*, Allahabad, 1958, p. 65, vv. 1-4.
142. *Tol. Porul*, 116.
143. *Nar*, 39:1-3.
144. *Ibid.*, 15:9-10.

145. *Ibid.*, 15:7-10.
146. *Kurun*, 231.
147. *Ibid.*, 149.
148. *Akam*, 208:18-24.
149. *Nar*, 17.
150. *Tol. Porul*, 111:1-2.
151. *Nar*, 365:1-5.
152. *Akam*, 145:20-22, 203:8-9.
153. *Ibid.*, 221.
154. *Ibid.*, 203:4-6.
155. *Budd*, 2:26.
156. *TTP*, p. 48.
157. *Avim*, act 2. pp. 50-51.
158. *Ibid.*, act 3. p. 62.
159. *Ibid.*, act 3. p. 66.
160. *Kuma*, 5:52, 63-64.
161. *Ibid.*, 6:91.
162. *Ragh*, 6:80.
163. *Ibid.*, 7:25.
164. *Abhi*, act 1. p. 26.
165. *Ibid.*, act 1 v. 31.
166. *Ibid.*, act 2 v. 11. p. 54.
167. *Kural*, 1094.
168. *Mala*, act 3, pp. 56-58.
169. *Vikr*, p. 38.
170. *Puram*, 169:12-13.
171. *Akam*, 102:4-9.
172. *Ibid.*, 118:13.
173. *Puram*, 218:5-9.
174. *Ibid.*, 219.
175. *Kurun*, 89; *Kali*, 41, 42.
176. *Kurun*, 89.
177. *Kali*, 40.
178. *Ibid.*, 43:29-31.
179. *Kurun*, 33. See Swaminathaiyar's Commentary.
180. *Cilap*, 3:8, 8:64.
181. *TTP*, p. 18.
182. *Ibid.*, p. 50.
183. *Mala*, p. 30. act 3.
184. *Megh*, U. 26.
185. *TTP*, p. 77.
186. *Ibid.*, p. 81.
187. *Ibid.*, p. 83.
188. *Vikr*, act 3.
189. *Kali*, 94.
190. Surendra Nath Shastri, *The Laws and Practice of Sanskrit Drama*, Varanasi, 1961, pp. 313-14.

Chapter 5

The Harlots

Even a heroine of much beauty, culture and charm is often not able to keep the hero faithful to her for life. Both the Tamil and Indo-Āryan societies seem to have tolerated polygamy. This tolerance as well as the position of the courtesan or harlot is depicted in most of the poems and dramas depicting love. Neither polygamy nor the company of courtesans and harlots is mandatory, for we have heroes in both Sanskrit and Tamil literature who are faithful to their wives. Ollaiyūr Tanta Pūtappāṇṭiyaṉ for example, considers it a great misery and disgrace to be separated from his queen,[1] while Chola king Nalaṅkiḷḷi thinks it most degrading and disgraceful to embrace the loveless harlots.[2] Udayana would not think of a marriage with Padmāvatī even to save his country and people, till his wife's death is faked. Aja would have happily followed his wife in her death, if it were not for reasons of propriety and a sense of duty to his country. Rāma has always been considered to be the symbol of fidelity in love and marriage. All Caṅkam heroes of the *mullai* poems are shown to be thinking only of their wives at home, and sometimes the child as well, on their journey home. This, as well as the emotion for the *mullai* poems, *iruttal* or chastity, suggests that the patient waiting is mutual. But the societies depicted in both literatures, though accepting the norm suggested by the above-mentioned heroes, do not seem to have blamed or looked down upon those who did not measure up to the ideal. They allowed the men more sexual freedom than the women from respectable families who were chosen to be wives. The same standard of morality was not enforced for both sexes. As long as he did not forsake his wife or the family, the man was not considered to have gone aganist *dharma* or *aṟam* if he cherished women other than his wife.

Some might have even thought that it was good from the point of view of sensual pleasures (*kāma* or *iṉpam*). A Caṅkam poet sings that if soldiers die in action, they enjoy the favours of faultless women in heaven.[3] A life with plenty of wine and women is mentioned as pleasurable and some poets bless kings with words like the following:

> Great One !
> May you live joyously
> drinking the cool, fragrant wine
> offered in golden goblets
> by women decked with bright bangles.[4]

But these women need not necessarily be his wives, for many a poem sings of a king's association with other women as a way of singing his pre-eminence in love. A *Patiṟṟuppattu* poem praises a Chera king's generosity. Then it describes how he begs his wife to give him the little, red *kuvaḷai* flower that she is about to throw at him because of her anger at his having danced with other women and fails to get that flower. It then ends in a note of wonder for how could such a king succeed in overcoming other kings and capturing their forts with sky-scraping walls?[5] The aim of this poem is to sing the king's generosity (*koṭaic ciṟappu*), his pre-eminence in love (*kāmac ciṟappu* or *iṉpac ciṟappu*) and his victory in war (*veṟṟic ciṟappu*). This tradition is also found in Sanskrit literature, especially while describing the kings sporting in the rivers or lakes. They are said to sport with many women from the inner or women's apartment (*antaḥpura*). At the *svayamvara* of Indumatī, the maid appointed to relate the characteristics and greatness of each of the suitors present, shows to the princess, Suṣeṇa, the king of the Sūrasenas, whose fame had spread even in the next world and is the light (*vaṃsadīpam*) of his father's and mother's line. Then she speaks of the sacrifices he had performed and his valour and adds that the waters of the Yamunā change colour because of the sandal paste that is washed off from the bosoms of his women from the inner apartment (*avarodha*) during water-sport.[6] This too, is obviously mentioned as showing his eminence in the performance of his religious duties, in valour and his love-life. These two instances may be an indication that such descriptions are not necessarily a depiction of the particular king's actual life but a traditional way of singing a king's greatness.

Apart from such general references to the hero's association with women other than his wife, we have instances of kings as well as heroes from other social or caste groups who seek the company of other women. Five *Puranāṉūṟu* poems are devoted to advising King Pēkaṉ to return to his home and his wife Kaṇṇaki and not to tarry longer at Nallūr with his new-found companion.[7] All poems in the *marutat tiṇai* deal with the sulks and anger of the heroine or her friend, the *tōḻi* because of the hero's infidelity. The epic *Cilappatikāram*, though deifying Kaṇṇaki, evolves round Kōvalaṉ's attraction for the *kaṇikai* Mātavi. Agnimitra and Duṣyanta fall in love in spite of having married more than once previously. Cārudatta too is attracted by Vasantasenā. These suggest that extra-marital relations or polygyny was existent in both societies. The monogamous heroes mentioned above and their aversion to such relationships show that monogamy must have been accepted as the ideal, though an ideal not attained by many men. Even the *Kāmasūtra* which specialises on *kāma* or sexual enjoyment states, 'union with women who are of a lower caste or who are excommunicated or with those once married and later deserted or widowed or with courtesans is neither commended nor condemned since this relationship is entered into for mere pleasure.'[8] This may be accepted as the general view of both societies, though Tamil literature refers to all women other than the heroine or wife as *parattaiyar* or harlots. These *parattaiyar* are of many types.

Kāmakkiḻattiyar

Of the Tamil poems under study, none mentions that a hero took a mistress or sought the company of other women for the sake of having children or male heirs. The wife is always depicted as a mother as well, and referred to as the *talaivi*. She is also called the *illakkiḻatti* or the mistress of the home. But some heroes seem to have taken a mistress or *kāmakkiḻatti* (the mistress of desire).[9] Though the mistress too loves the hero, behaves like the heroine in checking his faults and misses him when he goes on long journeys,[10] her position is never exalted in Tamil literature to that of a wife. When the hero feels annoyed with his chief wife for having pointed out his faults or chided him for them, the secondary wife sometimes takes her side and points out to him that the mother of his children has the right to chide him for his faults and to make him a better man. She tries to pacify him and to make him realize the rights of his wife.[11]

Unlike in Sanskrit literature, the wife and the mistress in Tamil literature are always shown as living in separate establishments, but often close by, for there are references to the latter playing with the hero's son and even carrying him and going to visit his mother.[12] Sometimes when the husband spends a great deal of his time in the company of harlots and the wife is hurt or annoyed about it, the mistress tries to pacify her. One such woman says:

> Do not be annoyed with him.
> You are a woman of beauty and goodness.
> But people do not call him a man.
> They say he is like the bee
> that sucks honey
> even from the flowers
> that bloom in the tanks at night.[13]

By this she tries to make the wife realize that if he courted new women each day, it is not because of any defects on her part but simply because he has his weakness—women—and he has to be accepted as he is, weakness and all. The exact manner in which the hero distributes his time between his wife and the mistress or mistresses is not known. But in each case the chief wife knows of the mistress if there is one and in the course of time she gets used to the idea and does not seem to have grudged his absence from home occasionally on her account, for she even thinks of her as a mother of her own child and considers her as one like herself.[14] Tolkāppiyar generally talks of one *kāmakkilatti* and when talking of the chief wife and mistress, refers to both of them as 'the two' (*iruvar*).[15]

When looked at from this point of view, Sanskrit heroines like Mālavikā and Śakuntalā cannot be classified as heroines for Dhāriṇī and Vasumatī would be the heroines as the chief wives while Mālavikā and Śakuntalā, being women loved by the heroes of the respective plays, can only be considered as mistresses or at best secondary wives. But Sanskrit literature usually treats them with more respect than Tamil literature does. In both the dramas, *Mālavikāgnimitram* and *Abhijñānaśākuntalam*, Irāvatī and Haṃsapadikā are, however, given their actual status as secondary wives or *kāmakkiḻattiyar*. True to Sanskrit tradition, they are depicted as being proud of their youth and given to sensuous pleasures. When Irāvatī comes to know of Agnimitra's love for Mālavikā she is openly angry, hurt and jealous and in an attempt to stop the affair, she complains to Dhāriṇī.[16] Dhāriṇī, on the other hand, is anxious to stop it too but tries to do so in a more mature and dignified manner.[17] The younger queen is angry over the king's breaking his promise to be with her in the garden[18] while the Chief Queen wishes that he would show the kind of ingenuity he showed in love affairs to affairs of the state as well.[19] Similarly, in the *Abhijñānaśākuntalam*, Vasumatī does not wish to butt in and create a scene over Śakuntalā's painting, when she hears that Duṣyanta is busy with his duties as king.[20] Haṃsapadikā, on the other hand, is conscious of her youth and beauty which offers far more sensuous satisfaction than that of the Chief Queen. She subtly compares herself to the mango blossom, the king to a bee and his relationship to his Chief Queen as the mere dwelling of a bee in a lotus.[21] This vanity of hers is comparable to that of the *parattai* or harlot in some Tamil classical poems, who compares the heroine or the hero's wife to an old kingfisher who is incapable of catching fish, or of the other harlots who show off their beauty by taking a walk in the district where the wife lives.[22]

Even from the religious or ceremonious point of view the position of the wife and the mistress or secondary wife in Tamil literature seems to have been quite different from that of their counterparts in Sanskrit literature. The Sanskrit dramas do not throw much light on the ceremony that formalised the union of the hero and the heroine who is to become the secondary wife. The *Raghuvaṃśam* states clearly that Kuśa, the son of Rāma, marries Kumudavatī according to proper rites. The brother of the Nāga princess gives her away in marriage (according to rules) and Kuśa takes her hand in front of the holy fire.[23] Thus a regular marriage ceremony seems to have been conducted so that the new lady-love of the king also acquires the status of a wife. In Tamil literature under study, no such clear instance is to be found. A *marutakkali* poem mentions the marriage or *maṇam* of the hero to other women. The wife or heroine, seeing her husband return home after associating with harlots tells him that she is unable to sleep peacefully because of his loud festivities. When she tries to close her eyes she is awakened by the beats of his marriage drum (*maṇamuḻavu*) that comes from the wedding-house (*maṇamaṉai*). She also complains that the sound of the chariot that brings women to the house (*neṭunakar*) and the sound of those women's relatives who sing and dance the *tuṇaṅkai* also disturb her sleep.[24] This reference to the *maṇamaṉi* and *maṇamuḻavu* may be a reference to some sort of ceremony that the hero might have gone through by way of accepting her as his mistress or merely an exaggeration, by the hurt and angry wife, of the song, music and dance that he indulges in with his new companions. If it is a ceremony, it certainly does not seem to have had acceptance like the one performed for Kuśa. Another *Kalittokai* poem mentions that the actual wedding ceremony is *perumaṇam* which follows *aṟam* or virtue. This poem too consists of the words of the annoyed wife who is told by her philandering husband that he went horse-riding. Using the word horse she retorts that she knows it is not the horse he obtained by marriage which is respectful and performed in the presence of many according to rules of tradition. By this she means that she is aware of his extra-marital activities and that there is no need for him to find excuses. By 'the horse he obtained in marriage', she must have meant herself as his lawfully wedded wife.[25] Thus even if there were another *maṇam* it certainly would not have been of social or religious importance. Neither did the women achieve the status of wives.

Parattiyar or Veśyās

These harlots or *parattiyar* of Tamil love poetry are usually surrounded by the bards (*pāṇar*) and their wives (*viṟali*) as well as their troupe. These *pāṇar* or *viṟali* act as go-betweens and arrange for the rich men to meet the harlots in their homes. A *tōḻi* or friend of the chief wife addresses a *viṟali* as, 'O woman who has promised to win for our lord, new women for the morrow.'[26] The *pāṇaṉ* or bard too, because of his persuasive speech is able to win over rich men to patronise those whom he claims are more beautiful, youthful or better versed in song and dance. A *Kalittokai* poem mentions that a washerwoman also acts as a go-between for the harlots and the possible patrons or lovers.[27] The harlots however do not depend entirely on these people to arrange for meetings with rich or otherwise desirable men. Some of them stand at the entrance to their houses, well dressed with the intention of attracting the attention of those who pass by.[28] A favourite haunt of these women seems to have been the sites of the various festivals that are celebrated in their districts. A *tōḻi* says:

She has come alone.
She looks with feigned modesty.
She wears fragrant paste in her hair.
Her shoulders are slim like the bamboo.
Her teeth are straight and bright;
her thighs, close-set.
She wears a leafy garment
and stands there
adding beauty to the district that celebrates.
Let us save our men from her.[29]

A mistress tells her friends that were her husband to see the harlot dressed in a leafy garment at the festival, he is sure to be attracted by her. Therefore she plans to attend the festival herself and to stop him from seeing or meeting her if possible.[30] When the husbands are afraid to return home, the *pāṇaṉ, viṟali* or the charioteer (*pākaṉ*) goes to the wife to seek her permission for the hero's return. They always try their best to placate her. A *pākaṉ* tells a chief wife in a *Kalittokai* poem, 'You are the only woman for him', and tries to hide the fact that the husband had been disloyal to her. The *pāṇaṉ* says, 'He did not go anywhere secretly. Wouldn't I tell you if he did?' If necessary a musician even vows by his lute that he is not telling her a lie. If it is the friend who goes instead of the charioteer or the musician, he praises the husband before her and indirectly makes her realize his goodness in spite of his weakness and disloyalty.[31] The very fact that he sends someone to pacify the wife shows that the husband admits his infidelity and that he begs to be forgiven and be allowed to return home without further sulks or angry outbursts from the wife. The harlots also have maids to wait on them and to do the work around the house.[32] They are cared for and advised by their mothers who were probably harlots themselves and are now too old to practise on their own. So they set themselves up as advisers and guardians of the younger women especially their own daughters.[33]

The harlots are usually portrayed as being young and attractive. They are said to possess the beauty that is considered ideal by the ancient Tamils.[34] There is evidence to infer that a great deal of art was employed to enhance their beauty. A woman tells her husband,

> Why should she bear children like us
> and live without you
> in the home rich in paddy grains?
> What duty has she to do so?
> Poor woman!
> She cried, spoiling the painted beauty of her face.[35]

It seems that the harlot's beauty is the concern of the mother who cares for it and dresses her up accordingly.[36] The harlot is vain, especially so if she knows that the wife of her lover is not in the prime of her youth. One harlot, angered by the wife's accusations that the husband spends more time with her, says that she would do nothing about it but invites her friend to accompany her on her walk. She will go to the district where the wife lives. The wife can see for herself that the youth and beauty of the woman her husband has chosen, is better than that of the wife herself. The wife will then beat herself in self pity and agony. While referring to the hero, she mentions that he is the head of the country where the old kingfisher that could not fly has come slowly to the tank where lotuses bloom like flames and the fishes, like fried paddy, swim in the water. By this she obviously compares the wife to the old kingfisher that is not able to fly now but is greedy to eat the fish that swim in the tanks. The wife is too old to be a source of pleasure to her husband. He has therefore chosen a woman of youth and beauty of which the wife is jealous. By going for a walk near her home she thinks she would be able to let the wife see that for herself.[37] Another says:

> His women (*peṇṭir*) seem to be saying what they please
> about me.
> They would feel sorry indeed
> if I were to go to their *cēri*.[38]

Obviously she means that they would then know that they stand as no comparison to her and would be sorry on account of this. Often the wife knows about the harlots and their vanity. One wife tells her husband:

> The woman you have just won

is indeed silly.
I do not compare her with me.
Yet she compares me to her
and prides over her greater beauty.[39]

A wife asks her husband:

Who was she who caught hold of you
and prevented you
from coming to your rich home
to see your child?[40]

This could have been a normal question from the hurt wife. But it is also possible that the harlots stop the men from going back to see their wives and children. They might do it without making any secret of it, for one harlot says,

Let him come here.
I shall seize his garland and his upper garment
and tie him down to me
with my long tresses.[41]

Sometimes they even seem to threaten the men into stayir.g back by saying that they would go to the wife and tell her all what happened. Then the hero would be in a position to beg the wife for forgiveness. This is certainly a plan by which they hope to have the company of the hero for a longer time. Were the wife to know of it she would, out of anger and hurt, refuse to admit him to her house and the poor man would have no other alternative but to stay in the harlot's house till he manages to pacify his wife.[42]

Apart from the beauty they maintain with great care, they also have to their credit their knowledge of dance and song. They have the *pāṇaṉ* and the *viṟali* for company and the sound of the various types of drums and tabors is heard in the areas where they live. They also dance as shown by the *Akanāṉūṟu* poem:

We danced joyfully
to the sound of the large drum (*muḻavu*)
when the chief of the district
came to the section of the town [43]

says a harlot. A mistress declares:

He spent his time with another woman
to the accompaniment of song,
the lute played by the bejewelled maids
and the beat of the large drum.[44]

Maturaikkāñci describes harlots as women who dance happily to the music of the lute and the large drum. They are also said to visit the spacious houses where weddings take place and where the gods are honoured. It is possible that these women who can dance well are invited to perform at the rich feasts or banquets given in honour of the married couple or as part of the wedding celebrations. They are also said to make the celestial women who dance, suffer with envy. This again points out that the courtesans who are pretty are also accomplished dancers.[45]

These harlots can be classified broadly. Some of them go with the army to the war tent. According to Tolkāppiyar, *kulamakaḷir* or the lawfully wedded wives of those who indulge in war do not accompany them to the battlefield.[46] Yet the men in the tents are allowed to keep company with 'other women' (*puṟattōr*), which indicates that they are harlots.[47] *Mullaippāṭṭu* mentions that there are women in the army tents. They go about lighting the lamps at dusk. It is possible that the women taken to the war tents also attend to the little duties around the tents besides keeping the soldiers comfortable and cheerful.[48]

Iṟparattaiyar

Then there are the *iṟparattaiyar*. The name suggests that they are 'harlots of the house'. There are poems that mention the charioteer bringing home new courtesans.[49] They are certainly not brought to the house where the wife lives. It is possible that a separate house is built by the husband who sets up a harlot of his choice as mistress, in the new house.[50] It is interesting to note that an *Akanāṉūṟu* poem mentions a woman being brought (home) by the chariot, who then speaks ill of another harlot. The 'wronged' one says, 'They say that the woman brought by the chariot talks ill of me.' For this poem the explanatory comment at the top says that it is said by a *nayappupparattai*[51] of an *iṟparattai*.[52] These women are often faithful to the men who set them up as mistresses in a house and are less greedy for their wealth or money. They even take an interest in their men's welfare and care for the children of the chief wives. They even give away some of their jewels as presents for the children. Whenever they meet them, they adorn the little ones with whatever jewels they can. *Akanāṉūṟu* shows how a young harlot seeing her lover's son on the road calls him 'my life' and hugs him. The wife seeing this goes to her and says, 'Do not worry. You are also his mother.' At this the young woman puts down her head in shame and the wife cannot help liking her in spite of the fact that she is her rival for her husband's affections.[53] In the *Kalittokai* we come across harlots who give their lover's son rings and other ornaments out of affection for the little boy.[54]

Cērripparattaiyar

The other section of harlots are generally called *cērripparattaiyar*. The term *cēri* seems to denote a section of a town or city. Some commentators are of the opinion that it denotes a collection of houses.[55] Thus a *cērripparattai* must be one who lives in the section of the town where the harlots live. They must be living together in the same area and one of the main differences between them and the *iṟaparattai* is that they live in their own homes and the men visit them there. They might be paid each time they are visited and there is no obligation on either side to be loyal. The *iṟparattai* on the other hand is in charge of a house which, in reality, belongs to the man who has set her up and maintains her. This gives her the sense of obligation to be loyal to the man, who though not her husband, provides for her regularly. These *cērripparattaiyar* are also known as *nayappupparattaiyar* or *kāma-pparattaiyar*—those who are desired. Even among the *cēri-pparattaiyar* we do find some who are loving and loyal. But the mothers are usually against such attachments for this would be detrimental to their aim of getting rich at the expense of those who come to see their daughters. One young harlot tells the musician:

> Your lord came to our *cēri* on horse back.
> He won me
> with his handsome garland and chaplet
> and made me love him only.
> But mother is angry;
> She holds the bamboo
> with the close joints (to cane me).[56]

This shows that the general rule is to get what they can from the men and then to desert them in favour of richer men. Love and loyalty do not fit in with their way of life. The *Puṟanāṉūṟu* refers to them as women who do not love but who have thick, long tresses. The Chola king Nalaṅkiḷḷi vows that he would defeat his enemies or he would spend his time with women who have no love in their hearts. By this he shows that he does not like the company of these loveless women. He even hates it and considers it disgraceful.[57] The *Maturaikkāñci* is the only work of the Caṅkam times that brings out the true nature of the harlots. The author says that they embrace the rich youths from far and near with pretended ardour, tell many charming lies and keep their thoughts to themselves. They get from the youths all the wealth there is to be had from them and desert them like the bee that sucks honey from the fresh blooms and discards the old ones. They are also likened to the birds that go in search of trees laden with fruits. Since they receive wealth or take away the wealth of those who befriend them, they are known as *koṇṭimakaḷir*.[58] The *Puṟanāṉūṟu* refers to them as women who receive payment for their charms, *vilainalappeṇṭir*.[59]

Such harlots or *veśyās* are not found in the Sanskrit texts under study. But the *Kāmasūtra* classifies women, other than the legal wife or wives, with whom a man may have sexual relations, into nine groups. They are:

1. *Kumbhadāsī* or a woman who does menial work.
2. *Pañcārikā* or a woman who attends to her master.
3. *Kulaṭā* or one who is a debauch and goes to the house of another person for physical pleasure with another man because she fears her husband.
4. *Svairiṇī* or one who is disgusted with her husband and therefore seeks physical pleasure with another man, either in her own or in his house.
5. *Naṭī*, or a dancing girl or actress.
6. *Śilpakārikā* or the wife of an artisan.
7. *Prakāśavinaṣṭā* or one who, during her husband's life or after his death, is kept as a concubine and who openly indulges in physical pleasure with other men.
8. *Rūpajīvā* or a woman living on her beauty. (*Pañcārikā* and *Prakāśavinaṣṭa* are also included in this category).
9. *Gaṇikā* or the regular courtesan, well-behaved and following her profession with fitting dignity.[60]

This list suggests the variety of women who could attach themselves to the hero. One basic difference in the division of these harlots is that Tamil literature divides them on the basis of the woman's relationship to the hero and pays no attention whatsoever to her family status or other connections. The *Kāmasūtra* on the other hand divides them on the basis of their original family or profession.

The Tamil epics as well as some of the Sanskrit *kāvyas* and dramas under study deal with the *gaṇikā* or *kaṇikai*, who is a courtesan and therefore belongs to the ninth group in Vātsyāyana's classification. In the *Cilappatikāram* which depicts city life in detail, the *kaṇikaiyar* or courtesans enjoy a certain social position, especially in the large cities of Pukār and Maturai. They live in the rich and fashionable section of the town where the kings live. In this epic, the courtesans are said to have lived in the more affluent section of Pukār where the king, the rich merchants, the landed gentry and other such people live.[61] In Maturai, the district in which they live is happily patronised by the rich youths and the kings who protect the earth.[62] They are associated with the gay and attractive *Urvaci* (*Urvaśī*) by descent and there is a change in their social functions as well. They are not merely women who offer sexual services to those who pay them but are accomplished companions as well, who provide every sort of entertainment—good food, good company, good song and dance and good sport. Often they are trained in singing and dancing, are polished in manners, clever, provocative and very attractive, for they study besides dance and music, the art of make-up and beauty as well.[63] They are in fact trained in the sixty-four arts which are not listed in the *Cilappatikāram* but some are mentioned in the *Maṇimēkalai* and the *Kāmasūtra*.[64] They are, like the hetaerae of Athens and the Geishas of Japan, social companions. They go about the town during the various festivals, well-dressed and well-decked. Their beauty is such that they are referred to as the army of the Formless One (Kāman),[65] the Indian god of love.

The best, though only example, of such a character in the Tamil literature under study, is Mātavi and in Sanskrit literature is Vasantasenā. Both are courtesans (*kaṇikai* or *gaṇikā*) with the knowledge of the arts but there is a basic difference in their situation of life when each one meets the hero. Mātavi is young and has just completed her maiden performance. As such she knows no other man except Kōvalaṉ. Vasantasenā, on the other hand, is a famous and sought-after courtesan by the time she meets Cārudatta at the festival though Bhāsa shows her as being in love with Cārudatta and therefore desirous of giving up her profession.[66]

According to the *Maṇimēkalai* in which the heroine, though from the family of courtesans, had become a Buddhist nun, the courtesan is expected to know the *Ōviyac ceṉṉūl,* [67] the treatise for *kaṇikaiyar.* Her grandmother, who is anxious that the Prince should succeed in wooing Maṇimēkalai out of her nun's garb persuades him by explaining that she is a courtesan and that is how she would have to live. She says:

We are not chaste women.
It is our way of life
to take the wealth of many for ourselves.
We are like the lute
which does not die with the musician
but changes hands.
We are like the bees
that suck the honey
and discard the withering flowers.
We are like the Goddess of Wealth
who deserts
those devoid of fortune.[68]

This, however, is not the universal opinion. The *Tirukkuṟaḷ* denounces association with the harlots as one that is fit only for those who do not wish to be associated with the Goddess of Wealth and Good Fortune[69] and it uses a whole set of ten couplets to point out that the harlots or courtesans are loveless and care only for a man's wealth. Even in the *Cilappatikāram,* Mātavi herself, in spite of her love and loyalty for Kōvalaṉ is made to say that the life of a courtesan is the meanest of all, for the sages, the educated and those endowed with good sense treat them like plague and do not even look at them.[70] She, therefore, refers to her daughter as the daughter of Kaṇṇaki, so that at least Maṇimēkalai would be free from the disgrace and sin of being a courtesan.[71]

In the ancient Tamil poems, these mistresses or harlots are found chiefly in the poems of the *marutattiṇai,* pertaining to the agricultural regions. These are the regions dotted with cities and towns, where the landed gentry, enjoying comparative wealth, live in luxury and comfort. The chief emotion of the *marutam* poems is *ūṭal* or the sulkiness of the wife caused by the philandering behaviour of the husband. It is a generally accepted opinion that the association of the hero with harlots has been treated as one of the five aspects of love because of the emotion of *ūṭal*, which strictly speaking, is the playful love-quarrels which serve as a foreplay to love and union. In these poems, the *ūṭal* is caused not by the intensity of their love but by the infidelity of the husband. Besides, there are many poems that deal with the feelings or emotions of the *parattai* or woman other than the heroine who is often sincerely in love with the hero. Some poems show her as being hurt and angry with the wife or those close to the wife who might have blamed the *parattai* for the hero's irresponsible behaviour.[72] Others show her pride in her youth and beauty which she believes are superior to that of the heroine.[73] One such harlot, hurt over the hero's disloyalty and his insatiable nature in matters of love, says that if he does not change his ways many would be the women whose shoulders would grow slim, eyes shed tears and thereby waste away like withering flowers because of their love for him.[74] Another is annoyed over the fact that her lover is doing everything to please his wife (or the mother of his son) and so compares him to a puppet in her hands.[75] The *Kalittokai* also portrays some of them as being fond of the hero's son and giving him various jewels that they had been wearing.[76] One young *parattai* speaks of her loyalty to her lover (*orumaiya neñcam*) and her mother's anger at her loyalty.[77] Whether the emotion expressed by the harlot is one of love, loyalty, hurt or pride, it has as its basis, her relationship with the hero. The characters that usually speak in the *marutam* poems are the wife, the *tōḻi* or the *parattai* and the hero is usually portrayed as a pathetic figure, trying to make up with his angry wife. Quite often he is not allowed into the house by his wife (*vāyil maṟuttal*) and he wishes that some visitors would come by, so that the wife would forget her anger in the process of showing them the due hospitality.[78]

This situation contrasts sharply with the *ūṭal* as found in the *Tirukkuṟaḷ* which, being an ethical work, denounces the relationship with harlots and courtesans. In this work *ūṭal* is said to be caused by the wife's misinterpretation of words uttered by the husband and her suspicion that perhaps he may be connected with some other woman.[79] In these couplets, the husband is always shown to be the more confident and patient of the two and after his clearing the misunderstanding or suspicion, their love is further intensified. There is no extra-marital relationship that taunts the wife. This would seem to be the *ūṭal* that should be found between a couple whose love is reciprocated (*aṉpiṉ aintiṇai*). Thus it is rightly argued by V. Swaminathaiyar[80] and V. Sp. Manickam that these *marutam* poems have been included in *akam* poetry not to depict *ūṭal* or the patience and chastity of the wife but as an acceptance of a fact of ancient life. The latter even goes further to show that the *marutam* poems and Tolkāppiyar's verse which ordains that the hero shall not leave the heroine for the first twelve days after her menstrual period is an attempt at regulating this evil found in society.[81]

REFERENCES

1. *Puram,* 71:5-6.
2. *Ibid.,* 73:11-14.
3. *Ibid.,* 287:10-11.
4. *Ibid.,* 24:31-33. Also see 56:18-21, 367:6-9; *Porun,* 84-87; *Maturaik,* 779-81.
5. *Pati,* 52.
6. *Ragh,* 6:48.
7. *Puram,* 143-47.
8. *Kāma,* Part I. Chapter 1:1-3.
9. *Tol. Porul,* 144:49, 145:36.
10. *Ibid.,* 144:37-38.
11. *Ibid.,* 149:4-8.
12. *Ibid.,* 149:9-10.
13. *Nar,* 290:6-9.
14. *Tol. Porul,* 172.
15. *Ibid.,* 144:37.
16. *Mala,* act 4. p. 90.
17. *Ibid.,* act 4. p. 88.
18. *Ibid.,* act 3. pp. 82-86.
19. *Ibid.,* act 1. p. 32.
20. *Abhi,* act 6. p. 196.
21. *Ibid.,* act 5 v. 1.
22. *Akam,* 106, 216.
23. *Ragh,* 17:86-87.
24. *Kali,* 70:1-18.
25. *Ibid.* 96:32-34. Nacciṉārkkiṉiyar explains that this refers to the *Kāmakkiḷatti*

whom he married according to proper rites, but there is no evidence for such interpretation.

26. *Nar,* 310:4-5.
27. *Kali,* 72:13-14. *See also* chapter 1.
28. *Ibid.,* 97:15-17.
29. *Nar,* 170.
30. *Ibid.,* 390:5-7.
31. *Kali,* 71:9-18.
32. *Aink,* 79; *Akam,* 256.
33. *Akam,* 276:15.
34. *Ibid.,* 176; *Kali,* 97, 98.
35. *Akam,* 176:18-22.
36. *Ibid.,* 146:13, 276:15.
37. *Ibid.,* 106.
38. *Ibid.,* 216.
39. *Aink,* 67:1-3.
40. *Ibid.,* 66.
41. *Akam,* 276.
42. *Nar,* 100.
43. *Akam,* 76:1-2.
44. *Ibid.,* 186:9-12.
45. *Maturai,* 578-85.
46. *Tol. Porul,* 172.
47. *Ibid.,* 173.
48. *Mullaip,* 45-49.
49. *Akam,* 316:18, 336:11-12.
50. *Kali,* 70:13, 17.
51. See next paragraph.
52. *Akam,* 336.
53. *Ibid.,* 16.
54. *Kali,* 82.
55. A. Narayanacami Iyer, *Naṟṟiṇai,* Madras, 1956, p. 461.
56. *Nar,* 150:7-11.
57. *Puram,* 73:9-14.
58. *Maturai,* 569-76.
59. *Puram,* 365:8.
60. *Kama.* Pt. 6, chapter 6; Sutra 54.
61. *Cilap,* 5:50-51.
62. *Ibid.,* 14:144-45.
63. *Ibid.,* 3:8-9.
64. *Mani,* 2:18-32; *Kama,* Pt.6, chapter 6; *Also see* T. Tambimuttu, *India Love Poems,* New York, 1954, p. 34.
65. *Cilap.* 8:10-11.
66. These two characters have been discussed in the chapter on 'The Heroine'.
67. *Mani.* 2:18-32.
68. *Ibid.,* 18:15-22.
69. *Kural,* 920.
70. *Cilap,* 11:179-83.

71. *Ibid.*, 27:105-106.
72. *Akam*, 216.
73. *Ibid.*, 106.
74. *Nar*, 315:9-12.
75. *Kur*, 8.
76. *Kali*, 80.
77. *Nar*, 150.
78. *Ibid.*, 102.
79. *Kural*, 1301-20.
80. Swaminathaiyar, *Kuṟuntokai*, Madras, 1962, p. 71.
81. V. Sp. Manickam, *Tamiḻk Kātal*, Madras, 1962, pp. 275-92.

Chapter 6

The Confidante

The personal nature of the emotion of love and the various restrictions society and convention placed on the hero and the heroine from a cultured background, made it necessary for them to confide in someone who would be sympathetic and helpful. The texts under study, make use of the *tōḻi* (Tamil) or *sakhī* (Sanskrit) as the special and close friend of the heroine and the *pāṅkaṉ* (Tamil) or *vayasya* (Sanskrit) as the friend who would advise, help or console the hero.

THE HEROINE'S FRIEND

Family Background

The heroine is usually accompanied by her friend or confidante, (the *tōḻi* in Tamil and the *sakhī* in Sanskrit). In Caṅkam poetry she is depicted as the daughter of the heroine's foster-mother (*cevili*). An *Akanāṉūṟu* poem shows this very clearly when we hear of the foster-mother bewailing the elopement of the heroine. She addresses the *tōḻi* thus:

> My daughter,
> Look at me who was so close to her.[1]

The *Tolkāppiyam* states categorically that the *tōḻi* is the daughter of the foster-mother.[2] But her importance is due, not to this relationship but to her being the heroine's friend and confidante.[3] Being the daughter of the *cevili*, of course, gives her the opportunity to stay with the heroine and this makes it possible for her to help the heroine with her secret meetings with the hero, or to stay up with her and console her at night.[4] During the day they spend their time playing in the fields[5] or guarding the field.[6] This very close relationship and affection is brought out by a *Naṟṟiṇai* poem. The heroine who has met and fallen in love with a youth does not reveal her love to her friend but pines away on her own. Seeing this change in her, the friend tries to find out the reason for her paleness. When she fails, she breaks into tears and begs the heroine to take her into her confidence, reminding her that they share the same soul though they possess two separate bodies.[7] As in the case of the Caṅkam hero and the heroine, there is no caste division for the *tōḻi*. Neither are there special names based on the geographical division of land. Only the term *tōḻi* is used in all the poems and colophons. But we may assume that she belonged to the same geographical division as the heroine.

The *Cilappatikāram* does not mention a *tōḻi* in the strict sense of the term, but we have Tēvanti who is like a friend to Kaṇṇaki, especially in her sorrow of separation. They seem to have been intimate enough for the usually very reticent Kaṇṇaki to admit to her that she is confident of Kōvalaṉ's return and to relate to her the ominous dream.[8] Tēvanti, unlike Kaṇṇaki, must be from the Brāhmaṇa caste for she was married to Cāttaṉ who, though a deity, took the form of the son of a Brāhmaṇa, the husband of Mālati, out of compassion for Mālati.[9] After eight years of married life with Tēvanti, he related the story of his 'incarnation' and disappeared, asking her to go to his temple.[10] Being separated from her husband, her situation in life is the same as Kaṇṇaki's and is therefore an understanding friend who knows her sorrow. She cares enough to pray for Kaṇṇaki's reunion with Kōvalaṉ.[11] Vacantamālai seems to be a witness to all the important events in Mātavi's love-life and participates in most of them. She was with her at the beach, holding the lute on that fateful evening when Kōvalaṉ, misunderstanding Mātavi's song, walks away from her life.[12] It is Vacantamālai who takes her letter full of love and sensuous beauty, to inform him of the pain of those separated during the spring season.[13] But she is not a friend of equal status, merely a maid who is faithful and trusted, besides being close enough to be entrusted with such personal matters. Sometimes she is identified as the hunchback (*kūṉi*) who sold the garland of emeralds to Kōvalaṉ soon after Mātavi's maiden performance.[14] But we have no textual evidence for this identification. We shall see that she is in fact an attractive woman. Sutamati who accompanies Maṇimēkalai to the garden to pick fresh flowers[15] is a Brāhmaṇa woman, the daughter of Kaucikaṉ. Enamoured by her, a *vidyādhara* carried her away but later abandoned her at Kāvirippūm paṭṭiṉam.[16] Though she is actually a friend of Mātavi, she also becomes a friend of Maṇimēkalai.

Aśvaghoṣa's works do not mention any characters who may be called the heroine's friend, for the stress in both his works is not the development of the love theme but the final renouncement of life itself. Not all the plays of Bhāsa deal with love either and of those that do, *Pratijñāyaugandharāyaṇam* merely reports the love and elopement of Udayana and Vāsavadattā and the *Svapnavāsavadattam* deals with their separation with her consent and the arranged marriage of Udayana and Padmāvatī. The latter play, however, mentions a maid of Padmāvatī, who is intimate enough to know that, although she is sought after in marriage to Vāsavadattā's brother, the Prince of Ujjain, Padmāvatī is not interested in that proposal of marriage because she has heard of the virtues of Udayana and fallen in love with him.[17] Madanikā is a slave maid of Vasantasenā but with the same intimacy, for she could question her mistress for not wearing any jewellery and thereby discuss Cārudatta with whom she has fallen in love.[18] Though the drama *Avimārakam* presents three friends and attendants of the princess, Kuraṅginī, (Nalinikā, Māgadhikā and Vilāsinī), only one of them, Nalinikā is the real friend in whom the princess confides. She is the daughter of a nurse who takes care of the princess[19] and she herself admits to her mother that the princess tells her everything.[20] Her caste is not mentioned but her status is certainly inferior to that of the princess whom she serves.

Some of Kālidāsa's works also mention the *sakhī*. Of the *kāvyas*, the *Kumārasaṃbhavam* shows the friends as being with Pārvatī even during her penance and Śiva's visit to the grove in the guise of a young hermit. Of all the friends, she is the one who knows the secrets of Pārvatī's heart.[21] Nothing however is mentioned of her birth or family background. The plays, dealing chiefly with the love theme, naturally make use of the *sakhī*. In the *Mālavikāgnimitram* we have two such characters . . . Bakulāvalikā who is a maid of Queen Dhāriṇī but a friend and confidante of Mālavikā[22] and Nipuṇikā who is a maid of Irāvatī, intimate enough to know and to help in her affairs of love.[23] Even if we have to bear in mind that Mālavikā is introduced as a maid herself and therefore the social position of Bakulāvalikā is apparently the same as that of Mālavikā, it does not raise her social status in any way, when Mālavikā is established as the Princess of Vidarbha.[24] But as two maids in the service of the Chief Queen, they must have been close friends for Bakulāvalikā to say, 'You are indeed as dear to me as my own body.'[25] Here too the background of the two maids, Bakulāvalikā and Nipuṇikā is not known. In the *Vikramorvaśīyam*, Citralekhā, being an *apsarā* herself, may be assumed to be of the same background as Urvaśī but not as important in the court of Indra. The concept of the friend as seen in the Caṅkam poems is best seen in the *Abhijñānaśākuntalam.* The caste, parentage or the circumstances of the birth of Anasūyā and Priyamvadā are not found in the play but they have grown up together with Śakuntalā in the hermitage and this provides them with the same background as the heroine.[26] There is no distinction of the mistress and the maid in this play for they enjoy equal status in the hermitage, though Śakuntalā is the favourite. In the case of Vacantamālai of the *Cilappatikāram* and the other friends of the heroines of the Sanskrit works, though mutual affection and a close friendship are found, they are not of equal status as the heroines for they are actually maids who are employed as servants or kept as slaves to serve their mistresses.

Age

The development of the love theme requires an easy companionship between the heroine and her friend and it is certainly essential or at least convenient that both are nearly of the same age. The *tōḻi* of the Caṅkam poems is always depicted as being of the same age as the heroine. They play together on the mountain slopes,[27] picking flowers,[28] bathing in the mountain streams[29] or keeping the birds away from the millet fields.[30] The ages of the friends in the two Tamil epics is not found in the works concerned. But we may assume that Tēvanti, having been married for a short period and then separated from her husband, is nearly of the same age as Kaṇṇaki. While it is difficult to form any opinion regarding the age of Vacantamālai, Sutamati is certainly older to Maṇimēkalai for she is said to be as old as Mātavi herself.[31]

In Bhāsa's plays, the age of Padmāvatī's maid is difficult to ascertain but Nalinikā in the *Avimārakam* should be as old as Kuraṅginī for she is the daughter of Kuraṅginī's nurse,[32] a relationship that may be compared to that found in the Caṅkam works. Madanikā too must be in her youth to have fallen in love herself with Sajjālaka.[33] Kālidāsa's works do not reveal clearly the age of the *sakhī.* We are told that Pārvatī's friend is her *vayasya* i.e. her friend of the same age.[34] Bakulāvalikā may be assumed to be as young as Mālavikā, from the way she discusses the love of Mālavikā for the king, teases her and encourages her like a youthful companion of the same age.[35] Nipuṇikā, suspicious and crafty like Irāvatī[36] is as old as her mistress. Citralekhā like Urvaśī is ageless. In the case of Anasūyā and Priyamvadā we know for certain that they are of the same age as Śakuntalā (*sama vayo. . .*).[37]

Beauty

This young friend is also depicted as being beautiful. In an *Aiṅkuṟunūṟu* poem, the hero asking his beloved to keep a tryst the following day as well, says:

> Bless you maiden.
> If loving me, you also take pity on me,
> then do come,
> bringing your Toṇṭi-like qualities,
> walking gently with the friend
> who has upper arms resembling the bamboo
> and a lovely forehead.[38]

The bamboo-like upper arms and a lovely forehead are clear indications of her beauty. The physical beauty of Tēvanti is not described in the *Cilappatikāram* and her situation in life is such that even if she were beautiful, she would not have cared to maintain her beauty. Vacantamālai is described as a woman with 'lance-like eyes spread with (thin) red lines'.[39] An idea of her overall beauty may be obtained from the following lines:

> The forest-residing deity
> filled with passion and
> hoping he too would love in return,
> appeared in the form of Vacantamālai.
> Like a quivering creeper,
> she fell at his feet,
> shedding false tears.[40]

The word creeper conveys a picture of a dainty and charming woman. Sutamati must have been a beautiful woman to have attracted, or at least aroused the desires of a *vidyādhara*.[41]

In the Sanskrit works, the physical charms of the friends or maids are not described. Even Citralekhā's appearance is not described as being beautiful. Although we have to accept the tradition that *apsarās* are beautiful beings, Citralekhā cannot be compared to Urvaśī. Anasūyā and Priyamvadā are, however, clearly stated to be equally attractive as Śakuntalā herself and this could be due to their position as equals (*sama vayorūpa ramaṇīyam*).[42]

Her Role

The role of the friend in love poetry is important, especially from the point of view of the heroine's modesty which prevents her from talking about her love or admitting it to others. Both Tamil and Sanskrit poetry accept this function of the friend. She is a spokeswoman for the heroine and generally acts in her interest. In the *Svapnavāsavadattam* she is useful in voicing the feelings of Padmāvatī who is in love with Udayana's virtues, though she has not met him.[43] In the case of Vasantasenā the *gaṇikā*, she needs no such help to safeguard her modesty. But Madanikā is one who could discuss her mistress' lover and thereby reveal her emotions to the audience.[44] Nalinikā's role in the *Avimārakam* is not very clearly defined. She and her mother meet Avimāraka and invite him to the palace that night to be united with Kuraṅginī.[45] The two together make it possible for him to stay on in the women's apartments without the knowledge of the king or the queen. But most of the maids in that part of the palace seem to be aware of his presence.[46] Pārvatī's *sakhī* has the definite role of explaining the love of Pārvatī for Śiva. After the young hermit offers half the religious merits he had acquired himself so that Pārvatī could add them to her own so as to win the husband she desires, he requests to know details about him.

> She thus addressed by the Brahmana
> who had penetrated the innermost secret,
> could not speak out the desire of her mind (through modesty).
> So she, with eyes devoid of collyrium,
> looked at her friend standing beside her.[47]

Her look, obviously, is a signal to her friend that she may tell him about her love for Śiva. But we find the friend giving a detailed though artistic account of Pārvatī's love as well as the torments experienced by her because of her inability to win Śiva's love.[48] Later, it is the friend who also gives him a message from Pārvatī that her father has the authority to give her in marriage, implying that Śiva should ask her father for her hand.[49]

In the dramas of Kālidāsa, the friends help by making the heroine talk of her love. This is something within the bounds of modesty and at the same time, most useful in depicting the emotion of the heroine. Bakulāvalikā encourages Mālavikā's love for the King by telling her that he too loves her and she is ready to help her achieve her heart's desire. The King who overhears their conversation praises her saying:

> Surely she (Bakulāvalikā) holds her (Mālavikā)

to her purpose
by the words which are spoken after ascertaining
her feelings
and which effectively answers all her objections.[50]

In the *Abhijñānaśākuntalam* the two friends themselves admit that they are ignorant of such matters and whatever they happen to know is from the legendary stories. Yet they are eager to be of service to Śakuntalā. Though they suspect her love for the king they make her admit it. Then after considering briefly what they could do to help Śakuntalā, quickly and secretly, they decide that she should write a letter. They also promise to deliver the letter to the King. They are resourceful enough to think of handing it over to him along with some remains of offerings made to some deity and this is certainly a very good excuse for the girls to give something to the guest in the hermitage. They, being aware of the king's love for her feel justified in encouraging her.[51] Their loyalty and care for Śakuntalā make them conceal the incident of Durvāsa's anger and his curse, from her.[52] Of all the Sanskrit works under study, the *Abhijñānaśākuntalam* seems to portray the *sakhī* (though there are two of them in this drama) as someone really important and a true friend though the usual role of spokesman is made unnecessary.

In the love poetry of the Caṅkam age, the friend has a much more important role to play. She is consulted in all matters by the heroine and her advice is heeded. From the moment she comes to know of the heroine's love for the hero, she becomes the guardian of her love-life as well. She acts as a steadying hand on the heroine even after marriage. Being a close and constant companion, she is always the first to know the mental and physical changes wrought by love on the heroine. She persuades her to talk of it and her suspicions are always confirmed. She may ask the heroine directly, reminding her of their intimate friendship as when she says,

You do not tell me
though your body has lost its lustre
like a lamp held in daylight;
the beauty of your forehead is
like the moon concealed by Rāhu.
But since to you, I am
as one sharing the same soul

I have noticed.[53]

This is also seen in the *Abhijñānaśākuntalam* when the two friends, Anasūyā and Priyamvadā noticing Śakuntalā wasting away, question her, though they suspect the actual cause. The reason they give for questioning her is that 'grief (*duḥkham*) shared with affectionate friends (*snigdhajana*) becomes bearable'.[54] In both these instances, apart from the anxiety of the friends, their true desire to help by making the heroine confident of their affection and loyalty is clear. At other times, if she feels that a direct question might hurt the heroine, she would speak of the landscape in such a manner that the heroine would feel that her friend knows or guesses something.

O Maiden with pretty, plump upper arms
and dark eyes spread with red lines
that resemble the arrow of the hunter
who had killed while protecting the field
and plucked out the arrow!
The parrots steal away
the fat ears of grain.
But they know not that they are noticed
by the peacock in its nest
on the lofty mountain
where the blooms of the *vēṅkai*,
with many small fruits,
fall like sparks from the metal beaten by a smith.[55]

Here she seems merely to describe the hillslope with the *vēṅkai* tree, the peacock in its nest and the parrots eating the grain in the field. But the friend actually makes the heroine know that her clandestine love for the hero is like the stealthy act of the parrots who think that no one watches them. They do no realise that the peacock, though in its nest, has a better view of the hillslope and since it is not involved in any activity of its own, is able to see and know everything. The friend compares herself to the peacock which is in a position to observe what is going on and thereby makes it easier for the heroine to talk about her love.

The friend also takes upon herself the responsibility of testing the youth's intentions or the strength of his love. She tries to discourage him, giving him various reasons. She may, for example, tell him that the heroine is young and is easily frightened and as such, she is too innocent to know of love.[56] A *tōḻi* from the maritime tracts tells a hero who asks for her help in obtaining the love of the heroine:

> This girl is the daughter of the fisherman
> who lives in the lovely little house
> near the maritime park.
> He sails out to cast his net
> as if churning the vast, blue waters.
> You are the beloved son
> of the wealthy owner of fast chariots
> living in the ancient town,
> where tall flags flutter along shop-lined streets.
> What is to be gained by us?
> We keep away birds from pieces of shark flesh
> spread out to dry.
> Please go away, for we smell of fish.
> Our modest, good, living made from the large ocean
> is not comparable to yours.
> Among us too, there are rich people.[57]

In both these instances, the intention of the *tōḻi* is not to send him away for good but to see if he loves the heroine enough to persist further. Though trying to point out the difference in wealth, she is careful and loyal enough to make him realise that though they live in a small house, it is beautiful and in good surroundings and that she comes from a family where heroism is the source of their livelihood. The men return with huge sharks, the meat of which is more than enough for their daily consumption and so the remainder is spread out to dry. Since they live by killing, they can be heartless and cruel. Such information would frighten away one who does not care enough for the heroine. Sometimes she also tells him that if he were really that interested in her he might as well marry her[58] meaning that she is not happy to encourage his secret love.

Once she is convinced of his character and sincerity, she talks to the heroine and encourages her. If the heroine pretends not to know about him or to be disinterested, she carefully gives her own opinion which is always sound and practical. A *tōḻi* tells her friend who feigns innocence:

> You do not believe me
> when I say, 'The chieftain of the hill

suffers because of his love for you.'
See for yourself.
Deliberate with your people.
Only after deciding should you unite with him.
His requests are not to be rejected easily.
My friend!
Good people get together after considering
(each other's worth).
They consider not after befriending them.[59]

Here she tries to convey the idea that the hero is a good and reasonable man and that there is no reason to discourage him. She also tells the heroine indirectly that since she herself has accepted his love and friendship, though without the friend's knowledge, she has no choice but to continue the relationship she has started.

The meetings of lovers which are always of a secret nature, are usually arranged by their friends. In the *Avimārakam,* Nalinikā, though with the consent and help of her own mother, arranges for Avimāraka to meet the princess in her apartments without the knowledge of the King and Queen.[60] In the *Mālavikāgnimitram,* we find that though Bakulāvalikā does not actually plan the meeting of Mālavikā and the King, in the *samudragṛha,* she accompanies Mālavikā there at the *vidūṣaka's* request and is prepared to hide herself from the sight of others so that the King and her friend may be left to themselves in the pavilion.[61] The *tōḻi* is much more resourceful and she normally has an ultimate reason for arranging the tryst in a particular spot. There are, no doubt, instances where she simply informs him of a suitable meeting place.

The pond is near the village.
The rivulet, not far from the pond.
The park (nearby) is deserted
but for the white cranes looking for food.
We shall go there to get sand for (washing) our hair.
The modest maiden would also come.[62]

In the above poem, the friend clearly indicates the place for their meeting and the suitability of the park that is deserted except for the cranes which too would not look their way because they search for food. But mostly, the invitation to meet the heroine at a particular spot is not as innocent as it may seem. In the *Akanāṉūṟu,* a *tōḻi* informs the hero who has been meeting his beloved at night, that the path he takes during his nocturnal visits are dangerous enough for even those who are accustomed to it to falter, and that the heroine would not live if any mishap were to occur. Then she adds:

Even if you come during the day
to the bower of gloriosa
in the dense clump of fruit-laden trees
next to our garden
on the tall mountain slope
with honey-combs on high branches,
you would embrace the cool, gentle upper arms
of my friend cherished by my mother.
They are like the portion between joints
of the bent bamboo that grows on the broad hill.[63]

It certainly sounds like a suitable place for lovers to meet but she has her reasons for choosing the bower. The trees laden with fruits and the honey-combs would attract the mountain dwellers who collect them. As if that were not enough, the heroine is cherished by the foster-mother and as such she might come out often to keep an eye on her, especially because the bower is only next to their own garden. So there is also the danger of her seeing her with the hero. Like most poems that seem to suggest suitable places to meet, this too brings out the dangers of the clandestine meetings and hints to the hero that it cannot go on in this stealthy manner but should come to an end with marriage.

At times she informs the hero that there are proposals of marriage for the heroine from other youths through their elders. This offer of marriage may be true or imaginary, but the expected result is the same, namely, a definite proposal of marriage from him.[64] When such broad hints fail to make the hero think of marriage, she even complains about him to the heroine, making sure that he can overhear their conversation:

If you love the lord of the tall mountain
where the uneducated monkey trembles
because the sharp-toothed, modest she-monkey
with its young
is hidden by the clouds
on the slopes of high peaks,
then you would not listen to me.

Yet I shall speak.
Bless you my friend!
For long, he has not been praiseworthy.
He follows not the tradition of forefathers
who have pity in their hearts bound by affection.
Know this well.[65]

If he followed the tradition of the forefathers, he would be responsible enough to marry the woman he loves. Even the monkeys who are not educated to know such matters follow tradition so that they live with their families with love and affection.

One of the most difficult things a friend is expected to do is to inform the family of the heroine's love for the hero. Often it is fear of elders in the family that prevents them from doing so. Anasūyā faces this problem when Kāśyapa returns to the hermitage after his pilgrimage. She is not able to summon up enough courage to tell him of Śakuntalā's secret marriage to Duṣyanta and of her pregnancy. But her problem is solved by the verse recited by an incorporeal voice at the fire sanctuary of the hermitage.[66] Tamil poetry, not dealing with the supernatural, offers no such relief to the friend or the heroine. The only possible divine or supernatural aid is in the mother's belief that the daughter's malady might have been caused by Murukaṉ and that a *veṟiyāṭṭu* or ritual to pacify the deity would cure her child. Yet this belief only provides the situation in which she may inform the mother so that due to the relief the mother would experience, she may not become angry. The friend would ask the priest or priestess summoned to perform the ceremony, to sing the praises of the chieftain's hill.[67] Or the *tōḻi* may address Murukaṉ himself saying, 'You would indeed be foolish if you came to this place.'[68] She might even ask the priest:

O wise *vēlā*, who worships Murukaṉ,
Please do not be cross (with me).
I have something to ask.
If, together with rice of various colours
you kill a kid,
stroke this girl's forehead,
and make obeisance and offerings,
would his broad, bright-garlanded chest
that afflicts her,
eat it?

He is the chieftain of the great
heaven-touching mountain.[69]

The *tōḻi* makes it clear that the ritual is unnecessary for it is the hero's chest, a symbol of his valour, that has caused the paleness of the heroine and not Murukaṉ as the mother thinks. Though it is the *vēlaṉ* or the priest of Murukaṉ who is questioned, the information is certainly meant for the mother who will now realise that her daughter is in love and make the necessary arrangements. If the friend is consulted regarding the heroine's malady, then she might explain how the heroine met the youth and has been affected since then. The meeting is usually depicted as one caused by a dangerous situation from which the brave but kind-hearted youth saved them.[70] She may even put the blame on fate and talk as if they are helpless against the forces of providence.[71]

Yet there are some friends who are unable to face the mother and speak out the truth. At such times the friend encourages the lovers to elope. The hero might seem reluctant, thinking of the arid tracts the gentle heroine would have to cross, but it is the friend who persuades him, if necessary, to take the step. According to her the waterless desert would be sweet if the heroine were in his company.[72] It is usually the heroine who is most reluctant to take this step, for it would be against the norms of modesty. But in order to safeguard her chastity the friend finally persuades her to leave with the hero.

Bless you, my friend
He is the lord of the tall mountains.
There the large tiger with open jaws
and great strength
jumped on the beautiful face
of the leader of the elephant herd,
and reddening his white tusks
lay dead in a cave
like the branch of the black-trunked *vēṅkai*
with fading flowers
blown down by the west wind.
May you consider leaving with him.[73]

The dangers of the journey should not worry her for he is like the elephant that protects the herd without any difficulty and should therefore be able to take care of her. If she does not leave with him, then she may grow pale like the flowers of the *vēṅkai* or even be destroyed like the branch. The reference to the *vēṅkai* tree, the flowering of which is said to mark the beginning of the wedding season, might even suggest a possible marriage to someone else if she stayed.

The friend's anxiety for the heroine's welfare and happiness is one of the most important traits in her and this is shown in nearly all the texts that deal with her. Though she too has known the hero during the period of courtship, she is not involved herself and is therefore in a position to look at the relationship and the two people involved objectively and to study them, especially the hero. She is not blind to human weakness and to the evils of the society she lives in. Hence at marriage or elopement, she enjoins the hero to love and cherish the heroine under all circumstances. Anasūyā and Priyamvadā, knowing that Duṣyanta is already married to many wives, entreat him to 'favour her and preserve her life.' Anasūyā also adds:

> Friend, kings are said to have many favourite consorts.
> You must therefore act in such a way
> that our dear friend may not become a cause of grief
> to her kinsfolk.[74]

A *tōḻi* from the *Naṟṟiṇai* also feels anxious for her friend's future when she is about to leave with the hero whom she loves. So she requests the hero:

> Even when her erect, beautifully curved breasts
> droop,
> or her lovely, long, sapphire-like tresses
> that fall on her golden body
> turn grey,
> desert her not,
> O lord of flowering parks.
> . . . She has accepted your words
> as good and true
> like the spear of Paḻaiyaṉ, the lord of warfare.[75]

Since the heroine is leaving everyone, including her friend, all she has now is the hero himself and the love he has for her. So she makes it a point to stress on the good words that he had spoken while wooing her and reminds him that now he has to prove them true.

In the Sanskrit works the role of a *sakhī* seems to come to an end with the marriage of the hero and the heroine. But in the Tamil works it continues even after their marriage. The Tamil poems sing of separation before and after marriage, for various reasons. The hero might go away on duty or in search of wealth. Both these separations are considered necessary or unavoidable. If it were a journey he plans to undertake for the acquisition of wealth, the friend sometimes tries to persuade him to postpone the trip, making him realise that the heroine would not be able to bear the separation well.[76] There are times when she, realizing that the journey he proposes to make is necessary to lead a good, useful life, would like to give her consent on behalf of her friend, but fears that her friend would suffer. Then she would clearly explain the situation and advise him to return soon.

> You keep saying, 'I shall go.'
> But I fear to show displeasure
> and bid you leave.
> To say, 'Do not go,'
> I fear slander
> that prick like arrows on the chest.
> Hence go.
> Having gone complete your mission
> and stay not long.
> She fears at night, though you are by her side
> embracing her closely
> till the jewels leave their impressions (on the bodies).
> Don't you see the northern wind
> which has followed the cool, gentle clouds
> lightened by the shedding of rain?[77]

The poem portrays not only her own dilemma but also of the hero. The heroine's nature is not unknown to the hero, but the friend merely uses it to impress on the hero the necessity for his speedy return.

Being the friend and confidante, she is the one to share the heroine's sorrow in separation. She tries her best to console her and what she says or does depends on the thoughts and moods of the heroine herself, for the friend cannot be of help unless she understands the heroine's line of thought and advises or consoles accordingly. If the hero has left after promising to return by the rainy season (*kār*), when the trees and shrubs of the region flower, the heroine who has been patient till then becomes anxious and worried. Then the friend might tell her that though there have been showers and the *koṉṟai* and *kāyā* trees have bloomed, it is not the rainy season yet. The trees are foolish to have bloomed out of season.[78] If the heroine is anxious for the comfort and safety of the hero, then she tries to tell her that the path traversed by him cannot be dangerous or difficult.

Good is the path he has taken.
It has the bright, flame-like gloriosa
and the jasmine
brought forth by the cool showers.[79]

These words cannot be brushed aside as meaningless or improbable for we know that in the tropics there are showers in seasons other than the rainy season and the desert regions in the Tamil country are actually *mullai* tracts that have turned arid for want of rain. So with some rain the hero's path could become cooler and more comfortable.

When such words cannot wipe off the heroine's tears of anxiety and grief she reminds her of the necessity for the separation. One heroine is told:

O maiden with fine ornaments!
Do try to endure your grief.
Do not sob
causing your beautiful ornaments to slip off,
or complain saying,
'Now that he is gone
past the barren, deserted mountain
where lovely-petalled blooms
of the forest gmelina (*kumiḻ*)
that resemble bright, dangling ear-ornaments
may be heard falling decoratively on the path
winding through acacia trees,
my soul too will leave me.'
Consider.
Did he not go
desiring wealth for his friends
and ornaments to adorn your arms?[80]

Here the friend does not deny the aridity of the tracts he would cross, but points out subtly the duties of a householder. The head of the family has certain obligations to fulfil and these include generosity and the support of his dependants. The wife has to help him fulfil these obligations. It does not mean that the hero does not think of her. The fruits of the journey would help him provide her with luxuries as well. If all these means of consoling her are of no avail, then she might even take the heroine out of the house for a while, hoping that the change would do her some good. A good excuse for asking her out is to see for themselves if the hero's chariot is coming, implying that he should be returning soon.[81]

Apart from such legitimate separations caused by his duty to country or home, there are others caused by his desire for amusement or variety. When the hero is disloyal to his wife, then he has to reckon not only with the wife but also with her friend. It is in this situation that we see the extent of her rights and importance in Tamil love poetry. She is not restricted by the feelings of respect that the wife has for her husband. So she rebukes him in a manner suitable for the occasion and the person concerned. One *tōḻi* reminds the hero:

> You come here with signs of sport
> after dalliance with your group (of courtesans)
> who are adorned
> with clothes, ornaments, flowers and leafy garments.
> This town says,
> 'His was a life of poverty
> living on the food earned by a single cow.
> Now that the young wife
> of great beauty and goodness is here,
> there are festivities.'[82]

It is therefore most indecent and ungrateful of him to cause her sorrow. There is a subtle hint that the tears of such women who are the bringers of good fortune might cause misfortune to the home. Since such husbands spend most of their spare time outside their homes, and have no time for their wives and children, their relationship suffers. Hence another friend tells a hero,

> Though unable to ride,
> the children derive joy
> in dragging by hand, the little chariot with horses
> made by the carpenter.
> Likewise,
> deprived of the pleasure of
> touching the lord of good chariots and ponds,
> we nurtured his friendship (in our hearts).
> So the bangles are still tight.[83]

By comparing the heroine to the children who play with toy carts and horses and indulge in make-believe, she brings out the cruelty of the situation. The heroine is no longer a child or an inexperienced girl to live with mere thoughts. She is a woman who has her longings and desires which cannot be satisfied by thoughts alone. The selfishness and thoughtlessness of the hero has reduced her to that state and it is about time he thought of the woman at home. Another friend tries to make him realise the heroine's position by blaming the tradition of the family or section of society she is born in.

'The lord of rich villages,
rising at dawn and
harnessing his fast chariot,
went to embrace the woman
adorned with bright ornaments.
He is lustrous (with happiness).'
Thus reflecting, the mother of his little son
is distressed and confused.
It is indeed a misfortune to be born
in such a family (of chaste women).[84]

By thus referring to her family, she indicates that only the wife is loyal and therefore suffers on account of his disloyalty. The woman or women in whose company he spends his time and wealth have no such obligations and do not have to be eternally loyal to him. It would do him good to realise this and be loyal to his wife.

Whatever the situation, the confidante is always portrayed as a person with a good amount of common sense and the ability to put across her thoughts and ideas delicately but effectively. She is quick at repartee and even this is subtle, with thought-provoking words. A musician (*pāṇaṉ*), who has been keeping the hero company and perhaps been of help to him while he dallied with the courtesan, comes to the house to pacify the heroine, so that the hero can come back without having to face an angry outburst from his wife. The *pāṇaṉ* tries to tell her that the hero is a pleasant man (*iṉiyaṉ*) and asks her not to be angry with him but to show favour. To this the friend replies:

The lord of the fertile tracts
where the male bird with a hoppety walk
picks (with its beak)
the odourless, white flowers
of the sweet-stemmed sugarcane

to build a nest for its mate about to lay eggs,
is indeed the sweetest and most loving. . .
but only by the words of the *pāṇaṉ*.[85]

She thus brings out the irony of the situation where the *pāṇaṉ* is compelled to tell a suffering wife that her husband is a pleasant person. Besides, by choosing the right objects to describe the hero's country, she puts across much more than meets the eye. The reference to the female bird about to lay eggs suggests that the heroine is with child. If the male bird spends its time picking sugarcane flowers, it is to make the nest comfortable for her to lay the eggs in. But the hero, who is supposed to be sweet-natured, does not seem to have affection or sense of family responsibility the birds and beasts of his field have. He spends his time away from his wife who is to become a mother. The sugarcane blossom points out the nature of the harlots who are attractive but have no virtue (smell) and are useless for the continuation of his family or its good name.

During such separations the grief of the heroine is quite different from what she experiences during his journeys to distant places on account of duty. There is no anxiety for his safety but merely a feeling of hurt, inferiority and self-reckoning. Realising this and the hero's weakness, she consoles the heroine saying:

O lady with thistle-like teeth!
Do not be angry with him.
He is the lord of the country
where the fresh, white water lily
brought from the fields along with sheaves of grain
is eaten by the cow newly delivered of calf
and the worn-out bull eats the left-overs.
You are a woman of beauty and goodness.
But people do not call him a man.
They say he is the bee
which sucks honey from fresh flowers
that bloom in the deep tanks even at night.[86]

The description of his agricultural tracts no doubt, shows the abundance as well as the utility of even the weeds that grow there. But the choice of objects for description shows that the heroine has recently attained motherhood and this increases her status while the hero seeks women who are comparable to the bull. But more important than that is the character of the hero. If he seeks after new women each day, it is not due to any shortcomings on the part of the heroine but because of the inherent weakness of the hero himself.

Being a woman with such understanding of human nature, she gets annoyed if she feels that the heroine has relented too easily to the erring husband's pleas. At such times the heroine too is rebuked indirectly, though as usual it is the hero who bears the brunt of her annoyance.

> O lord of the country
> where the soft-spoken, modest daughter
> of the fearless forester
> tries to keep away the little green parrots
> from the millet on the terraces of dry cultivation!
> Though restrained with advice,
> many are the women ensnared in your net of lies.[87]

Again the description of the country has its specific purpose. It shows the futility of her attempts to protect the hero and the heroine. The hero is like the millet field that attracts many parrots (women) that would come there only as long as there is grain. The heroine is like the maiden who has to guard the field not only for the grain but also because it belongs to the family. But since she is gentle and modest, she is not able to make enough noise to keep the parrots away. On the other hand, when she says that many women are taken up by his untrue words, it also includes the wife who has given in easily. It is not the aim of the friend to see them unhappy or separated but merely to make her hold out long enough for him to realise his fault and repent, so that he would become a more responsible husband and member of society.

THE HERO'S FRIEND

The friend of the hero (*pāṅkaṉ* in Tamil and *vayasya* in Sanskrit) is found in both the classical literatures, but the importance given to this character in Tamil and Sanskrit is quite different. In the Tamil works we find him only in the Caṅkam poems where his function and role cannot be said to be important. We do find some colophons mentioning that the poems are utterances of the friend of the hero or the *pāṅkaṉ* but not all may be accepted as such.

> Lord of the tall hill
> where the long, white waterfall
> descends on the bright hill

sounding like the drums of experienced dancers!
Love should be shunned
for it also goes to those
who have no power of discrimination.
It is indeed foolish.[88]

In the above *Kuṟuntokai* poem which is usually accepted as the advice of the friend (*pāṅkaṉ*) to the hero who has fallen in love, we have no internal evidence for the colophon. We may also take it to be the words of the *tōḻi* who is trying to point out that in spite of the greatness of the hill that belongs to him, he is like the waterfall that comes downwards, attracting a lot of attention because of the noise it makes. He has fallen in love but has not the power of discrimination to decide when he should put a stop to his clandestine affair and marry her so that there would be no more gossip that brings down the name of the heroine. Hence on internal evidence, we can admit only very few poems as those dealing with the *pāṅkaṉ*, who is addressed as *eluva, naṇpa* and *tōḻa* (a direct masculine form of *tōḻi*).[89] Sometimes he is addressed as *kēḷir*[90] though this term is also used to denote relatives in general.[91] Though few in number, these poems give a fairly clear picture of the friend. The two epics, the *Cilappatikāram* and *Maṇimēkalai* do not mention anyone as a special friend of the hero.

In the Sanskrit works under study, the *kāvyas* on the whole do not concentrate on a friend. The only exception is Udāyin, the friend of Sarvārthasiddha in Aśvaghoṣa's *Buddhacaritam*. He is appointed by the king to be his son's companion,[92] and this is perhaps due to the king's intention of keeping the prince tied down to the pleasures of the palace so that he would not renounce his position. All dramas that deal with love as the main *rasa* deal with the *vidūṣaka*, irrespective of whether the hero is a king or not. The basic characteristics of the *vidūṣaka* are the same in all the plays, though the role and the extent of his involvement in the love-plot varies.

Though V. Swaminathaiyar in the introduction to his fourth edition of the *Kuṟuntokai* mentions that in Caṅkam poetry there are two classes of friends, Brāhmaṇas and others, we have only the evidence for Brāhmaṇa friends. It is not possible to say with any certainty if those who are addressed by the general terms like *eluva* or *kēḻir* are necessarily non-Brāhmaṇas. At least one *Kuṟuntokai* poem is addressed to the son of a Brāhmaṇa.

O son of a brahmin! son of a brahmin!

with the ewer slung low on a stick
of the red-blossomed *palāśa* tree,
stripped of its fibres!
Son of a brahmin!
eating (scanty) food of penance!
Among your words of unwritten texts (literally education)
is there any remedy
capable of uniting the separated?
It (i.e. what you say) is due to delusion.[93]

The Brāhmaṇa is thus portrayed as one who is educated so that the hero asks him if there is anything in the texts he has studied that can unite him with the heroine. Perhaps it is a reference to his Vedic education (the Vedic texts being considered not written by man) or perhaps to the oral tradition. Because of his knowledge and the high standard of education he is also called 'a friend of the poets' (*pulavar tōḻa*).[94] As regards his appearance, apart from the assumption that his preoccupation with education and his habitual fasts must have made him rather thin, the Caṅkam poems offer no details.

Neither does Aśvaghoṣa offer any description of his personal appearance. He is the son of the family priest (*purohita-suta*) and one who is wise (*dhīmaṉ*),[95] being skilled in the rule of policy (*nītiśāstrajña*).[96] Terms like *sakhā* and *mitra* are used to denote his relationship with Sarvārthasiddha. The *vidūṣaka* in the Sanskrit dramas is also a Brāhmaṇa. Apart from this single point of similarity, it is not possible to find anything else that is common to the *pāṅkaṉ* of the Caṅkam poems or Udāyin of the *Buddhacaritam* and the *vidūṣaka* of the dramas. The dramas of Bhāsa that deal with love have the *vidūṣaka* as a constant companion of the hero. It is certainly not possible for Vasantaka to keep Udayana company at Ujjain but he still makes it to the city as a beggar and is of help to him in arranging the escape.[97] In the *Svapnavāsavadattam,* he is the usual companion. The close friendship between the hero and the *vidūṣaka* is clear in the *Cārudattam* and the *Avimārakam* where he remains with the hero even in times of poverty and hardship. In fact in the latter play, Santuṣṭa is upset over the disappearance of Avimāraka; so he describes his feeling of loss as 'my own death-like sorrow'.[98] Judging from the relationship between Duṣyanta and Māṭhavya, they are like brothers, for Duṣyanta sends his *vidūṣaka* to stand in for him at a religious fast (*putra-piṇḍa-pālana*) observed by his mother.[99] Even Mātali, the charioteer of Indra, seems to be aware of this friendship to catch hold of Māṭhavya in order to anger Duṣyanta who will do anything to get him out of his sorrow.[100] Gautama in the *Mālavikāgnimitram* has been the friend of Agnimitra since childhood (*bālavayasyo 'smi*).[101]

The characteristics of the *vidūṣaka* may be said to be in contrast to those of the friend in the Caṅkam poems and in the *Buddhacaritam*. He is pictured as an odd-looking person and many of the dramas in translation call him the jester. Mānavaka in the *Vikramorvaśīyam* is said to look like a monkey (*vānara iva*).[102] He himself admits that the son of Purūravas who has lived in the hermitage need not fear him for the boy must be familiar with monkeys (*sākhāmṛgā*).[103] He is unashamedly greedy for food and this trait is brought out in every play. In the *Pratijñāyaugandharāyaṇam* he is introduced as a beggar running after a madman who has stolen his sweetmeats (*laḍḍu*).[104] While discussing the two queens in the *Svapnavāsavadattam*, he admits to Udayana, though jokingly, that both the queens are good but he prefers Vāsavadattā because she had often given him sweetmeats.[105] In the *Cārudattam*, he openly discusses his plight, for, Cārudatta is poor and so he is unable to eat the type of food that he has been accustomed to, 'and must live like the pigeons, running elsewhere for my food before I come here.'[106] Santuṣṭa tries to get himself invited for a meal, being a Brāhmaṇa[107] and later, as soon as he and Avimāraka enter the palace, he asks the maid outrightly to bring in food for him.[108] In the *Abhijñānaśākuntalam*, he is unhappy that the king is so lost in his thoughts of Śakuntalā and his unfair repudiation of her to the extent of being unmindful of his meals which obliged the *vidūṣaka* also to go hungry.[109] Mānavaka is happy that the queen is observing fasts for it would mean gifts of sweets (*modaka*) for himself.[110] Only Gautama makes use of his greed for the *modaka* as an excuse to detain Mālavikā longer on the stage so that the king can have a better look at her.[111]

Though a Brāhmaṇa, he is pictured in the plays as being uneducated and foolish. He is often called a fool (*mūrkha*) and he himself describes his intelligence as that of a lump of clay (*mṛt-piṇḍa-buddhi*).[112] In the *Avimārakam* this is further illustrated when a maid shows him a seal with her name on it and asks him to read it. The *vidūṣaka* is not even able to read the name.[113] Perhaps this is the reason why he speaks Prākṛt in spite of being a Brāhmaṇa and a close friend of the king. Another unusual and astonishing fact is that culturally too, he does not seem to have reached the level that is expected of people who keep a *nāgarika* company. Of all the characters in the drama, he alone swears at people. In the *Abhijñānaśākuntalam*, forgetting that he is within the sacred grounds of the hermitage, he uses words like *dāsyāputra* even on a general.[114] Though C.R. Devadhar translates this term as 'the son of a slave girl' it also has the very derogatory meaning of 'the son of a prostitute'.

Often, in spite of his foolishness, his words contain the truth, though expressed in a comical manner. For instance in the play *Pratijñāyaugandharāyaṇam* he informs the two ministers of Udayana's love for Vāsavadattā and adds, 'Troubles come in shoals'. This seems most appropriate, for the three of them are trying to free their king from the prison in Ujjain and the king, to add to their problems has fallen in love with the daughter of the enemy king.[115] King Agnimitra, eagerly awaiting the beginning of the contest performance and anticipating Mālavikā on the stage seems impatient. The *vidūṣaka* cautions him saying:

> Friend, the honey of your eyes has come.
> But the wasp is close by. So be watchful,[116]

meaning that though Mālavikā has appeared on stage, Queen Dhāriṇī who has control over her is also with him and any undue attention on the king's part would bring about more obstacles to his meeting Mālavikā.

The *vidūṣaka* is also portrayed as a very timid person, afraid of the dark,[117] and easily frightened.[118] He can never keep a secret and the queens as well as their maids seem to know this quite well. The maid in the *Avimārakam* easily tricks him into divulging the truth about Avimāraka's birth and lineage.[119] In the *Vikramorvaśīyam*, the maid of Queen Auśīnarī finds out easily enough the name of the woman the king is enamoured by.[120]

The chief function of the hero's friend is to advise him but the nature of the advice given varies greatly. The *pāṅkaṉ* in Tamil classical poetry is a true friend according to the standards set by the *Tirukkuṟaḷ*. He does not always agree with the hero to humour or please him, but checks him and tries to get him out of his lovelorn condition, so that he would be his noble self again. Since there are no poems attributed to the friend himself, we know of this function from the poems which are utterances of the hero to his friend. One hero says:

> O friend who rebukes!
> It would be comforting if you can
> control (this pain) as your own.
> This disease is difficult to bear

for it spreads
like melting butter on a hot rock
made hotter by the sun's rays
guarded only with his eyes
by a dumb man without arms.[121]

Thus in spite of the rebukes from the friend, the hero continues to love the heroine. These rebukes make him profess his love openly and perhaps this is a help in itself. The hero may describe the heroine who has won his heart[122] or the intensity of his love that desires not to live any longer if only he could be united with her for a single day.[123]

In a *Kalittokai* poem, we find that the friend (*tōḻaṉ*) of an erring husband does not consider the hero's fault even after hearing that he has forsaken his wife for the company of harlots. Instead he praises the virtue of the hero to the wife. So on the hero's return home, the angry wife tells him that she wishes the friend was there to see him return after his dalliance with the harlots.[124] The mention of the friend along with the charioteer and the *pāṇaṉ* who are party to his extra-marital activities suggests that the role of the friend in the *Kalittokai* is different from that found in the other Caṅkam poems and in a way comparable to that of the *vidūṣaka*. He does not seem to be independent but one who forms a part of the hero's train.

In the *Buddhacaritam*, Udāyin himself explains the characteristics of a friend (*mitra-lakṣaṇa*). They are three in number, namely, to prevent the hero from doing anything improper (*ahita*), urge him to do what is good (*hita*) and not to forsake him in misfortune.[125] He also adds that it is therefore his duty to see that he does not turn away from love which is one of the aims in life (*puruṣārtha*) and continues to advise the hero on the right conduct with women.[126] Though the advice is just the opposite of that given by the *pāṅkaṉ*, the purpose or aim is the same, which is to put the hero on the 'right' path.

The role of a friend or *vidūṣaka* in Bhāsa's plays does not seem to be important. In the *Pratijñāyaugandharāyaṇam* he merely furnishes information regarding the love of Udayana for Vāsavadattā. Apart from questioning Udayana so as to draw out the innermost feelings about his two queens, he does not do anything for the development of the love theme in *Svapnavāsavadattam*. The love of the hero and the heroine in the other two plays, the *Cārudattam* and the *Avimārakam*, do not depend on the *vidūṣaka*. Of the three plays by Kālidāsa, *Mālavikāgnimitram* is the only play in which he is important. He is referred to by Agnimitra as 'the minister who looks after another matter',[127] meaning love and truly enough he manages to incite a quarrel between the two teachers of dance so that a dance performance is arranged to decide who is the better of the two. Since Mālavikā is taking dancing lessons from one of the teachers and is considered to be the best pupil, she is sure to be chosen to represent her teacher. This gives the king the opportunity to see her in person.[128] Later, when she is imprisoned by Queen Dhāriṇī it is the *vidūṣaka* again, who, pretending to be bitten by a snake, obtains the queen's signet ring and frees Mālavikā so that she can meet the king in the *Samudragṛha*.[129] But even in this play the final union of the lovers does not depend on the friend of the hero.

REFERENCES

1. *Akam*, 369:1.
2. *Tol. Porul*, 123.
3. *Ibid.*, 124.
4. *Akam*, 298:22-23.
5. *Kurinji*, 100-106.
6. *Akam*, 92:6-7.
7. *Nar*, 128:1-6.
8. *Cilap*, 9:44-54.
9. *Ibid.*, 9:5-8.
10. *Ibid.*, 9:22-36, 30:85-87.
11. *Ibid.*, 9:40-44.
12. *Ibid.*, 6:170-73.
13. *Ibid.*, 8:69-71.
14. *Ibid.*, 3:167, 171.
15. *Mani*, 3:170-71.
16. *Ibid.*, 3:32-41.
17. *Svap. TTP*, p. 48.
18. *Caru. TTP*, p. 85.
19. *Avim*, p. 65.
20. *Ibid.*, p. 51.
21. *Kuma*, 5:62.
22. *Mala*, p. 53.
23. *Ibid.*, p. 67-69.
24. *Ibid.*, pp. 145-49.
25. *Ibid.*, p. 64.
26. *Abhi*, p. 25.
27. *Kurinji*, 100-106.
28. *Ibid.*, 61-99.
29. *Ibid.*, 55-56.
30. *Ibid.*, 38-45.
31. *Mani*, 11:126-27.
32. *Avim*, p. 65.
33. *Caru. TTP*, p. 98.

34. *Kuma*, 5:51.
35. *Mala*, p. 71.
36. *Ibid.*, p. 67.
37. *Abhi*, p. 25.
38. *Aink*, 175.
39. *Cilap*, 8:72.
40. *Ibid.*, 11:171-75.
41. *Mani*, 3:30-41.
42. *Abhi*, p. 25.
43. *Svap. TTP*, p. 48.
44. *Caru. TTP*, p. 85.
45. *Avim*, p. 56.
46. *Ibid.*, p. 82.
47. *Kuma*, 5:51.
48. *Ibid.*, 5:52-61.
49. *Ibid.*, 6:1.
50. *Abhi*, act 3. pp. 72-80.
51. *Ibid.*, act 3. pp. 75-78.
52. *Ibid.*, act 4. p. 95.
53. *Nar*, 128:1-5.
54. *Abhi*, p. 74.
55. *Nar*, 13:3-9.
56. *Ibid.*, 379.
57. *Ibid.*, 45.
58. *Aink*, 196.
59. *Nar*, 32:3-9.
60. *Avim*, p. 82.
61. *Mala*, act 5. p. 113.
62. *Kurun*, 113.
63. *Akam*, 18:13-18.
64. *Kali*, 114.
65. *Nar*, 233.
66. *Abhi*, act 4. p. 102.
67. *Kurun*, 23.
68. *Nar*, 34.
69. *Kurun*, 362.
70. *Kurinji*, 153-65; *Kali*, 39.
71. *Kurun*, 366.
72. *Ibid.*, 388.
73. *Ibid.*, 343.
74. *Abhi*, pp. 83-85.
75. *Nar*, 10.
76. *Aink*, 301, 302, 305, 306.
77. *Nar*, 229.
78. *Ibid.*, 99.
79. *Aink*, 440.
80. *Nar*, 286.
81. *Kurun*, 275.

82. *Ibid.*, 295.
83. *Ibid.*, 61.
84. *Ibid.*, 45.
85. *Ibid.*, 85.
86. *Nar*, 290.
87. *Aink*, 283.
88. *Kurun*, 78.
89. *Ibid.*, 129.
90. *Ibid.*, 58, 280.
91. *Akam*, 279:1.
92. *Budd*, 4:62.
93. *Kurun*, 156.
94. *Ibid.*, 129.
95. *Budd*, 4:8.
96. *Ibid.*, 4:62.
97. *TTP*, pp. 22-28.
98. *Avim*, act 4. p. 97.
99. *Abhi*, act 2. p. 62.
100. *Ibid.*, act 6. pp. 206-208.
101. *Mala*, act 4. p. 96.
102. *Vikr*, act 2. p. 26.
103. *Ibid.*, act 5. p. 152.
104. *Prat*, act 3; *TTP*, pp. 22-24.
105. *Svap*, act 4. *TTP*, p. 56.
106. *Caru*, act 1. *TTP*, p. 75.
107. *Avim*, act 2. p. 46.
108. *Ibid.*, act 5. p. 110.
109. *Abhi*, act 5. p. 186.
110. *Vikr*, act 2. pp. 86, 88.
111. *Mala*, act 2. p. 40.
112. *Abhi*, act 6. p. 180.
113. *Avim*, act. p. 17.
114. *Abhi*, act 2. pp. 40, 50.
115. *Prat*, act 3. *TTP*, p. 27.
116. *Mala*, act 2. p. 34.
117. *Caru*, act 1. *TTP*, p. 80.
118. *Mala*, act 4. p. 114.
119. *Avim*, act 2. p. 47.
120. *Vikr*, act 2. p. 28.
121. *Kurun*, 58.
122. *Ibid.*, 129.
123. *Ibid.*, 280.
124. *Kali*, 71:17-20.
125. *Budd*, 4:64.
126. *Ibid.*, 4:64-82.
127. *Mala*, act 1, p. 16.
128. *Ibid.*, act 1 and 2.
129. *Ibid.*, act 4.

Chapter 7

Relatives

The Foster-Mother

In both Tamil and Sanskrit classical literature we find the foster-mother (*cevili* in Tamil and *dhātrī* in Sanskrit), taking care of children, and both the literatures suggest that she is a wet nurse employed by or attached to rich families to nurse and care for the children. A *Kuṟuntokai* poem mentions how the hero and the heroine, being neighbours, quarrel as children, pulling at each other's hair. It is not easy for their foster-mothers to separate them. But love blossoms between them when they grow older.[1] The foster-mothers seem to have been entrusted with the duty of bringing up the children. The *Buddhacaritam* also mentions a *dhātrī* for Siddhārtha. When the king arrives with the wise men to see his son, he carries him from the side of the *dhātrī* and Aśvaghoṣa describes the baby lying next to the *dhātrī* as Skanda beside Devī.[2] Thus in the growth and upbringing of the child, the foster-mother seems to have been important. But love poetry is not concerned with the foster-mother of the hero. It is interested in the foster-mother of the heroine, for, it is the heroine who is protected by the foster-mother, her own mother, as well as the other members of her family. In the Tamil texts, she is the friend of the heroine's mother[3] and the mother of the *tōḻi*.[4] The *Tolkāppiyam* gives more importance to the foster-mother than to the natural mother and though the term mother (*aṉṉai, tāy, yāy*) is used interchangeably for both the mother and the foster-mother, certain conventions show that it is the foster-mother who is important. The mother, busy with the overall management of the household, and other relevant duties, has little time or less time with the child compared to the foster-mother. In fact, the *Tolkāppiyam* mentions that it is the *cevili* who imparts education to the heroine and therefore is called 'mother'.[5] This does not necessarily mean any formal education but the teaching of values and family traditions. She does this by giving advice and preventing the heroine from doing wrong. The lives of people in the past and present and a discussion of what could happen if some value or tradition is not observed, helps in this education.[6] The relationship between the foster-mother and the girl is naturally closer than that between a foster-mother and a boy and it is this closeness and affection that we find in the Caṅkam love poems. The *cevili* feeds the heroine as a child and she has such rights over the child that she would threaten the girl with a stick, though a flower-soft one, into drinking the milk.

Holding in one hand
the glittering gold vessel
filled with sweet milk mixed with honey,
(the foster-mother)
shook a little, thin, flower-soft stick
bidding her drink.
The playful girl, refusing it,
toddled about the shed
causing the pearls in her gold anklet
to tinkle.
The (other) foster-mothers,
their hair finely streaked with grey,
grew weary unable to catch.[7]

She sleeps next to the heroine, perhaps a habit continued from childhood, and embraces her while sleeping.[8] The care over the heroine's food and well-being continues as long as she is with them. Sometimes, she sends the heroine and her friend, the *tōḻi*, to guard the millet fields and this gives them the opportunity for play while keeping an eye on the field.

Her love and constant care for the heroine makes it possible for her to notice the changes in the heroine when she falls in love. There are various ways in which she tries to find out the reason for the change. She may ask her own daughter, the *tōḻi*, as to what has happened. This gives the *tōḻi* an opportunity to inform the foster-mother of her friend's love for the hero as in the following poem:

Long may you live, mother !
Please listen to my words.

You ask (why)
your daughter, not even drinking milk,
suffers greatly and turns pale.
I myself do not know for certain.
One day, while plucking flowers
from the gorgeous branches of the *vēṅkai*,
we shouted, 'Tiger, Tiger'.
(A youth) wearing a garland
made by threading with needle
the bright, lovely water-lilies
which bloom like eyes,
stood before us.
In his hair was a chaplet of ixora
and his chest, worthy of being embraced,
was adorned with the red sandal paste.
With his decorated bow drawn
and a selected arrow in hand, he asked,
'Which way did the animal go?'
Feeling shy, we tried to hide ourselves
one behind the other.
He asked,
'O modest maidens with dark shiny hair
divided carefully into five parts
and beautiful foreheads !
Do your mouths utter falsehood?'
Then the lord of the mountains
drove his chariot, controlling the pace of the horses.
Before leaving,
he looked into the surm-lined eyes
of your daughter.
At the end of the day, at sunset,
she looked in the direction he went and said,
'My friend, he is indeed a man.'
For the discerning it may mean something.[9]

The pallor of the heroine, her disinterest in all that she had enjoyed doing before and her listlessness worry the *cevili* so much that thinking it is due to some serious malady, she invites the priest or priestess of Murukaṉ to cure the girl.[10] The *tōḻi* tells the heroine:

Ignorant (of the true cause),
and thinking 'she is afflicted by Murukaṉ,'
mother too is distressed.
So it is cruel not to inform her
that the illness that spreads pallor
over the surm-lined eyes
resembling choice (blue) lotuses
is caused by the lord of the faraway hills.[11]

If the *cevili* happens to see the heroine go out at night she does not go out at once to catch her red-handed. Perhaps she suspects something, but out of regard for the heroine's modesty she keeps quiet and later enquires from her own daughter about the heroine's movements. She may even sound harsh and threatening, for a *tōḻi* tells her:

Mother, do not harass us saying
'At midnight, in the dense darkness,
quiet after the heavy showers that came
with thunder (and lightning)
I saw her descend from the upper floor
with her heavy earrings flashing
like lightning.
Her plait of thick, wavy hair loosened,
she moved like a peacock descending the hillslope.'[12]

The *tōḻi* might feign innocence, as in this poem, or admit the truth. But the foster-mother is ever careful about the heroine.

Usually the foster-mother comes to know of the heroine's connection with a youth through other women in the village or neighbourhood, for they gossip. This gossip angers the foster-mother but there is nothing she can do to stop this gossip except to prevent the heroine from meeting the youth. She may try threatening the heroine and the friend with a stick, thinking that being afraid they would stay away. One girl laments:

Hearing the words of the women
who gossip in the street,
mother took a little stick
and threatened me.

I am deeply distressed, my friend.[13]

The only other alternative she has, is to keep the girl indoors and thus prevent her from going out or meeting him, though it gives rise to complaints like:

Listening to the women of this village
who are possessed by the demon of gossip
and speak only evil,
mother guards me at home saying,
'In this large port,
on the sands as white as the moonbeams,
a chariot yoked with beautiful horses
chosen carefully by the charioteer
roams day and night.'[14]

Though the foster-mother thinks this is effective enough to put an end to gossip, it is not necessarily so. The hero comes to see her in spite of the difficulties. The friend of a heroine tells within hearing distance of the hero who has come:

Bless you my friend!
The lord of the cool ports
who sported with us on the beach of fine sand
has come stealthily
in spite of mother's strict guard.[15]

It is such strictness that causes greater fear and inability on the part of the girls to communicate with her on this matter or to persuade her into accepting the heroine's choice and so this leads to elopement.

On the other hand, when the heroine goes away, her anger disappears and in its place we find her intense love for the girl she has brought up. Some incidents, though small and had seemed to have no importance, begin to have meaning. For instance, one foster-mother says that once when she embraced the heroine, she was not pleased and tried to brush away the foster-mother saying that she was perspiring. Now that she is gone with the hero, the then unsuspecting mother realises that, being in love and used to the stealthy embraces of the hero, the heroine did not welcome that of the mother.[16] She may accept the departure with equanimity and inform her friend, i.e. the heroine's natural mother, about it. Then she will have to be careful in the way she puts it to her so as not to cause her any grief, or only the minimum possible. So she may say:

> With the beat of the drum
> and the sound of conches
> the friendship of (your) bangled maiden
> with the youth wearing the heroic anklet
> and carrying the bright red-leafed spear
> is proved true,
> like the good works of the Kōcar of Nālūr
> deliberating in the village open
> under the old banyan tree.[17]

By talking of the drums and conches which are usually sounded at weddings, she stresses on the marriage of the daughter which would please any mother. In this way she hopes to reduce the shock and grief of the mother at her daughter's silent departure. It does not mean, however, that she is free from grief or anxiety herself. She prays to the deities that nature be kind to the couple so that their journey may be pleasant.

> May the arid tracts
> crossed by the modest, dark maiden
> who, leaving us,
> went with the youth who carries
> a bright, long spear,
> have cool showers.
> May the sun not shine brightly.
> May there be shady trees and sand
> on the narrow, mountain path.[18]

Many Caṅkam poems dealing with the elopement of the hero and the heroine, depict the *cevili* as going in search of the girl. What her intention is we are not sure, but most of the poems mention her anxiety for the girl's safety and comfort. None of the poems show her meeting the girl during the journey, but all portray the great sorrow of the mother. One such foster-mother braving the scorching sun and the summer heat, is tired and disappointed that all her efforts are in vain. She laments:

> My legs falter.
> My eyes, constantly looking out
> have lost their brightness.
> In this world are many others.
> They outnumber the stars
> in the broad, dark sky.[19]

This poem shows how much she is prepared to suffer in order to save the heroine from such suffering. She also asks the wayfarers or recluses who come from the opposite direction if they have seen her daughter with a youth.[20] The mother of the heroine does not go out to look for her daughter. Likewise, it is the *cevili* who visits the heroine in her new home after marriage and reports to the mother, the happy life the girl is leading. The *Aiṅkuṟunūṟu* contains a number of poems dealing with this role of the *cevili*. For example, one *cevili* informs the mother that:

> The lord of the beautiful *mullai* region
> where the honey-collecting bee
> hums around pollen-rich flowers,
> sat happily embracing his wife,
> while the lovely, dark-eyed son played.[21]

Thus, the foster-mother is more important than the mother in the life of the heroine in her parents' home.

The role of the *dhātrī* in the Sanskrit works does not seem to be so important, and of the works under study, only the plays of Bhāsa depict the foster-mother as having a role, however small, in the love affair of the heroine. Some translators, however, seem to prefer the word nurse to foster-mother.[22] Her role in some ways, is similar to that of the *cevili* in the Tamil poems. In the *Svapnavāsavadattam* it is Padmāvatī's foster-mother (*dhātrī*) who informs her of the decision taken regarding her marriage.[23] Later, the foster-mother of Vāsavadattā comes to the palace of Udayana with the portraits of Udayana and Vāsavadattā. Like the *cevili*, she has come to the house of her daughter, though Vāsavadattā is reported dead. She carries a message to Udayana from the Queen of Ujjain which also reveals the fact that the Queen, along with the King, is responsible for the decision regarding the marriage of the lovers and their meeting in the first place.[24] The *dhātrī*, thus acts as the mouthpiece and representative of the mother in such matters. In this play we are not able to get a clear picture of the relationship between the foster-mother and the heroine but the two small incidents are enough to show that the communication between the young woman and her foster-mother is better than that found between her and her own mother.

Gautamī in the *Abhijñānaśākuntalam*, though a hermit woman (*tapasī*), is like a foster-mother to the girls brought up at the hermitage. She is addressed with respect as *ārye* (vocative of *āryā*) or lovingly as *jāte* (vocative of *jātā* meaning mother), though she is normally referred to as *āryā gautamī*. She seems to have taken over the responsibility of caring for them and teaching them good manners and behaviour like any other mother or foster-mother. She is so much like the *cevili* when seeing Śakuntalā listless and pale, is anxious for her health, but being a woman of the hermitage, is unaware of the true cause for the girl's affliction. She resorts to religious help, for, she brings a vessel of water, perhaps from the sanctuary, and sprinkling some of it on Śakuntalā's head, says:

> With this water mixed with *darbha* grass,
> your body will be relieved of pain.[25]

She reminds the girls, especially Śakuntalā, to be respectful to Kāśyapa[26] and to pay reverence to the various deities at the hermitage (*tapovanadevatā*) before she leaves for her husband's home.[27] Being a quiet woman, she merely stands by while Kāśyapa advises Śakuntalā on her duties to her husband and her behaviour in the palace. Then she confirms all that he has said with the words:

> This is the (proper) advice for wives.
> My child, be sure to remember all of it.[28]

Yet in the palace, still maintaining the quiet dignity of a woman from the hermitage, she is fearless enough to point out to King Duṣyanta that both he and Śakuntalā have erred. Neither of them has observed tradition and consulted the elders. This naturally brought about problems. When all her attempts to make Duṣyanta remember fail, she is not angry with Śakuntalā but pities her instead. Her confidence in Śakuntalā is not shaken and she is convinced that Duṣyanta is her husband.[29] But her position as a woman of the hermitage makes her powerless to protect Śakuntalā.

The *dhātrī* or foster-mother in the *Avimārakam* stands out as an unusual mother or foster-mother compared to the foster-mothers we see in the other texts under study, for, she alone brings the lovers together. She has her doubts, for she is not sure of Avimāraka's family and lineage and is therefore worried that the Royal Family will be disgraced. But finding that Kuraṅginī is listless with no desire for food, clothes, cosmetics or even the various pastimes with her friends, the *dhātrī* decides to invite Avimāraka to enter the palace stealthily. Her fears and doubts find some solace and excuse in 'a voice' off-stage, which she feels has a divine quality.

> I feel a thrill through my whole body.
> Surely a heavenly being spoke. I am now
> convinced that he is no ordinary man.[30]

To make his entry into the palace easier, she explains to him the lay-out of the palace and promises to manage everything that has to be seen to within the palace. Thus she is one who definitely helps the heroine and the hero, not worrying about the consequences and keeping the secret from the heroine's parents as well.

The Mother

In the Tamil and Sanskrit literature dealing with love, the mother of the hero or the heroine does not have any particular role worthy of mention. She is usually in the background and the mother of the hero seems even less important than the mother of the heroine. In the Caṅkam poems, the heroine's mother and her foster-mother are not distinguished for both are referred to as mother (*aṉṉai, yāy, tāy*), but some colophons use the term *naṟṟāy* to denote the mother. Most of the poems that portray the feelings of the mother are those that sing of the elopement of the heroine with the hero, and the mother's sorrow at her daughter's departure and the pity for the gentle and protected girl who traverses the dry, waterless path with the hero. Some poems do provide internal evidence to show that the term mother actually refers to the natural mother and not to the foster-mother. A mother bewails the departure of her daughter, who

Making desolate the splendid mansion
with walls that touch the clouds,
and not thinking even of me
who gave birth to her,[31]

has gone away. Here it is obvious that the mother is the *naṟṟāy*. In other poems the reference to the parents naturally indicates that it is the natural mother who is mentioned. For instance another mother thinks of the way she had cared for her child.

Even when she ran about gaily
with her anklets tinkling
in the broad, glorious mansion,
playing ball with her playmates,
I call her, 'Won't you come'?
Then holding a vessel of milk
resembling the white flower
of the broad-leafed *pakaṉṟai* filled with dew
fed her saying,
'If you take one (mouthful) for me,
then take this for your father.'
I have cherished and cared for her
since the day she was born.
Now my little girl with gold bangles
has left with the man devoid of goodness.[32]

A heroine wishing to send word to the hero that her parents would be away and that it would be easy for them to meet, tells her friend:

I wish we could get a loyal person
who would walk fast
over the long-stretching path
with a message
to the lord of the cool, extensive beaches
that
My father, his wounds
suffered while killing sharks,

healed,
has gone out to the large, blue ocean.
My mother too has gone to the salt-beds
to barter salt for padi.
So it is easier to meet now.[33]

In these two poems it is clear that the mother who is referred to is the heroine's and not the *tōḻi's.* There are yet other poems where the foster-mother refers to the mother as *tāy* and says that the heroine would not drink the sweet milk that she and the mother (*yāṉum tāyum*) gave the girl.[34]

From most of the poems we gather that the mother is actually kind and understanding and does not get angry when she hears of the love of her daughter. She is the one to convey the news of the daughter's choice to the father and the brothers in such a way that they do not lose their temper,[35] though she herself is anxious for her daughter's happiness. A heroine herself feels uncomfortable to be in the presence of the mother, for, she feels that the mother knows of her clandestine love but keeps quiet. Unable to say it out herself or bear her own sorrows, she tells her friend:

May you live long, my friend.
My forehead slowly turns sallow.
My tender, shoot-like body grows thin.
Thus my sorrow becomes evident, for many to see.
What else would all this do
but take away my life?
The wicked women of this town
enjoying gossip
do not realise that women are anxious
for those who cross numerous paths
where groups of bears eat
the abundant tubular flowers resembling hailstones
which fall from their bunches on the *mahua* tree,
with spotted trunk and bubbly stem.
They talk ill (of me).
But saying,
'It does not conform to my daughter's behaviour,'
mother prays (to the deities).
How am I to continue like this in her presence?

She knowing me (and my love) is calm.[36]

Thus parental disapproval is not always met with.

However, when the heroine leaves, both the mother and the foster-mother are grieved but tradition prevents the mother from going out in search of her. She laments the separation from her daughter and her sorrow increases or returns whenever she sees the toys the heroine had played with or the trees under which she used to play. She hugs these things and sheds tears.[37] She is anxious to have her back at home though she is also conscious that her daughter would have to set up home on her own. The return of the daughter is something that she longs for but is not sure of. So she resorts to omens and shamanism. A mother tells the crow:

Little black crow with faultless feathers!
I shall give you
good food of raw, tender flesh
in a gold vessel
to eat with your loving relatives.
Just caw that my daughter with lovely tresses
comes with the spear-bearing youth
of valour and victory in battle.[38]

She hopes that the cawing of the crow which is usually considered to be an omen that informs us of guests to come, would mean the home-coming of her daughter with the hero. Another mother asks the priest of Murukaṉ called the *vēlaṉ,* to foresee if the hero would bring the girl back to her home.

I hear that his mother,
expecting my young daughter with large upper arms,
who has crossed the difficult tracts
together with the youth bearing a good spear,
prepares happily
painting the walls with red clay,
spreading sand in the courtyard
and hanging garlands.
Even if he does not favour me
for the affection of having borne
the modest maid with gazelle-looks,
I have also helped care for her and her beauty

mounting her on my hips
or combing her tresses.
It would be beneficial if he knew that.
O *Vēlā* who utters wise words and knowing the future!
You wear a long hair-knot that touches your clothes
and carry a bent, forked staff
hung with a small satchel.
With your molucca beans
divine for me his intentions.
Will he bring her first to our house
so that my eyes shedding continuous tears
even at night, will sleep,
or will he take her to his?[39]

Though her displeasure is usually directed towards the hero who, she feels, has persuaded her innocent little girl with false or untrue words, her anger is also directed towards his mother. At times she even curses the hero's mother.

May she come to grief,
shedding tears each time she remembers. . .
the mother of this youth.
He is a skilled archer
carrying a bow made of new bamboo.
It is he who took my daughter
through the cruel desert,
where the male deer with forked horns,
having escaped a tiger,
calls its mate.[40]

This angry outburst does not however last long, for her chief concern is the happiness of her daughter. One mother, anxious to perform the usual ceremonies is prepared to send a message to the hero's mother.

Won't you tell the mother of the youth
with a victorious spear,
wearing a faultless, bright heroic anklet
and adept at lying,
'Even if you hold in your house

the anklet-removing ceremony
why not have the wedding in ours?'[41]

Thus the mother and her feelings become important only when there is an elopement. She does not otherwise play an important part in separating them or in bringing them together. She is however useful in giving us a picture of the life of the heroine in her childhood surrounded by her relatives and friends and also the home where there is love and luxury.

In the epics, the parents of both Kōvalaṉ and Kaṇṇaki are mentioned, but apart from getting them married and helping them set up a home of their own,[42] they have not done anything. Through Kaṇṇaki we learn that his parents felt sorry for her[43] but they do not seem to have advised their son or interfered in any way. Mātavi in the *Maṇimēkalai* is basically responsible for instilling into the mind of Maṇimēkalai her desire for her to become a Buddhist nun and to avoid the attentions of Utayakumaraṉ though she too feels attracted to him.[44] Utayakumaraṉ's mother does not seem concerned that her son is interested in a Buddhist nun born of a *gaṇikā*. But when he is killed for having behaved dishonourably towards Maṇimēkalai she is angry and seeks to take revenge. She does not propose to do this openly. She hides her feelings of anger and revenge from her husband, the king, and from Maṇimēkalai. She gets an uneducated and uncultured youth to molest Maṇimēkalai and spread the news in town so that the people will no longer regard her as the Buddhist nun who saved many from hunger but look down on her as an immoral woman. This, she feels, would disgrace Maṇimēkalai who is saved from such a fate by her supernatural powers.[45]

In the Sanskrit texts too, the mother does not play an important role. Māyā, in the *Buddhacaritam*, is described as a good woman worthy of being the mother of a Bodhisattva but she does not live long enough to bring him up.[46] Instead, she goes up to heaven so that she does not die and Sarvārthasiddha is cared for by his mother's sister as if he were her own child.[47] But she too is not important in his love relationship or his marriage. Mothers seem to be out of the whole drama of love and have nothing whatsoever to do with the love of the hero or the heroine. The Queen of Ujjain, the mother of Vāsavadattā acts as the chief communicator between the heroine and the father. She does not, however, relate the daughter's love for Udayana, which she may not have been aware of, but only her desire to learn to play the *vīṇā*. Like all mothers she is anxious to get her daughter married but is sad at the thought of having to send her to her husband's house.[48] Together with the king, she makes decisions regarding the choice of a suitable son-in-law. As soon as she hears of the capture of Udayana, she announces: 'Then we will not affiance Vāsavadattā to anyone at present.'[49]

In the *Svapnavāsavadattam,* we learn that she actually has intended Udayana as the husband for her daughter and that the music lessons have been arranged to bring them together and develop their love. This is clear from the message she sends to Udayana through the foster-mother of Vāsavadattā.

> Vāsavadattā has passed away. To me and to Mahāsena you are as dear as our Gopāla and Pālaka, for, from the very first we intended you to be our son-in-law. That is why you were brought to Ujjain. Under the pretext of learning the *vīṇā* we gave her to you with no ritual fire as witness. In your impetuosity, you carried her off without the auspicious nuptial rites. So we had portraits painted of you and Vāsavadattā and therewith celebrated the marriage. . .[50]

This is an unusual role for a mother when compared to that of the mother in the other texts under study. Thus we may say that she is at least partly responsible for the love between Udayana and Vāsavadattā, for though Udayana sees the princess on the way to the temple, the music lessons gave them the opportunity to meet, cultivate their love and perhaps plan their elopement. The mother of Padmāvatī, being a widow, lives in the hermitage.[51] All her obligations and duties towards Padmāvatī, especially her marriage, are carried out by her son's wife who is now the queen (*bhaṭṭinī* or *bhartṛdhārikā*) who wants to hold the marriage on the very day of the betrothal for the day is auspicious.[52] The Queen of Vairantya, the mother of Kuraṅginī is happy that there are proposals of marriage and like the mother of Vāsavadattā, is eager to get her daughter married and yet regards her daughter as a little girl.[53] Obviously she has entrusted the care of her daughter to the *dhātrī* for even when she hears that the girl has just been saved from a wild elephant, she stays on at court till the king suggests that she consoles Kuraṅginī.[54] This is further proved by the fact that she has not discovered the presence of Avimāraka in her daughter's apartments for more than a year[55] and we do not know her reactions when she finds out later. Though she is keen in obtaining Viṣṇusena (Avimāraka) as her son-in-law,[56] she is not present when the final decision is made.[57]

Vasantasenā's mother is only briefly mentioned and as is expected of a *gaṇikā's* mother, she is merely interested in making her daughter serve and please men of wealth, position and influence. So when the brother-in-law of the king sends ornaments and wishes to have the company and services of Vasantasenā, she sends those ornaments to Vasantasenā bidding her dress up and come at once to his presence.[58] We do not know what her feelings or reactions are on hearing of her daughter's love for Cārudatta who is poor.

In the works of Kālidāsa, only Menā, the mother of Pārvatī and Menakā, the mother of Śakuntalā are mentioned. Menā is the mind-born daughter of the *pitṛs,* equal to Himavān, respected by sages[59] and always self-restrained.[60] Though aware of Pārvatī's feelings at being unsuccessful in winning the love of Śiva with her beauty, Menā tries to dissuade her daughter from performing austerities, for, in her opinion, as a mother, Pārvatī's body is too tender for *tapas.* She says, 'The delicate śirīṣa flower can bear the tread of a bee, but not that of a bird.'[61]

But she has to give in to the insistence of the daughter especially when Himavān himself grants her a place suitable for her penance. She is present when the Śaptarṣis and Arundhatī arrive to ask for Pārvatī's hand in marriage.[62] A typical mother, her eyes are blinded by tears while tying the sacred thread and has to be helped by the foster-mother.[63] But emotion does not make her forget propriety or duty. She makes Pārvatī worship the tutelary deities (*kuladevatās*) and pay homage to the chaste ladies present, before leaving her apartments for the marriage ceremony.[64] Here we have a mother who is quiet and happy for there is nothing for her to be anxious about, regarding the choice of a husband for Pārvatī. All there is to be known about him is known to all and there cannot be a more desirable son-in-law for her.

Menakā's appearance all of a sudden shows that she has been keeping a watchful eye over the life of her daughter. But her role is merely limited to taking Śakuntalā to a hermitage where she is cared for and protected till she meets Duṣyanta.[65] Apart from helping the daughter at the most awkward and needful hour, she is in no way useful to the development of her love for Duṣyanta or its fulfilment.

The Father and the Brothers

Usually the responsibility of finding a suitable husband and getting the daughter married rests with the father (*tantai* in Tamil and *tātaḥ* in Sanskrit). The father, and in his absence, the brother or brothers have the final authority in accepting or rejecting a proposal of marriage. Most often he is not aware of the love affair of the daughter and is informed by his wife, who would have heard of it from her friend, the foster-mother. The heroine is afraid to go out to meet the hero, for, she fears her father. The father (or brother) being brave himself is easily provoked and the heroine and her friend are aware of this. When her mother questions the movements of the heroine saying that she saw the heroine go down the stairs at night, a *tōḻi* explains that she could not have done so because she is afraid of the dark.

Besides,
Father with his Murukaṉ-like fury
and great strength,
though without his hounds
resembling a pack of tigers,
is home.
Won't she be afraid to do so?[66]

This fear may actually prevent the heroine and the friend from keeping their tryst with the hero whenever the father is around the house. But it can also serve as a means of exaggerating the dangers of clandestine meetings so as to make him marry the heroine and thereby put an end to such meetings. A *tōḻi* tells a heroine within hearing distance of the hero

The chieftain of the hills
where the fearless boar
having eaten the soft ears of millet
sleeps on the slopes of firm rocks,
is afraid that father would know.

That is why he did not come (to the appointed place.)[67]

The hero is not necessarily afraid of the father, but the friend makes it clear that it is not easy for them to keep such appointments. Another *tōḻi* from the agricultural tracts asks the hero:

O owner of the farmlands
where the male water-fowl in the tanks
answers the call of its mate,
let me ask you.
You come every day to the tall mansion
where people sleep.
Are you not afraid of her father's spear?[68]

The fear for the father and his valour and ability is not always mentioned clearly. A mere description of the work he does is given, leaving the reader or listener to infer his qualities. For instance, a friend tells the hero that she is the daughter of the fisherman who goes out to sea and returns with huge sharks whose meat cannot be consumed by the family so that they spread out pieces of the shark flesh to dry.[69] This gives the impression that he is fearless and strong. One of the poems in the *Aiṅkuṟunūṟu*, usually accepted as the words of a hero on his return after a journey before marriage, sounds very much like the subtle hint or invitation of a *tōḻi* to a hero that he may come and ask for the heroine's hand in marriage.

Her father's town is in the fields
with tanks and dense shade,
where the warrior-like, broad-horned buffaloes
laze with their women-like mates.
She has a beautiful, bright forehead
resembling the lotus that blooms in tanks.[70]

The comparison of the buffaloes and their mates to warriors and their wives is a suggestion that the people of the village or town approve of love and marrige and therefore he need not fear rejection. His coming with a proposal would make the heroine happy. Such suggestions usually have the desired effect for a hero promises to go to the father's place, with a proposal of marriage.

Maiden with bright bangles!
If I can obtain you (in marriage)
I shall come to your father's village
where the black-horned, red-eyed she-buffalo
newly delivered of calf,
feeds her beloved young
with udders flowing (with milk).[71]

In spite of his valour and the fear and respect the daughter and her friends have for him, the father is very fond of his daughter. Many poems depict this by referring to the heroine as the 'beloved, modest daughter of the forester' (*kuṉṟak kuṟavaṉ kātaṉ maṭamakaḷ*).[72] She is even considered precious because the father had prayed to the deities and begged to have her.

The forester of the hills
worshipping God, prayed
to obtain this young girl
wearing bright bangles.
Far away is the country you go to
causing her long eyes, spread with red thin lines
to shed tears.[73]

Sometimes the terms *taṉṉaiyar* or *tamar* are used in the plural to denote the elder, male members of the family, usually the father and brothers of the heroine. Their reaction to a proposal of marriage from the hero is not always favourable. This uncertainty makes the heroine and her friend pray to deities along with the mother, though the mother and the girls pray for different favours.

'Long live Ātaṉ! Long live Aviṉi!
May his enemies be subdued.
May his years be more.'
Thus prayed mother.
We prayed,
'May the lord of cool waterfronts
at large, lotus-blooming tanks
marry her.
May father too give his consent.'[74]

Instances are not wanting where the father and mother hear of the love of their daughter for a particular youth from her friend and later when he comes with a proposal, accept it and arrange to get their daughter married to him. A *tōḻi* relates how she conveyed to the heroine's father and mother in such a manner that they accepted the secret love between the young couple. When the chief of the mountains came to ask for the heroine's hand, they agreed and the whole town which was busy with gossip, then united in wishing them well.[75] But the knowledge of the heroine's clandestine affair seems to anger and vex the father and the brothers at first. However, after some reflection on the whole matter they get calm and realise that it is only natural and nothing is amiss. A *Kalittokai* poem relates how the friend informs the mother of the heroine's love for the youth who saves her from the swift waters of the mountain stream. The mother too conveys the matter to the father and brothers with care and with such words as to make it more acceptable to them. Yet their eyes redden and for the whole day they keep looking at their bows and choice arrows, angry and impatient. Later they become calm and saying, 'Neither is to be blamed,' hang their heads as if ashamed at their hasty anger.[76]

The Caṅkam poems also show that the father and brothers (*tamar* or *taṉṉaiyar*) sometimes disapprove of the union and even if the heroine elopes with the hero, go in search of her. On such occasions, it is the hero who, out of love and consideration for the heroine, hides himself so that no confrontation or regrettable incidents would take place. A heroine remembers such an incident that took place on the way during their elopement.

It happened long ago,
but revolves before my eyes as if today.
The parasol-shaped flowers
of the soft petalled *kōṅku,*
bright like stars before dawn,
beautified the thickets of the flower-fragrant forest.
Along that path,
you feared not the robbers who clashed noisily
wearing armlets
and living by the sharp, practised arrows.
You defeated them in battle.
But when my people approached

you hid yourself in that forest.[77]

In this poem, she refers clearly to the brothers and others following her and her lover. But the hero, though heroic and capable of putting the enemies to flight, is reluctant to show enmity towards the members of the heroine's family. A hero, taking his beloved from her father's house without his consent, tells her on the way:

My dark-hued beauty!
You have come,
crossing the bounds of your father's house,
moving gracefully like a walking doll.
Play for a while,
watching the deep red cochineal insect
that spread over the forest
made lovely by the first showers.
I shall hide near the sand bank
behind the *vēṅkai* with thick trunk
rubbed against by young elephants.
If robbers come,
I shall drive them away fearlessly.
If your brothers come,
I shall stay hidden.[78]

Though the father and the brothers are hasty enough to follow the couple they do not actually bring her back. When they see him hide himself, they cannot help realising his decency and the helpless and forlorn condition of the heroine if they were to be separated.

As in the Tamil works, the Sanskrit works too, give the father importance as the head of the family, but his actual role in the love of his daughter is negligible. Like the father in Tamil love poetry, he too is loving and protective towards his daughter and though anxious to get her married, is careful to give her only to one who is suitable. We find this indulgence, love and anxiety in King Mahāsena of Ujjain towards his daughter Vāsavadattā. In his anxiety to choose the best possible man as the son-in-law, he refuses nobody and favours none,[79] though keen on getting her married. He is also aware that when a girl marries, she has duties and responsibilities and therefore would have no time or opportunity to indulge in her own likes and dislikes. So, knowing that Vāsavadattā is keen on learning to play the *vīṇā*, he gives her the Goṣavatī, the *vīṇā* of Udayana who has just been captured.[80] Only in the play *Svapnavāsavadattam* we come to know that he and his queen had planned to get her married to Udayana who is brave, beloved of his people and has all the qualities they look for in a son-in-law. This perhaps explains the affection and respect Mahāsena shows towards his young prisoner.[81] His son is mentioned as a suitor for Padmāvatī in the *Svapnavāsavadattam* but not even his name is mentioned till later in the play when we hear the message sent by the Queen of Ujjain to Udayana. Here we are told that there are actually two sons—Gopāla and Pālaka.[82] But we are not sure which of these two is Padmāvatī's suitor. In the absence of Padmāvatī's father, her brother Darśaka[83] arranges her marriage with Udayana who is believed to be a widower. The reason for his choosing Udayana and offering his sister on his own is given by Padmāvatī's *dhātrī*.

> He (Udayana) came here on some other business. When our king observed his nobility, wisdom, youth and beauty, he offered her (Padmāvatī's) hand of his own accord.[84]

The *Kumārasaṃbhavam* depicts Himavān as a doting father to whom his daughter is the favourite child.[85] In the case of Pārvatī, there is no need for fear, for her love is not forbidden or even feared to be so. Ever since Nārada foretold that she would be the wife of Śiva,[86] both Pārvatī and her father have not thought of another person as her husband. Yet the love of the father and his esteem of the daughter is such that he cannot offer her to Śiva, though he is Devadeva, unsolicited.[87] So he takes her along with two of her friends to the place of Śiva's penance, and worshipping him with customary offerings, asks the girls to serve and propitiate him.[88] He is full of sympathy for Pārvatī when Śiva burns Kāma and vanishes from the presence of women. He takes her in his arms in sympathy to protect her from shame and the wrath of Śiva. But love and concern for Pārvatī does not blind him to the greatness of Śiva, so that when she asks for permission to do penance, he knowing her love for Śiva is only delighted to grant her permission to do penance.[89] He is very pleased when the Śaptarṣis arrive with Arundhatī to ask for his daughter's hand in marriage to Śiva but also seeks his wife's approval.[90] Thus the father in the *Kumārasaṃbhavam* is one who approves of the choice even before it is consciously made and Pārvatī has his help and support in her endeavour to win the love of Śiva.

Śakuntalā has never known her father Viśvāmitra but does not lack fatherly affection because of Kāśyapa whose hermitage is her home. The fear and respect for him is present but Kāśyapa being a sage is gentle and seems to communicate better with her than the other fathers do with their own daughters. He too is concerned with the marriage of Śakuntalā and knowing that her future holds some adversity (*daivam pratikūlam*), he goes to Somatīrtha on a pilgrimage to remove or at least lessen the adverse effect of her fate.[91] He is away during Śakuntalā's period of courtship and marriage and comes back only after the king has left for his palace. He is overjoyed at hearing the incorporeal voice announce that Śakuntalā is married and with child. So embracing her he says:

> Though his sight is obstructed by smoke, the offering of
> the sacrificer has fallen into the sacrificial fire.
> My child! Like knowledge imparted to a good pupil,
> you are not to be lamented over.
> This very day I shall send you to your husband, escorted
> by hermits.[92]

He also sheds tears at parting with Śakuntalā and gives advice regarding her behaviour in her husband's house. This is something not found in any of the other works under study. Kāśyapa wonders if he, a hermit, were to feel such sorrow at having to send a daughter away to her husband's house, how much more would a real father suffer at his separation from his child.[93] He blesses Śakuntalā:

> May you be cherished by your husband as Śarmiṣṭā was
> cherished by Yayāti; and may you bear a son as she did Puru,
> who shall be sovereign of the world.[94]

The advice he gives her is traditional, asking her to be respectful to her elders, polite and friendly towards her co-wives, obedient to her husband and courteous towards servants so that her humility and good behaviour will be an honour to her family.[95]

Though he finds it difficult to check his tears[96] and wonders how his grief (*śokaḥ*) will cease, he is nevertheless relieved at having fulfilled his duty.

> A daughter, actually, is another's property; and having today sent her to her lord, I find my soul has become tranquil as after restoring a deposit.[97]

He is not important after Śakuntalā is sent to her husband's palace and though he is said to know everything through the power of his penance,[98] he does not do anything further to mitigate the severity of the curse or their suffering.

Mālavikā's father being dead, her brother Mādhavasena arranges a marriage between her and Agnimitra. Even though there is a political reason for the marriage it turns out to be a marriage for love as well.[99] By arranging the marriage and sending her to his capital, he prepares the *parivrājakā* and perhaps Mālavikā for the love between her and Agnimitra. Otherwise he is unimportant and is only reported on stage.

REFERENCES

1. *Kurun,* 229.
2. *Budd,* 1:4, 6.
3. *Kurun,* 15.
4. *Tol. Porul,* 123.
5. *Ibid.,* 122.
6. *Ibid.,* 151.
7. *Nar,* 110: 1-8.
8. *Kurun,* 356: 6-7.
9. *Akam,* 48.
10. *Aink,* 249.
11. *Ibid.,* 242.
12. *Akam,* 158: 1-7.
13. *Nar,* 149: 3-5.
14. *Akam,* 20:8-13.
15. *Aink,* 115.
16. *Kurun,* 84.
17. *Ibid.,* 15.
18. *Ibid.,* 378.
19. *Ibid.,* 44.
20. *Kali,* 9; Aink, 386.

21. *Aink*, 406.
22. Muller, A.C. Woolner and Lakshman Sarup, J. Masson and M.R. Kale.
23. *TTP*, pp. 48-49.
24. *Ibid.*, pp. 66-67.
25. *Abhi*, act 3. p. 88.
26. *Ibid.*, act 4. p. 110.
27. *Ibid.*, act 4. p. 112.
28. *Ibid.*, act 4. p. 120.
29. *Ibid.*, act 5. pp. 142-58.
30. *Avim*, act 2. pp. 50-55.
31. *Akam*, 35:1-2.
32. *Ibid.*, 219:1–9.
33. *Kurun*, 269.
34. *Nar*, 179: 5-6.
35. *Kali*, 39: 20-21.
36. *Akam*, 95.
37. *Ibid.*, 165: 6-13.
38. *Aink*, 391.
39. *Akam*, 195.
40. *Aink*, 373.
41. *Ibid.*, 399.
42. *Cilap*, 2:84-88.
43. *Ibid.*, 16:74-80.
44. *Mani*, 29:1-4.
45. *Ibid.*, 23.
46. *Budd*, 1:15-19.
47. *Ibid.*, 2:18, 19.
48. *TTP*, pp. 19-22.
49. *Ibid.*, pp. 19-20.
50. *Ibid.*, p. 67.
51. *Ibid.*, p. 41.
52. *Ibid.*, p. 49.
53. *Avim*, pp. 33-34.
54. *Ibid.*, p. 38.
55. *Ibid.*, p. 82.
56. *Ibid.*, p. 115.
57. *Ibid.*, act. 6.
58. *TTP*, p. 97.
59. *Kuma*, 1:18.
60. *Ibid.*, 1:22.
61. *Ibid.*, 5:4.
62. *Ibid.*, 6: 84.
63. *Ibid.*, 7:24.
64. *Ibid.*, 7:27.
65. *Abhi*, act 7. pp. 240-42.
66. *Akam*, 158:15-18.
67. *Aink*, 261.
68. *Ibid.*, 60.

69. *Nar,* 45.
70. *Aink,* 94.
71. *Ibid.,* 255, 256, 258-60.
72. *Ibid.,* 92.
73. *Ibid.,* 257.
74. *Ibid.,* 6.
75. *Kurun,* 374.
76. *Kali,* 39: 20-25.
77. *Nar,* 48.
78. *Ibid.,* 362.
79. *TTP,* pp. 17-18.
80. *Ibid.,* p. 21.
81. *Ibid.,* p. 22.
82. *Ibid.,* p. 67.
83. *Ibid.,* p. 41.
84. *Ibid.,* pp. 48-49.
85. *Kuma,* 1: 27.
86. *Ibid.,* 1: 50.
87. *Ibid.,* 1: 52.
88. *Ibid.,* 1: 58.
89. *Ibid.,* 5: 6, 7.
90. *Ibid.,* 6: 85.
91. *Abhi,* act 1. p. 10.
92. *Ibid.,* act 4. p. 102.
93. *Ibid.,* act 4. v. 5.
94. *Ibid.,* act 4. v. 6.
95. *Ibid.,* act 4. v. 17.
96. *Ibid.,* act 4. v. 5.
97. *Ibid.,* act 4. v. 21.
98. *Ibid.,* act 7. p. 244.
99. *Mala,* act 5. pp. 143-45.

Chapter 8

Dependants and Others

The heroes of both literatures being financially well-to-do and enjoying a high social position, have a number of dependants in their service and comparatively, the Tamil love poems use them more than the Sanskrit works to develop or depict certain aspects of the love between the hero and the heroine. They usually have no role in the first meeting or the subsequent clandestine meetings between the lovers but are important after the lovers marry and set up a home. Hence they feature in the *mullai* and *marutam* poems and only to a much lesser extent in the other poems.

The Musician

One such dependant is the *pāṇaṉ* or musician. The musicians on the whole are depicted as being poor and as a result go in search of patrons.[1] They carry a *yāḻ* or lute on which they play sweet music which is used as a standard of comparison to the voice and words of a heroine which stand out as sweeter than the sound of the strings made by the *pāṇaṉ*.[2] They are happy to become the companions of rich men who appreciate music. They play music to the hero and the heroine at home.

> The musician sang the *mullai* tune.
> The bejewelled, bright-foreheaded wife
> wore *mullai* flowers.
> The hero sat happily with his son
> with malice towards none.[3]

Obviously, when the hero is away on duty or business, there is not much for the *pāṇaṉ* to do. But he certainly notices the sorrow of the heroine at home and sometimes listens to her words of pain and sorrow. Then he may decide to go to the war camp or battlefield where the hero is on duty, to let him know of her plight and bring him back.[4] A hero tells his charioteer how the *pāṇaṉ* seeing his mistress shed tears which redden the dark, petal-like eyes, comes of his own accord to inform the hero of the sorrow he is causing her. This news of his wife's sorrow makes him want to return home to her.[5] A *pāṇaṉ* himself tells his friends:

'On the long, broad gravel path
as red as lac
lie faded blooms of the *kāyā*.
Cochineal insects crawl about making it seem
like a mixture of sapphire and coral.
This path winds through mountain-forests
where the stag with twisted horns,
embracing its mate
grazes and frisks about.
In the pastoral regions
the cowherds, allowing their herds to graze
on the extensive grasslands
amuse themselves by plucking and stringing
fragrant flowers from nearby hillocks.
The cows with firm footsteps,
after feeding on the *harialli* grass,
their udders flowing with sweet milk,
return to their sheds calling their calves.
If our lord does not return
even at this hour of sunset
what would my condition be at sunrise,
O *pāṇa*?'
Thus asked the mistress.
Unable to answer her and full of sorrow
I played the tune called *cevvaḻi*
and worshipping God, set out to his place.
Then I saw the tall decorated chariot
of the chief who was at the camp
arrive with fast horses
that overcome all obstructions
and the wheels knocking against stones
sounding like thunder.[6]

Usually he has a message for the hero or at least is able to give him the latest, first-hand news of the heroine. The hero eagerly asks the *pāṇaṉ* to repeat what she had said in her pale and sorrowful condition.[7] To him the words of the heroine though repeated only by the *pāṇaṉ* are sweet enough to offset the cold north wind.

> Tell me dear bard,
> the message of my beloved
> with cool flower-like eyes.
> It is sweet (to hear) each time you repeat,
> now that the cold, cruel north wind
> laughs at my loneliness in a distant land.[8]

The musician's relationship with the hero is such that he gets annoyed with the hero when he is touched by the pain of separation felt by the heroine and perhaps finds that the hero could expedite his duties and return earlier to remove that pain. This annoyance is sometimes seen in his conversation with the hero.

> I am not your bard
> and you are not my chief.
> You do not show favour even after hearing
> of the tears shed by the surm-lined eyes
> resembling wet petals
> and the sorrow of your beloved at home
> who loves you so.[9]

This, however, is merely a means of making the hero who is so intent on his duty, realise the plight of the wife he has left behind at home. As a means of consoling her, the hero may send the *pāṇaṉ* himself to go ahead and keep her company with news of him promising to be back soon.[10] This implies that he would leave his camp shortly and the *pāṇaṉ*'s return would herald the return of the hero.

The *pāṇaṉ* does not always enjoy a good relationship with the heroine or her friend. In the poems that deal with the hero's extramarital activities, the *pāṇaṉ* is usually an aide and companion. He provides the hero and his 'other women' music for their entertainment. When an erring husband returns a *tōḻi* tells him:

We do not care.
While your *pāṇaṉ* skilled in playing
various tunes on his good lute
played to the beat of tightly drawn drums,
you drank spirituous liquor with joyful companions
and their relatives.
You did not return to our home.
You stayed instead in 'your' home,
and the young bangled maiden of that house
was certainly happy.[11]

Thus a *pāṇaṉ* is quite indispensable for the hero's life of leisure and love.

The *pāṇaṉ*, however, does not admit to the heroine or her friend the hero's infidelity or the part he played in the hero's extramarital activities. He tries to pacify the angry or sulking heroine, speaking well of the hero. Sometimes he swears by his lute that had the hero seen any other women, he himself would tell the wife about the hero's infidelity.[12] At other times he assures her that he is good and sweet-natured.[13] But whatever he says, the heroine and her friend are aware of his ability to lie for the hero's sake. They mock the *pāṇaṉ* and call him a liar. A *tōḻi*, hearing the *pāṇaṉ* trying to convince them that the hero is good and loyal, calls out to the crier of the town or village who is announcing a festival to be held, to inform the women of that place that the *pāṇaṉ* is a liar and that they should be careful of him.[14] A heroine tells a hero:

Lord of the country with *kāñci* trees!
You have fields with ponds
where the *keṇṭai* fish, having escaped the herons
fears even the white lotus bud nearby.
Since your one *pāṇaṉ* is a liar
all musicians seem liars
to women separated from you.[15]

Another heroine tells the musician himself, within hearing distance of the disloyal hero:

O musician!
My clothes are soiled

with the oil, smoke and surm
used to bathe and adorn my child.
My breasts are full of milk
and my shoulders have the peculiar smell
of women in confinement.
I am not good enough for him
who visits the dwellings of those
who are always brightly ornamented.
Therefore take your chief away.[16]

On such occasions, the *pāṇaṉ* with his loyalty to the hero is in a difficult position. It is made worse by the fact that being a musician he himself spends time with other musicians, perhaps including those in the courtesan's house and this would make the heroine and her friend more suspicious of him and his intentions. The text of conventions, the *Tolkāppiyam* mentions the *pāṇaṉ* as one of the many who may approach her as a mediator or pacifier (*vāyil*).[17] But his own role as musician makes him more vulnerable to their insults, sarcasm and angry outbursts.

The Sanskrit texts under study do not have any characters who may be compared to the *pāṇaṉ*.

The Charioteer

The charioteer (*pākaṉ* or *valavaṉ* in Tamil and *sūtaḥ* in Sanskrit) is usually a silent character, hardly saying anything. He seems to have been responsible for transporting the hero from one place to another. One Caṅkam poem mentions that the hero's chariot is yoked with lovely horses chosen by the charioteer.[18] He is adept at driving chariots and managing the horses by means of their reins, (*kaiyuṭai valava*).[19] He obtains this skill not only by practice but also by the study of texts and treatises on horse-lore. A hero who has completed his duty and is returning home by chariot tells his charioteer:

O *pāka* with a knowledge of the texts (on horses)!
There is the city with flags waving
on walls that reach the sky.
The lamps lit on them by the night guards
resemble the stars in the firmament.
In that city, difficult for the foes to enter,

in the prosperous mansion
is my beloved
like a goddess with spotless chastity,
cool, dark eyes spread with fine, red lines
and upper arms like the bamboo.
Drive in that direction,
the chariot yoked with horses bridled in gold.[20]

It is the hero who speaks to him and asks him to drive faster, overtaking all other chariots.[21] The impatient hero wishes to see his waiting wife at once,[22] or to reach home by sunset when the sound of the cowherds bringing home their cattle can be heard in the town.[23]

The *pākaṉ* does drive fast and thus he is one who is responsible for uniting the hero and the heroine after the separation. The hero is grateful and appreciates the ability of his charioteer. An *Akanāṉūṟu* poem describes a scene that takes place outside the hero's house as soon as his chariot stops there. He praises the charioteer, saying:

'The king at camp completed his war victoriously.
I too remember ascending the large chariot
with great love.
But I know not how I reached here.
I am surprised to hear you say,
"May you descend,"
after halting the chariot
before the house of my gentle beloved,
in the small pastoral town
where young rabbits hop about
and thick ears of millet grow.
Tell me charioteer,
Did you harness as horses
the wind that blows in the sky?
Or did you harness your mind?'
Asking thus, the great one
clasped him closely to his mountain-like chest
and took him into the house.
The bejewelled maiden too
obtained the opportunity to welcome guests.[24]

Mostly the poems from the *mullai* division of love poetry that deal with the *pākaṉ* are useful in describing the hero's impatience to reach home and the condition of the heroine as he imagines her to be. They also contain the anticipated joy of his reunion with his beloved wife.

The poems in the *marutam* division, on the other hand, depict the *pākaṉ* as being unfavourable to the heroine because he drives the hero to the homes or meeting places of other women. A heroine relates to her friend how the hero having dressed himself, set out in his chariot to meet a harlot. But his son, toddled out wishing to see his father. The hero, asking the charioteer to stop, descended from the chariot, carried the boy and entered his house and did not go out to meet the harlot as planned.[25] Thus the *pākaṉ* usually knows the movements of the hero. When necessary, he too seems to pacify the heroine. A *Kalittokai* poem relates how the *pākaṉ* swears by touching his chariot, 'He has no other woman but you,' in an attempt to convince the heroine of her husband's loyalty. This is the only poem that contains the actual words spoken by a charioteer.[26]

We do come across charioteers in Sanskrit works, especially in Kālidāsa's dramas. The charioteer is instrumental in driving Duṣyanta to the hermitage where he meets Śakuntalā, but like the *pākaṉ* in Caṅkam poetry he hardly speaks anything. He merely agrees with whatever Duṣyanta says, and obeys instructions.[27] When Duṣyanta is reunited with Śakuntalā the charioteer is not with him, for Mātali, the charioteer of Indra drives him to and from Indraloka and it is on his return journey that he stops at the hermitage of Marīca where he is reunited with Śakuntalā.[28]

Religious People

Apart from the hero, the heroine, their friends, relatives and dependants, there are also other characters who contribute to the love theme. They may either help the young people in love, give their support or blessing or merely accept their love. We do not come across people who hinder their love or secret meetings on purpose. Similarly the religious people in both poetry seem to accept their love and think that it is only right and natural.

In the Caṅkam poems we have the *antaṇar* who are usually Brāhmaṇas or those with compassion and graciousness of heart. They are addressed as *antaṇir*. They are followers of *aṟam* or *dharma*, well-versed in the *Vedas* and always think and do only what is right.[29] They carry the trident staff and ewer on their shoulder and seem to be people who travel a great deal on foot, through arid regions. Hence they carry an umbrella and some water in the ewer.[30] The things they carry seem to be quite identical with what the *pāṅkaṉ*, also a Brāhmaṇa, carries.[31] But they do not seem to be the ordinary brāhmaṇas who live in their own homes in a different section of the town or village.[32] Since they are also said to be people who have their mind and senses under control,[33] they must be hermits or *sanyāsins* who have renounced the ordinary way of life. Tolkāppiyar does not mention *antaṇar*, but only *pārppār* and *aṟivar*.[34] Of these the *antaṇar* are probably the *aṟivar* mentioned for they are said to know the *maṟai* or *Vedas*. In a *Kuṟuntokai* poem a *tōḻi* wishes such a person carrying an ewer, abundant food and water for the ewer from a single house and enquires of him when the north wind (*vāṭai*) would blow, for that is the time the hero would return.[35] The poem does not mention any particular term used to address the person but the reference to the ewer suggests that he is of the same category as the *antaṇar* described in the other poems and is one who knows the seasons.

In the Tamil love poems they do not play an active role in bringing the lovers together, or in separating them. They are merely people who meet the eloping couple on their way. But they do not frown on young love. In fact they accept it as something natural and good. One such *antaṇar* tells a foster-mother:

> We did see her on the desert path.
> She passed the high, dense hills
> caressed by her loving husband,[36]

implying that she has made the right choice for he is loving and therefore she is happy. Another *antaṇar* not only tells the foster-mother that he saw her but also advises the foster-mother not to go in search of the girl for it would only bring sorrow (*evvam*) to the girl who has done the right thing.

> We did not miss them.
> We saw them on the arid path.
> You seem to be the mother
> of the modest, bejewelled maiden

who chose (to traverse) the shadeless desert
with the youth
of masculine beauty and goodness.
Of what use is the sandal paste
mixed with other fragrant things,
to the mountain on which it grows
but to those who use it?
So is your daughter to you.
Of what use is the lustrous white pearl
to the ocean in which it was born
but to those who wear it?
So is your daughter to you.
Of what use is the music of the seven strings
to the lute from which it emanates
but to those who play on it?
So is your daughter to you.
Hence do not bring sorrow
to the maiden of excellent chastity.
She went, honouring a good man.
That is the way of righteousness.[37]

Out of the goodness of their hearts, these hermits seem to carry messages to people. A maiden who is leaving with the youth she loves, meets an *antaṇar* on the way and asks him to take a message to her friends though she is not acquainted with the hermit.

O recluse with gentle walk
and a distant destination!
I beg a favour of you.
At my village,
please give this message to my friends
with slender wrists and forearms.
'She crossed the difficult tracts
so that her beauty
lovingly nurtured by her mother
is further enhanced.'[38]

The *Cilappatikāram*, too, deals with some characters comparable to these *antaṇar*. On the way to Maturai with Kavunti Aṭikaḷ, Kōvalaṉ and Kaṇṇaki meet a Brāhmaṇa from Māṅkāṭu *(māṅkāṭṭu maṟaiyōṉ)* who is proficient in the *Vedas* (*māmaṟaiyāḷaṉ*)[39] and tends the sacrificial fires, (*tīttiṟam purintōṉ*).[40] While giving his reason for coming that way, he explains that he has a great desire to see Tirumāl reclining at Śrīraṅgam and standing at the Vēṅkaṭa hills. So after his pilgrimage to these two places he is on his way back to his place of origin. Thus he is in a position to direct them to Maturai describing the three different paths they can choose from. Later, Kōvalaṉ alone meets the Brāhmaṇa, Kōcikamāṇi, who is sent by Mātavi with a letter for Kōvalaṉ. It cannot be called a love-letter in the usual sense but the Brāhmaṇa could not have been aware of the contents. We are given no indication as to whether he is a recluse or not. Neither is his purpose for coming that way made clear in the epic. If he has come to deliver the letter, then it is difficult to explain how he came to know of the whereabouts of Kōvalaṉ. Hence it is possible that he is also a pilgrim. The same phrases like *tīttiṟam purintōṉ* are used to refer to him also. He relates to Kōvalaṉ all that took place at Pukār after he left the city with his wife. Apart from furnishing this information, he is most useful in removing the suspicions or misconceptions Kōvalaṉ had regarding Mātavi. After his meeting with Kōcikamāṇi, he is able to realise that she is not at fault but he is. Finding the letter suitable to be sent to his own parents, he bids Kōcikamāṇi to take it back to his parents at Pukār.[41] We come across another Brāhmaṇa well-versed in all the four *Vedas* (*nāṉmaṟai*), leading a life of virtue with malice towards none. He too travels to places of worship like the Potiyil hills and Kaṉyā Kumārī, though his place of residence is Talaicceṅkāṉam.[42] His travels of pilgrimage take him not only to Maturai in the Pandya country[43] and Vañci in the Chera kingdom,[44] but also to the banks of the Ganges where he goes to wash away his sins.[45] In spite of his extensive travels, he too is familiar with the events of Kōvalaṉ's life especially at Pukār and fills in the information regarding the charitable acts of the hero. He is also useful in building up the character of the hero just before he is killed unjustly.

More important than these Brāhmaṇas, from the point of view of the hero and the heroine, is Kavunti Aṭikaḷ, the Jaina nun whom they meet in a Jaina temple, just outside the city of Pukār.[46] Since she too is interested in visiting Maturai, she offers to go with them.

These tender feet, fit to wear anklets
cannot bear the sharp, rough gravel.

She is not capable of crossing
the districts covered with forests.
But who knows (what is in store)?
Though unfit for travel,
you will not abandon the journey
even if I asked you to.
Since I too wish to visit faultless Maturai
in the good, southern Tamil country,
to pay homage to Ar̲ivan̲
by listening to words of *dharma*
taught by the wise men,
who, having discarded cruel words
hear only what is blameless,
I shall go with you. Let us go.[47]

Kōvalan̲ is relieved and happy because she would be a suitable companion for Kaṇṇkai. Kavunti, though a *sanyāsinī* who has attained the power to curse, has not attained the calm compassion of forgiving. Neither is she free from attachments, for when an immoral couple, hearing her refer to Kōvalan̲ and Kaṇṇaki as her children, retorts,

O learned one!
Can children of the same parents
live together as man and wife?

she is enraged and curses them saying,

Be old jackals
roaming the thorny forests.[48]

Her renunciation has for its basis only her great faith in Jainism and she is quick to denounce other religions and their practices, praising her own.[49] She is yet to achieve actual detachment.

Kavunti enters the life of Kōvalan̲ and Kaṇṇaki at the most difficult period of their lives. Kaṇṇaki had been separated from her husband due to his careless selfishness and disloyalty. Though he has now come back to her and she is unselfish enough to forgive and forget, there is still the ominous dream, a part of which has come true with their leaving Pukār for a new city. He having spent all his wealth on the sensuous and leisurely life he liked, suspected Mātavi of becoming disloyal to him, though there is no cause for this suspicion. He returns home, and for the first time is filled with remorse for his cruelty to his virtuous wife and the way he has squandered the family wealth. He decides then and there to leave for Maturai with his wife but just after reaching the outskirts of Pukār he realises the difficulty his gentle wife will have to undergo before reaching their destination. It is at this point that they meet Kavunti, who is able to talk to them of God and fate. For the couple who has suffered and hardly had any time to resolve their differences, Kavunti is a great help. Her knowledge of the various stories and her ability to relate them in a suitable manner helps them. For instance, she relates in brief the story of the *Rāmāyaṇa* and the *Nalopākhyāna*—both stories of heroes who had to leave their comfortable homes and enter the forest with their wives. The suffering they underwent is explained as having been caused by fate (*ūḻ*).[50] These stories certainly help to console both of them, so that they can accept the past with equanimity, the present with a sense of gratitude, for at least they are not separated in the forest as the hero and the heroine in the two stories were and to look to the future with hope that they too would return to their city to live happily. Even though Kavunti accompanies them on their way to Maturai, she too meets them, like the *aṟavōr* or *aṟivar*, on the way, after the hero and the heroine have left their home stealthily, without the knowledge of even their parents. The only difference is that in this case, the hero and the heroine are already married with the approval and blessings of the parents.

The Sanskrit texts under study do contain many characters who may be called religious people but only the Parivrājakā of the *Mālavikāgnimitram* may be said to be important from the point of view of the love theme. She alone renders help for the meeting of the hero and the heroine. She is the widowed sister of Sumati, the minister of Mādhavasena. So she accompanies King Mādhavasena's sister Mālavikā to Vidiśā but is separated from the princess due to an attack on their group by robbers. Her brother, the minister, dies in the battle with the robbers and so she comes to Vidiśā and becomes a nun. There is no clear indication as to what religious order she belongs. She merely says:

> Then, having cremated my brother's body, and the sorrow
> of my widowhood renewed, I came to your country
> and took to these red (or brown garments).[51]

The word *kaśāya* merely means red or brown and since it is in the dual, it refers to two such garments. Both Hindu and Buddhist *sanyāsins* wear this colour and though the possibility of women joining the Buddhist Saṅgha is greater, it is doubtful if Buddhist nuns were allowed by their Saṅgha to stay in the palace. Her role in the drama is important, for unknown to everyone else in the palace, she has been of help in bringing the king and the princess together. It is very clear that Queen Dhāriṇī objects to the dance contest being held. But the Parivrājakā, in spite of being her friend and confidante, supports the king's idea of holding it. It is she who suggests: 'Your Majesty! The dramatic art is a practical art. What is the use of mere verbal arguments?'[52]

Only at the end of the play we realise that she behaved thus because she knew of a proposal of marriage (though for political reasons) between Agnimitra and Mālavikā. Hence she merely brings together two people already destined to marry and as such is not going against anyone's feelings or wishes, including Queen Dhāriṇī's.

She enjoys great respect in the palace and this is due, besides her orange robes, to her level of education in the various branches of knowledge. She is consulted regarding a dispute in dance and her detailed knowledge in the various rules and aspects of dancing is of great help in her decision.[53] Her ability to talk of music and the various notes show her to be a truly accomplished person, quite contrary to the accepted norms of education fit for an ascetic.[54] The queen seems to be aware of her capabilities, for she requests the Parivrājakā to dress Mālavikā in the bridal attire of the people of Vidarbha.[55] She also seems to know something about medicine for when she sees the *vidūṣaka* with the alleged serpent bite, she tells him in jest, knowing how easily he can be frightened, that the afflicted thumb should be cut off. She quotes from the texts that:

> Exicision of the bitten part, or the burning of it,
> or letting off blood from the wound—these are remedies
> to save the lives of persons just bitten (by a snake).[56]

Like Kavunti, she too relates interesting stories, though not to the hero and the heroine but to the Chief Queen.[57] Thus she is addressed as 'the learned Kauśikī' (*paṇḍita-kauśikī*).[58]

The only exception among the religious people is Durvāsas, for he alone is responsible for the separation of lovers. It is usually explained that the love of Duṣyanta and Śakuntalā begins with physical love that does not even wait for traditional approval of marriage. Besides, Śakuntalā, lost in her love, is careless of the usual duties of hospitality to guests, especially hermits. Hence the curse of Durvāsas that causes the separation. Suffering is essential to purify their love so that it rises above the physical attraction to a purer, spiritual level where this love becomes the basis of social duties and obligations. Yet it cannot be overlooked that a sage who is aware that she is thinking of the man she loves, is not able to find compassion in his heart to understand that the girl in love is not rude or careless but merely lost in her thoughts about her lover from whom she is separated for the first time. The sage's ego is actually responsible for her repudiation by Duṣyanta and their consequent separation. However, the sage and his anger are only reported[59] by the two friends of Śakuntalā.

A curse by another sage, but of Indraloka, is reported in the *Vikramorvaśīyam*. Urvaśī, being the danseuse and actress of the court of Indra, participates in the play *Lakṣmīsvayamvara,* playing the lead role of Lakṣmī. But like Śakuntalā, she too is lost in her thoughts. In the midst of the play, when Menakā in the role of Vararuṇī asks her:

> Friend, here are assembled the best men in the
> three worlds—the guardians of the spheres,
> together with Keśava. Towards whom does your heart incline?

she instead of saying, 'Puruṣottama', says, 'Purūravas'. This enrages their *guru,* Bharata who curses that she should lose her divine place. Since this means that she cannot live in Indraloka but descend to earth as a mortal, it helps to unite her with Purūravas.[60] Hence even a curse by a religious person is of use in uniting the lovers in the *Vikramorvaśīyam,* unlike in the *Abhijñānaśākuntalam.* But Indra, being a friend of Purūravas and aware of the love between him and Urvaśī, makes the curse into a blessing, saying:

> The *rājarṣi* on whom you have set your heart, my ally in battle, is entitled to my favour. So, stay with Purūravas as you desire, till he beholds the child you will bear him.[61]

So later when Purūravas meets his son Āyus, Urvaśī's period of stay on earth comes to an end, and there is about to be a permanent separation between them. Just at that time, Nārada arrives with a message from Indra granting her permission to stay on with Purūravas till his death.[62]

Nārada appears as a uniter of lovers in the play *Avimārakam* as well. The disguise of Avimāraka who is actually Viṣṇusena, the adopted son of Sauvira and Sucetanā stands in the way of the marriage of Avimāraka and Kuraṅginī and the traditional acceptance of their union by their parents. So Nārada arrives to explain to their fathers, especially Kuntibhoja, the curse that made the disguise necessary, and 'to dispel their grief'.[63] He also summarises their whole love affair and their meetings thus:

> Destiny gave her in marriage
> for he saved her from a mad elephant.
> Once he entered (the palace) with the bravery of heroes
> And once again with the silence of magic,[64]

thereby saving anger or embarrassment on the part of Kuntibhoja.

Wayfarers

The religious people mentioned by the Tamil works, be they recluses or Brāhmaṇas, may be included in the general and more varied group of wayfarers, (*vaḻippōkkar* or *kaṇṭōr*) for all of them are met with on the way either by the eloping couple or the *cevili*. The Caṅkam literature contains some poems attributed to them and others addressed to them, but as usual we depend on the colophons. There are some poems which may be attributed to other characters though the colophons say that they are the words of the wayfarers depicting their own feelings and opinions. But on the other hand, there are other poems which are unmistakably the words meant to be utterances of the wayfarers. A *Kuṟuntokai* poem that contains the thoughts of some wayfarers shows them wondering who the young people are.

The ankles of the bow-bearing youth
are adorned by the heroic anklet (*kaḻal*).
On the tender feet of the bangled maid
are anklets (*cilampu*).
Who are these good people?
They are to be pitied.
They have decided to traverse the arid tracts
dense with bamboo,
where the white dry seed of the *śirīśa*
beaten by the west wind sounds
like the drum at the pole dance of the Aryans.[65]

Most of the poems depict them as feeling sorry for the couple having to undergo privations and suffering during their journey but are happy to see their love which is sometimes compared to the love that exists between a pair of *makaṉṟil* birds.[66] Their concern is chiefly for the maiden who is young and unaccustomed to the hardships of such journeys though the husband is loving and understanding.[67] Other travellers, being sympathetic towards their youth and the strength of their love that prompted them to face such hardships, are helpful and protective towards them. Perhaps being experienced travellers who are used to the sounds of the perilous paths and the dangers therein, they warn them of those dangers and advice them to stop over for the night.

The sun is not shining anymore.
Harken to the sound of the drum
(of highway robbers)
moving about as in a battlefield
bearing tall spears decorated with rings,
because the caravan approaches.
Do not proceed,
O husband of (the maiden like)
a young she-elephant.[68]

Their advice against the two of them continuing the journey is due not to their lack of confidence in the young man's valour or strength but to their concern for the young woman. Hence they do not mention his ability but the new responsibility he has accepted by marrying her or proposing to do so.

Like the religious people, they too are accosted by the heroine who sends a message through them to her people in her hometown or village.

> Bless you wayfarers!
> Please tell my mother
> who took care of my beauty (literally the upper arm)
> and (nearly) ruined my life,
> 'Boarding a chariot with the fearless youth
> she has crossed many arid tracts
> leaving behind the hills
> with tigers that kill.'[69]

In this poem the term wayfarers (*āṟu ceṉ mākkaḷ*) is used to address them. They seem to comply with the heroine's request and inform the mother or the foster-mother, telling her clearly that the heroine has left with the lover she has chosen.[70] Often they answer the foster-mother who enquires them of her daughter[71] and like the *aṟivar* they too do not seem to have any objections to the step the young couple has taken.

Some Sanskrit texts also mention the wayfarers in the summer season. The *Meghadūtam* describes how their wives (*pathikavanitāḥ*) who wait for their husbands to return, take heart when they see the cloud, for it means that summer would soon be over and their husbands would return.[72] The *Ṛtusaṃhāram* depicting the passions and the effect the seasons have on them shows the traveller (*adhvagaḥ*) as a lover himself, separated from his beloved. His heart is touched with sorrow at the sight and scent of the mango blossom in spring.[73] Thus the wayfarers in most of the Sanskrit works seem to be people with their own thoughts and sorrow and as such are of no importance in the love of the hero and the heroine.

The only exception may be found in the *Avimārakam*. When Kuntibhoja discovers that Avimāraka has been living in the women's apartments for nearly a year he places the princess' palace under heavy guard. Avimāraka manages to escape unharmed. But while going out of the kingdom he is overcome not only by the heat of the summer but also by the sorrow of separation. Unable to bear the pain in his heart, he prepares to kill himself by jumping off a cliff. Just then a *vidyādhara* and his beloved passing by on their way to the Malaya mountains see him and come to his aid. He gives Avimāraka a ring which, worn on the right hand, would make him invisible and worn on the left, would make him visible again. With his supernatural ring he is able to return to the palace where he stays till his true identity is revealed and his union with Kuraṅginī, approved.[74] No doubt the *vidyādhara* and his companion are not comparable to the human travellers found in the Tamil poems. But their sympathy for the love of Avimāraka and the princess may be compared to their compassion for the young lovers.

Elders

Though love is accepted by the various sections of society, the traditional marriage is one that is conducted in such a way that the whole community, village or town knows about it. Hence it is referred to in Caṅkam poems as *nāṭaṟi naṉ maṇam*.[75] To conduct such a traditional marriage the customary preliminaries have to be observed. The elderly relatives of a youth interested in marrying a girl have to approach the parents of the bride and formally ask for her hand. One of the poems in the *Kuṟuntokai* pictures them as being old, with grey (literally white) hair, holding staffs or walking sticks (*taṇṭu*) in their hands. Since they bring together in marriage the hero and the heroine who love each other but are still separated, they are praised as 'men who unite those who are separated'.[76] We are not sure if any elderly women accompany these men. These people are usually the hero's relatives and they also accompany him to the bride's house for the wedding ceremony. They are knowledgeable in various matters and are therefore respected.[77]

In the *Kumārasaṃbhavaṃ*, when Pārvatī makes it known that she is still under her father's care and authority, Śiva summons with his thoughts (*smaraśāsanaḥ*) the Śaptarṣis together with Arundhatī, and requests them to go as emissaries to Himavān. They are Brāhmaṇas who have performed great *tapas* and wear sacred threads of pearls.[78] After praising Himavān and Śiva, they point out the glory Pārvatī would enjoy by marrying Śiva.[79] They are described as wearing gold bark garments and holding jewel rosaries (*ratnākṣara sūtraḥ*).[80] The difference between the elders in Tamil and Sanskrit poems seems to have been in the clothes, made necessary by their position in life, caste and relationship to the society. Besides, the Śaptarṣis, are accompanied by Arundhatī for Śiva himself feels the appropriateness of her going along,[81] while no specific mention is made of a woman accompanying them in Tamil poetry.

REFERENCES

1. See *Porun; Ciru; Perum; Paricirrurai* in *Puram* poetry.
2. *Aink,* 100: 3-4, 185.
3. *Ibid.,* 408.
4. *Ibid.,* 474.
5. *Akam,* 244:8-14.
6. *Ibid.,* 14.
7. *Aink,* 478.
8. *Ibid.,* 479.
9. *Ibid.,* 480.
10. *Ibid.,* 477.
11. *Akam,* 346:12-18.
12. *Kali,* 71:13-16.
13. *Kurun,* 85.
14. *Nar,* 200.
15. *Kurun,* 127.
16. *Nar,* 380:1-6.
17. *Tol. Porul,* 150.
18. *Akam,* 20: 12-16.
19. *Ibid.,* 344:11.
20. *Ibid.,* 114:7-16.
21. *Ibid.,* 44:3-5.
22. *Ibid.,* 334:15.
23. *Ibid.,* 120:13-15.
24. *Ibid.,* 384.
25. *Ibid.,* 66.
26. *Kali,* 71:9-10.
27. *Abhi,* act 1. pp. 6-14.
28. *Ibid.,* act 7.
29. *Aink,* 387:1-2.
30. *Kali,* 9:1-2.
31. *Kurun,* 156:1-4.
32. *Perum,* 297-301.
33. *Kali,* 9:4.
34. *Tol. Porul,* 191.
35. *Kurun,* 277.
36. *Aink,* 387:4-6.
37. *Kali,* 9:12-24.
38. *Aink,* 384.

39. *Cilap,* 15:34.
40. *Ibid.,* 11:57.
41. *Ibid.,* 13:57-99.
42. *Ibid.,* 15:11-20.
43. *Ibid.,* 15:5-14.
44. *Ibid.,* 30:145-47.
45. *Ibid.,* 27:110.
46. *Ibid.,* 10:35-45.
47. *Ibid.,* 10:52-61.
48. *Ibid.,* 10:225-233.
49. *Ibid.,* 11:152-164.
50. *Ibid.,* 14:46-55.
51. *Mala,* act 5. p. 146.
52. *Ibid.,* act 1. p. 24.
53. *Ibid.,* act 2. v. 8.
54. *Ibid.,* act 2. v. 21.
55. *Ibid.,* act 5. p. 133.
56. *Ibid.,* act 4. v. 4.
57. *Ibid.,* act 4. pp. 92-93.
58. *Ibid.,* act 1. pp. 22 and 25.
59. *Abhi,* act 4. pp. 94-99.
60. *Vikr.,* act 3. pp. 66-68.
61. *Ibid.,* act 3. p. 68.
62. *Ibid.,* act 5. p. 154.
63. *Avim,* act 6. p. 123.
64. *Ibid.,* act 6. p. 126.
65. *Kurun,* 7.
66. *Aink,* 381.
67. *Ibid.,* 382, 383.
68. *Kurun,* 390.
69. *Aink,* 385.
70. *Ibid.,* 386.
71. *Ibid.,* 388, 389, 390.
72. *Megh,* p. 8.
73. *Rtu,* 6:26.
74. *Avim,* act 4.
75. *Kurinji,* 232.
76. *Kurun,* 146.
77. *Kali,* 39:47-50.
78. *Kuma,* 6:4, 6.
79. *Ibid.,* 6:66-83.
80. *Ibid.,* 6:6.
81. *Ibid.,* 6:32.

PART TWO

NATURE

Chapter 9

Landscape

Nature has always been the background against which the human actors have enacted their drama. But in literature, the importance given to this geographical background, depends very much on the life of the people themselves, their geographical environment which moulds their culture and their traditions. In Sanskrit and Tamil classical poetry, the external world of nature is brought into direct relationship with human feelings so that nature and humanity co-exist. To depict this co-existence, the poets seem to have utilised the knowledge and experience that they had gleaned from close observation and understanding of nature in its various moods and seasons. Even if they followed certain set conventions and traditions, these must have had their beginnings in such observations which were later crystallised and accepted as conventions.

TAMIL LITERATURE

Tamil poetic convention, though recognising love as something personal and subjective (*akam*), classified it broadly into five different aspects or themes called *uripporuḷ*. The setting and description for each of these experiences consists of two parts—the *mutaṟporuḷ* which consists of place and time[1] and the *karupporuḷ* consisting of the changing and movable objects of environment.[2] For example, a poet singing of the first or subsequent meetings of lovers before marriage places it in the hilly region and uses the fauna, flora, deity (*teyvam* like Murukaṉ) food, musical instruments like the drum and the lute, occupation and the other aspects of environment found on the hills as the background to these meetings. The time of the day and season most suited to a particular emotion is also recognised. Thus the time for each aspect of love is again divided into seasons (*perumpolutu*) and time of day (*cirupolutu*). Land is divided into five regions, each with its peculiar vegetation, animals, peoples, their way of life and other such details that would differentiate one from the other. Since every landscape is made beautiful, expressive or capable of influencing human emotions under the illuminating effect of a particular period of year or day, ancient Tamil convention correlated the five geographical divisions of land with the five aspects of love and prescribed particular seasons and times of day for these emotions. The five regions are *kuriñci* or mountain region, *mullai* or pastoral fields, *marutam* or agricultural tracts, *neytal* or the maritime belt and *pālai* or the desert and their corresponding emotions are *puṇartal* or the meeting of lovers, *iruttal* or the patient waiting of the wife for the husband to return after completing his mission, *ūṭal* or the sulkiness of the wife due to the disloyalty of the husband, *iraṅkal* or pining in separation, and *pirivu* or separation, respectively. These emotions or *uripporuḷ* are most important for there may be poems without the mention or description of land, environment, season or time of day (i.e. *mutalporuḷ* and *karupporuḷ*) but there can never be an *akam* poem that does not deal with one of these emotions. If the emotion is not dealt with explicitly it is at least hinted at, for, without it there is no life in a poem and it becomes meaningless. For example, a *tōli* tells the heroine:

> Good is the path (your) lover has taken.
> It has the bright red gloriosa
> and the jasmine
> brought forth by the season
> of cool showers.[3]

Though this poem describes a path that has been made beautiful and refers to the season of cool showers, these are not the important aspects of the poem. They are the *karupporuḷ* and the *mutarporuḷ* respectively but the season of showers or *kār* suggests that it is the time of his return. The path being cool and comfortable, his journey would be pleasant and short. The words *puṇartal*, *iruttal* etc. are never mentioned in poetry but the use of the fauna and flora as well as the portrayal of the feelings of the dramatis personae concerned make this clear to the reader. The name for the region and division of love poetry is derived from the name of the most prominent flower of the region and now these names are sufficient to suggest the geographical division of land, fauna and flora, the types of people, their occupation and pastimes and most of all the aspect of love that was considered most suitably portrayed with that background.

Kuṟiñci

In the mountain regions the *kuṟiñci* (or *strobilanthus kunthianus*) the flower of a plant that blooms once in twelve years on the hills of South India, is one of the most significant flowers, for when they bloom they change the entire hills into beautiful gardens bearing dense clusters of purple, honey-filled flowers. Apart from this breathtaking beauty, the flowering season also seems to have brought wealth to the mountaineers in the form of extra honey. A *Kuṟuntokai* poem uses this flower to show the love of a heroine for her lover and the true nature of clandestine love. Their meetings are intermittent but exceedingly beautiful and sweet on account of their longing and separation. She says:

> Wider than the earth.
> Higher than the sky and
> Deeper than the vast ocean
> is my love for the lord of the hills
> where (bees) make abundant honey
> from black-stemmed *kuṟiñci* flowers.[4]

He is the lord of the country where plenty of honey (*peruntēṉ*) is obtained because of the black-stemmed *kuṟiñci* flower. By this she suggests that his coming to meet her is rare like the blooming of the *kuṟiñci* but their meeting is as sweet as that honey. This poem itself suggests that the aspect of love for *kuṟiñci* is *puṇartal*[5] or the meeting of lovers. This meeting takes place in the late winter or *kūtir* and the season of early dew or *muṉpaṉi* at midnight (*yāmam*).[6] Since the meeting of the lovers is clandestine in nature the season with incessant rain and the hours around midnight when everyone is expected to be back within the secure home is considered most suitable for such stealthy meetings. Besides, it heightens the feeling of anxiety that accompanies such clandestine meetings with the discomforts and dangers of the season and the hour of day. The darkness of the rainy night, the steep and narrow hilly paths the lover has to traverse to reach the place of their tryst, the wild animals and reptiles that might roam about in search of prey, the watchmen of the village and the ever watchful foster-mothers and mother as well as other members of the family add to the difficulty of the meeting. The whole situation seems to be a test of the strength of the hero's love and his courage to overcome or brave these dangers. But this is a source of anxiety to the heroine who says that her heart has gone away to hold his feet in case he slips at midnight along the path where the rain-water covers the deep holes.[7] Another *Akanāṉūṟu* poem refers to their meeting at midnight in the season of dew (*paṉiyaṭūu niṉṟa pāṉāṭ kaṅkul*).[8]

Mullai

The season of rain or the months when rain sets in (*kār*) and twilight or evening (*mālai*) are the most appropriate season and time of day for *mullai*.[9] This, too, is the name of a flower that blooms in districts where grass and shrubs form the chief natural vegetation. The *mullai* plant is a creeper that blossoms in the season of rain and unlike most flowers that bloom with sunrise, this blossoms at sunset (*mālai*) spreading its delicate fragrance around. This is why the heroine asks:

> O Pitiless *Pāṇa*!
> The thick clouds thunder
> with rain (*kār*).
> The delicate *mullai* creeper
> which the cowherds
> rich in cattle, collect
> blooms in season.
> Is there such pitiless evening (*mālai*)
> in the country he went to?[10]

The district is most beautiful during this season and time of day when the *mullai* blooms and so it has become the background for the aspect of love associated with it, *iruttal*[11] or patient waiting of the wife for the return of her husband who is away on business, duty (usually war or embassy) or education.[12] This season and hour are most suited for the portrayal of the quiet suffering of both the hero and the heroine. The birds and beasts return to their abodes to be safe from the rain and the darkness of night, and this reminds the heroine at home of the hero who has not returned yet and the hero, of the love and comfort that await him at home. The coolness, beauty and fragrance of this season and the sight of the animals and birds wooing their mates arouse longing in the heart of the hero who is busy, away from home and reminds him of his wife waiting for his return. She too is influenced by the exuberance of nature whose languor in the summer has been removed by the refreshing rain. Yet the heroine waits with trust and expectation. This has been accepted as the basis of chastity which is also the basis of a happy home. Hence *iruttal*, and most of all the flower *mullai*, is treated as symbolic of chastity. The purity of colour comparable to the western lily and the sweet fragrance have made poets describe virtuous women as

> the graceful and delicate young maiden,
> with chastity comparable to *mullai*.[13]

Its purity is brought out in a *Kuṟuntokai* poem which calls it the 'faultless divine flower of *mullai*'.[14] The time of day or *ciṟupoḻutu* ascribed to this *tiṇai* is *mālai* which is the time after sunset and Iḷampūraṇar explains it as early night[15] when the people as well as birds and beasts have returned and the *mullai* flowers have bloomed spreading their fragrance.

Marutam

The agricultural tracts (*marutam)* have love quarrels or *ūṭal* as their *uripporuḷ*. The hour for this is early dawn (*vaikaṟai*) but there is no special season ascribed to it.[16] This is the time when the infidel husband returns home after a festive night with a courtesan. The wife sulks or reproaches him as it fits her mood and sometimes refuses him admission into the house. But after his pleading with her, either in person or through his friends or hers, she forgives and accepts him. Quite often he enters the house with a guest in whose presence she is forced to behave normally with him. The agricultural region with a settled way of life, comparative wealth and the civilisation of towns and cities, seems to be the most appropriate location for such behaviour between the lovers, though it is by no means universal even in that region. What is really common in this region with abundance of water from the tanks and rivers is the *marutam* tree (*largerstroemia flosregina*) which grows chiefly along river banks.[17] The flowers are large and showy, usually of a pinkish or mauve colour, that attract the eye with their beauty even from a distance. This must have made the *marutam* tree the most conspicuous in that region. Besides, the very essence of the aspect of love for this region is based on the weakness of the hero for the physical attractions of the harlot whose nature it is to care for her beauty. When the hero returns home at dawn, the angered and hurt heroine sarcastically talks of her ability to enjoy the fragrance of his love and union at dawn (*vaikaṟai*).[18] She also compares him to the sun that has risen causing the lotuses to bloom while only one who has not been touched by the rays (herself) does not bloom but still has dew on it. Here the rising of the sun is a reference to the morning (*viṭiyal*) which is also a *ciṟupoḻutu* associated with this *tiṇai* or aspect of love.[19]

Neytal

The maritime tracts with the lady-love bewailing the long absence of the hero (*iraṅkal*) as its *uripporuḷ* has no particular season.[20] The appropriate hour is sunset (*eṟpāṭu*)[21] when the sea-birds return to their nests and the fishermen return with their catch. The dirge of the sea, most conspicuous after sunset, forms a befitting background to the despair and desolation of the lady, while the waves depict the restlessness of her loving heart. But there are not many poems that actually depict this emotion strictly for most of the poems classified as *neytal* deal with clandestine meetings and the subsequent separation between lovers. Yet this restlessness and sorrow is the most dominant emotion in these poems. This *tiṇai* is also named after a flower, that is found commonly in the backwaters and is therefore often referred to as *iruṅkaḻi neytal*[22] though its botanical name is *nymphae stellata*. It is bluish in colour and is very fragrant. The colour makes it a comparison for the eyes and since this emotion causes tears, this flower which is very common in that region is symbolic of the whole *tiṇai*. The *ciṟupoḻutu* for this aspect of love, i.e. *eṟpāṭu* is explained by Iḷampūraṇar as the last hours of day (*pakaṟ poḻutiṉ piṟkūṟu*)[23] when the sun has just begun to set. The poems depict this hour as one that causes sorrow as explained by a *tōḻi*. She tells the hero that at the hour when the white storks fly away against the red sky resembling a string of pearls worn by Murukaṉ, the day slowly ends, the sun reaches the west and the eyes of the heroine shed tears.[24] Thus intense sorrow that causes tears is said to be an emotion further intensified by sunset.

Pālai

The region with the largest number of poems is the desert. Strictly speaking, the Tamil country has no desert but certain parts of *kuriñci* and *mullai* become arid due to the want of seasonal showers.[25] Yet the region and *tiṇai* are named after a tree that is found in dry, sandy areas. It is the *pālai* or *wrightia tinctoria* with bright bunches of white flowers *(vāliṇar)* and fruits that look like a pair of pliers (*koṭiṟu*).[26] This is therefore the most prominent of the vegetation that is found in the arid areas. This *tiṇai* depicts the pining of the lovers in separation. The hottest half of the year, consisting of spring *(iḷavēṉil)*, summer (*mutuvēṉil*) and the late dewy season (*piṉpaṉi*), is suitable [27] for depicting this aspect of love, though summer, the hottest season and noonday, the hottest hour of the day are considered most appropriate. These show the heat of separation that burns the hearts of the lovers at its worst and is also symbolic of the heat of longing and unsatisfied passion. The lady-love imagines the various hardships the hero has to brave in the hot, dry season and this intensifies her own suffering. The time of day for this separation is midday when 'the earth cracks due to the fierce scorching rays like fire, the trees and vegetation shrivel and the rocks are hot enough to roast paddy scattered on them'.[28] The blazing sun shines blinding the eyes[29] so that the shade and comfort of the home is most welcome. This hour of day intensifies the sorrow of separation, which in Indian love literature, is also said to be hot and unbearable.

The correlation of the land divisions, seasons and time of day as seen in Caṅkam literature may be tabulated as follows:

Table 1

Land	*Aspect of love*	*Time of day*	*Seasons*
kuriñci	*puṇartal*	*yāmam, naṭunāḷ* (midnight)	*kūtir, muṉpaṉi*
mullai	*iruttal*	*mālai* (evening)	*kār*
marutam	*ūṭal*	*vaikaṟai, viṭiyal* (dawn)	-
neytal	*iraṅkal*	*eṟpāṭu* (sunset)	-
pālai	*pirivu*	*naṇpakal* (midday)	*piṉpaṉi* *iḷavēṉil* *mutuvēṉil*

These conventions that deal with the treatment of nature and love in Tamil classical poetry merely suggest the relationship between human emotions and nature and it is not to be supposed that these emotions are the only facets of love which everyone in love has to experience or that each region experiences only one particular aspect of love. In fact, each of these aspects has different facets of their own.

The Tamil Epics

The epics, being narrative poems, have not kept up this convention faithfully, but the *Cilappatikāram* has, to a certain extent, used this division, especially of land, people and their lives in these regions. The story of Kōvalaṉ and Kaṇṇaki is the story of a hero and heroine in the *marutam* region and the description of cities, life in the cities and Kōvalaṉ's indulgence in dance and music[30] are in keeping with the tradition of the five *tiṇais.* The *Kāṉalvari* with lyrics on the pining of a hero and then a heroine of the maritime tracts, follows the time, description and geography ascribed to this pining.[31] The journey of Kōvalaṉ and Kaṇṇaki to Maturai takes them to the arid tracts (*āriṭai attam*)[32] in summer where the priestess in a trance calls Kaṇṇaki a Goddess.[33] Reaching Maturai, Kavunti hands over the responsibility of caring for Kaṇṇaki to Mātari a shepherdess who takes them to her place. There Kōvalaṉ takes leave of his wife promising to return in the evening after selling one of her anklets.[34] This *iruttal* in the *mullai* region does not end as it should have for though there is trust and hope in Kaṇṇaki's heart, fate has interfered. This perhaps is useful in the epic to enhance the tragic elements. The description of *kuṟiñci,* the life of the people and the aspect of love pertaining to the region are found in the canto *Kuṉṟak Kuravai.* Aspects of *puṇartal* like the praising of the hero's hill[35] and *vēlaṉāṭal* or asking the priest to perform certain rites to propitiate Murukaṉ so that the heroine becomes well[36] are sung in this canto. All these, however, are not the main parts of the epic but incidents and places that are connected to the main story of the epic. The *Maṇimēkalai,* however, does not mention these divisions at all.

The time of day (*ciṟupoḻutu*) is not treated as faithfully in the epics. The only *ciṟupoḻutu* that seems important is *mālai* and the term *anti* is used frequently to denote this time of day. The

Cilappatikāram contains a whole canto (*Antimālaic ciṟappuc cey kātai)* in honour of this *ciṟupoḻutu*. It is described as the time when those who are united are happy while those separated are distressed in their loneliness, when *mullai* flowers bloom and women light up lamps.[37] This *ciṟupoḻutu* is used as a background to contrast the sad, unadorned Kaṇṇaki and the happy, well-adorned Mātavi. The ability of this time of day to evoke sorrow in the hearts of separated lovers is shown in phrases like *paṭarkūr mālai,*[38] *puṉkaṇ mālai*[39] and *puṉkaṇkūr mālai.*[40] Even the verses that deal with *iraṅkal* or pining on the seacoast use *mālai* as the time of sorrow and the time or term *eṟpāṭu* is not mentioned. *Vaikaṟai* or *viṭiyal* too is of no importance in portraying love in this epic. It is personified as a woman who is being awakened by the humming of bees.[41] *Yāmam* or *araiyiruḷ yāmam* is merely mentioned as a time when the city of Pukār is guarded, for Kāmaṉ parades in its streets. The love aroused by Kāmaṉ is not the type usually ascribed to this time of day in ancient *akam* poetry. It deals with the aspect of love concerned with jealousy and sulkiness due to the husband's disloyalty[42] and this in ancient poetry is normally ascribed to the city or agricultural regions. The *Maṇimēkalai* does not use these divisions of day except for *anti* or *mālai* which sets in with the sound of the *aṉṟil,* the return of cattle to their young in the sheds and the sounds of flutes played by cowherds. But the sorrow caused by this time of day is brought out by depicting evening as a widow.

> Like a woman
> losing her husband on the battlefield
> and entering the home of her people,
> Sunset,
> unable to bear the loss of the sun's rays
> and spread with pallor,
> entered the large city.[43]

Yāmam is merely a time at night when the king is praised.[44] Thus the conventions regarding *tiṇai* and the various details that make up a *tiṇai* are not followed in the epics. Instead they use descriptions of nature to beautify the poetry without necessarily conveying any particular or hidden meaning.

SANSKRIT LITERATURE

In Sanskrit literature too, we have the extensive use of nature, though the same type of division of land, day or love is not to be found. The geography of north India, watered by the two large river systems and bounded by mountains cannot create the same kind of interaction between man and nature as in the narrow, sea-bound south. Sanskrit literature sings of love (*śṛṅgāra*) as having two aspects, *vipralambha* and *saṃbhoga*. Of these, *vipralambha* is far broader than *pirivu* in Tamil classical poetry for it includes all the various types of separation mentioned in Tamil love poems in addition to others like, separations caused by a curse as in the *Meghadūtam* and the *Abhijñānaśākuntalam*. *Saṃbhoga* deals with love in union and includes the clandestine union or meeting (*kaḷavu* in Tamil) as well as the union experienced by them after marriage (*kaṟpu* in Tamil). It is therefore broader than *puṇartal* in Tamil love poetry.

Mountains

Certain relationships between environment (place and time) and love is also found in Sanskrit literature. Poems that deal with the description of mountains mention the mountain caves and groves as places suitably private for love dalliances, stealthy or otherwise. The clouds hanging over the entrances to the caves of the Himalayas, serve as screens to *kiṃpuruṣa* women who are shy because their garments have been snatched away by their lovers.[45] The stone-caves (*śilāveśma*) of Mount Nīchais near Vidiśā, the capital of Daśārṇa emit the scent of perfumes used by harlots (*paṇyastrī*) during their sport with the townsmen.[46] Mountain groves too, with their natural scenic beauty serve the same purpose, though normally are considered sacred to some deity or other. At the manifestation of the spring season in the grove where Śiva performs his penance, the *kiṃpuruṣa*, in the intervals of music, kisses the face of his beloved.[47] The arbours on the mountain Āmrakūṭa are places of enjoyment for the wives of foresters (*vanacaravadhūḥ*).[48] The commentary of Mallinatha states that the word *kuñjā* is a *latāgṛhā* or bower of creepers and reminds one of the bower of gloriosa creepers chosen as a suitable place for a tryst by a *tōḻi* in an *Akanāṉūṟu* poem.[49] Śiva and Pārvatī too are depicted as sporting on the Malaya mountains where the southern breeze (*dakṣiṇānilaḥ*) carrying the fragrance of sandal trees and *lavaṅga* blooms, removes the fatigue of Pārvatī.[50] Not all towns or cities, however, enjoy proximity to the Himalaya or Vindhya ranges, but a certain relationship must have existed between mountains and love-sports, for even in an urban setting, while describing an *upavana* next to a palace or the mansion of a rich *nāgarika*, a *krīḍaśaila* or pleasure mount is mentioned. The *Kumārasaṃbhavam*, describing how Tāraka harassed the three worlds, mentions that he uprooted peaks of the Meru mountain to build such mounts (*ākrīḍaparvatāḥ*) in his own residences.[51] In the *Meghadūtam* too, the pleasure mount is mentioned in the description of Alakā, near the Himalayas. Mount Kailāsa becomes one such mount for Gaurī when she walks about on the famous mountain in the company of Śiva who has discarded his serpent bracelet.[52] In the garden of the *yakṣa*, is the *krīḍaśailaḥ* made of sapphire[53] (a favourite spot of his wife).

Cities

The towns and cities are described as places where the women are well-versed in the art of coquetry. Though Sanskrit literature does not specify whether the chaste wife or the *gaṇikā* is referred to, the descriptions of the women seem to fit the *gaṇikā*. In the *Meghadūtam* they are referred to as *paurāṅganāḥ*[54] whose outer corners of the eyes are tremulous and dazzled by the lightning and, therefore, charming enough to delight those who see them. It certainly is a sight the cloud should not miss on its journey to the north. On the other hand, the eyes of the country women (*janapadavadhūḥ*) which moisten with affection are ignorant of sportive movements.[55] This difference and the fact that the accomplished *gaṇikā* enjoyed popularity and a social status that made it conventionally acceptable to treat her as the heroine in the *Cārudattam* and a *devagaṇikā* in the *Vikramorvaśīyam* suggest very strongly that extra-marital relationships are closely connected with city life. This relationship is not forgotten even while describing the love life of the people of Alakā. The men given to sensuous pleasures (*kāmin*) spend their time in the company of 'the women of gods' (*vibudhavanitāḥ*) but not their wives.[56] The harlots (*paṇyastrī*) of the capital of Daśārṇa country, Vidiśā, are mentioned as sporting with the men of the city in the caves of Mount Nīchais, but we have no indication as to whether these men are already married.[57] Even in the *Buddhacaritam*, King Suddhodana makes arrangements for a troupe of beautiful women, 'skilled in all the graceful arts, proficient in understanding the language of amorous sentiments and possessed of beauty and gracefulness',[58] to entertain his son Sarvārthasiddha in the Padmakaṇḍa forest, though the prince is already married to Yaśodharā.[59] The hour of sunrise is accepted as the time when the tears of injured women (*khaṇḍitāḥ*) are to be wiped off by the erring lovers or husbands. For this reason, the Yakṣa advises the cloud not to stand in the way of the sun who comes at dawn to wipe away the dew-tears of jealousy, anger and resentment on the face of the lotus.[60] It is significant that the term *khaṇḍitā* is used for it denotes a heroine or woman in love whose lover approaches her with obvious proof of his having spent his time with another woman, thus making her feel offended and sulky. The same idea is used in the *Raghuvaṃśam* when the sons of bards (*sūtātmajāḥ*) wake Aja in the morning. He is told that Lakṣmī, who is personified as his beloved, had spent the night like a *khaṇḍitā* or hurt and angry woman because he had been under the sway of sleep, also personified as a woman, implying that it is morning and he should return to Lakṣmī, i.e. his kingdom and his regal duties, and 'pacify' her.[61] This again is comparable to the time (early morning) and emotion (jealousy or sulkiness) depicted in the *marutam* poems of classical Tamil literature.

The Abhisārikā

In this connection may be mentioned the *abhisārikā* who, according to some writers, is a 'wanton woman' or one who indulges in extra-marital love.[62] But the *Amarakośam* defines *abhisārikā* as one of those women who choose their own husbands.[63] One characteristic that is highlighted in classical Sanskrit literature, is her secret tryst, which she keeps at night. The *Raghuvaṃśam*, describing the death of the demoness Rimā, who is smitten by the arrow of Rāma, says that she enters the abode of Yama just as an *abhisārikā* goes to her lover at an appointed place at night. The word used, however, is *niśācarī*, i.e. a woman who goes out at night.[64] The nights are invariably said to be dark, made darker by 'rumbling clouds'. The usual source of light seems to have been the flash of lightning.[65] The *Kumārasaṃbhavam* describes these women as knowing their way by the light emitted by the luminous herbs that grow in Oṣadhīprastha near the Himalayas.[66] In the Tamil poems, it is the light shed by the jewel on a cobra's hood that provides light at night. This light helps animals like the cobra itself and the tiger to look for their prey.[67] But such lights are considered detrimental to the secret meeting of lovers for it would light up the place and thereby rob them of the secrecy. A friend, trying to convince the hero of the helpless condition of the lady, tells him:

> To say that you would remove her sorrow
> at midnight,
> the lovely gem emitted by the cobra
> and washed down by the waterfall
> that has swept through the inky caves
> of the mountain slope,
> brightens the streets
> of the little village on the high slopes.
> The poor girl has lost that (opportunity) too.[68]

On the other hand, these gems provide invaluable light for them to meet in groves where the trees grow thickly and the gloriosa blooms in abundance.[69] Such bowers, being away from the village or in parts of the village that are hardly frequented by the villagers, especially at night, are private enough for the lovers.

The time, manner and season for the *abhisārikā's* tryst are similar to those found in the *kuṟiñci* poems. The place of meeting in the Tamil poems, however, is quite different. It is the hero who makes the dangerous journey to the heroine's village so that they meet near her house or sometimes in her own house or compound.[70] It is love that makes the girls brave enough to venture out of the house at that hour, forgetting their fear of darkness and thunder. Hence Ratī, while lamenting the death of her husband Kāma, says that it is he who enables these girls to reach the place of their tryst.[71]

The *abhisārikā* or the woman in love is pictured in both the literatures as being beautifully dressed when going out to meet her beloved. The *Meghadūtam* mentions the various flowers and ornaments the *abhisārikās* of Alakā use to adorn themselves before setting out on their rendezvous.

> Where the path pursued at night by women in love (*kāminī*) is

> indicated at sunrise by *mandara* flowers fallen from their hair, by the crushed petals of the golden lotuses that slipped from their ears and the threads from the strands of pearls broken on their expansive breasts, owing to the movement caused by their (rapid) gait.[72]

The Tamil poems too mention that the heroine is adorned with flowers and jewels. A youth thinking of his beloved coming out of her house to meet him at night says:

> I faltered,
> wondering if I should tell her or not
> of my secret love (for her).
> Then unable to contain myself
> I revealed it to her.
> Believing my sweet words
> she came stealthily at midnight
> in the pouring rain.
> her hair fragrant like the rainy season
> and her fine garments showing skilled workmanship.
> She came like the modest peacock
> surrounded by drizzling clouds.
> She wore cool scented flowers
> that bees followed her,
> and pretty, tinkling anklets bent like the bow,
> with their sound muffled.
> She came with fear
> at night when the village slept
> and embracing me she left,
> the dark, divine maiden with great chastity.[73]

But because of the stealthy nature of their meeting and the weather they have to brave, they cover themselves with suitably dark shawls or wraps so that they are partially hidden from the eyes of the passers-by or seem unrecognisable. Ūrvaśī in the *Vikramorvaśīyam* wraps herself with a blue garment with scanty ornaments and asks her friend how her *abhisārikaveṣa* suits her.[74] In her case there is no appointment to meet Purūravas but merely her own desire to see him unnoticed. A heroine from a *Kalittokai* poem tells her friend of her nocturnal meetings with her lover.

In the dark night when all beings slept,
wrapping myself well
with a pretty shawl of fine quality,
I stood at the appointed place
for him with a handsome chest
that removes affliction.[75]

The shawl is useful to hide her identity and to protect her from the cold of the rainy night.

Thus the difference seems to be in the place of the meeting. While the Sanskrit poems mention clearly that the women go to the houses of their beloveds, like the demoness Rimā entering the abode of Yama, the Tamil poems never show her as going to the district where her lover lives. They always meet near her home and sometimes, though rarely in her house or garden, so that the hero himself faces and overcomes any danger involved. This difference could have been caused by the difference in environment. The *abhisārikā* of Sanskrit classical poetry moves about in a well-guarded capital or city and there is no danger from climbing up mountain paths or of wild animals that are described in the *kuṟiñci* poems. Besides for the *abhisārikā* there is no specific mention of fear of her guardians finding out or preventing such meetings though it is not to be doubted that she too has to face the hazards of going out of the house at that time of the night. The season of course is similar in the *kuṟiñci* poems and the Sanskrit stanzas which deal with the *abhisārikā*.

REFERENCES

1. *Tol. Porul,* 4.
2. *Ibid.,* 20.
3. *Aink.* 440.
4. *Kurun.* 3.
5. *Tol. Porul.* 16.
6. *Ibid.,* 7 and 8.
7. *Akam,* 128.
8. *Ibid.,* 125.
9. *Tol. Porul,* 6.
10. *Aink,* 476.
11. *Tol. Porul,* 16.
12. *Ibid.,* 27, 30.
13. *Nar,* 142:10-11; *Akam,* 274:13-14.
14. *Kurun,* 108.

15. *Tol. Porul*, 6.
16. *Ibid.*, 9.
17. *Akam*, 36, 97, 34, 376; *Aink*, 31, 33, 72; *Kali*, 27; *Cilap*, 7:2.
18. *Kali*, 66.
19. *Ibid.*, 71:1-8.
20. *Tol. Porul*, 16.
21. *Ibid.*, 10.
22. *Kurun*, 9; Nar, 27, 47, 117, 138; *Akam*, 350, 170.
23. *Tol. Porul*, 10.
24. *Akam*, 120:1-6.
25. *Cilap*, 11:64-66.
26. *Nar*, 107.
27. *Tol. Porul*, 11 and 12.
28. *Akam*, 1:9-13.
29. *Ibid.*, 81:6-7.
30. *Cilap*, 3:158-75; 5.
31. *Ibid.*, 7.
32. *Ibid.*, 11:209.
33. *Ibid.*, 12:47-50.
34. *Ibid.*, 14:92-93.
35. *Ibid.*, 24 v. 3.
36. *Ibid.*, 24 v. 11-14.
37. *Ibid.*, 4:13-19.
38. *Ibid.*, 27:144.
39. *Ibid.*, 4:24.
40. *Ibid.*, 7. v. 33.
41. *Ibid.*, 4:72-76.
42. *Ibid.*, 4:66-84.
43. *Mani*, 5:137-41.
44. *Ibid.*, 7: 65.
45. *Kuma*, 1:14.
46. *Megh*, P. 26.
47. *Kuma*, 3:38.
48. *Megh*, P. 19.
49. *Akam*, 18.
50. *Kuma*, 8:25.
51. *Ibid.*, 2:43.
52. *Megh*, P. 63.
53. *Megh*, U.17.
54. *Megh*, P. 28.
55. Ibid., 16.
56. *Megh*, U.10.
57. *Megh*, P. 26.
58. *Buddh*, 2:9.
59. *Ibid.*, 3 and 4.
60. *Megh*, P. 42.
61. *Ragh*, 5:67.
62. S.A. Sabnis, *Kālidāsa: His Style and His Times*, Bombay, 1966, pp. 267, 129.

63. *Amarakośa*, 2, 6, 10.
64. *Ragh*, 11:20.
65. *Rtu*, 2:10; *Megh*, P. 40.
66. *Kuma*, 6:43.
67. *Akam*, 72: 13-15, 192.
68. *Ibid.*, 192:8-13.
69. *Ibid.*, 92:8-13.
70. *Ibid.*, 22.
71. *Kuma*, 4:11.
72. *Megh*, U. 11.
73. *Akam*, 198:1-12.
74. *Vikr*, act 3. p. 76.
75. *Kali*, 65:3-5.

Chapter 10

The Seasons

If Tamil classical poetry is closely connected to the fivefold divisions of land and time of day, Sanskrit poetry may be said to be closely connected to the seasons (*ṛtu*), a division of the year into six seasons. Tamil literature too, mentions the seasons (*perumpoḻutu*). But as is noticeable in Table 1 on page 199, the seasons do not fit in neatly with the five divisions of land and the *ciṟupoḻutu* or time of day. The division of the year into six seasons of two months each is identical in Tamil and Sanskrit, though the seasons could certainly not have been identical in the north and the south for obvious reasons, especially in the colder months.

TABLE 1

The Seasons

Tamil		*English*	*Sanskrit*	
iḷavēṉil	*cittirai*	April	*Caitra*	*vasanta*
	vaikāci	May	*Vaiśākha*	
mutuvēṉil	*āṉi*	June	*Jyeṣṭha*	*grīṣma*
	āṭi	July	*Āṣāḍha*	
kār	*āvaṇi*	August	*Śrāvaṇa*	*varṣā*
	puraṭṭāci	September	*Bhādrapada*	
kūtir	*aippaci*	October	*Āśvina*	*sarat*
	kārttikai	November	*Kārtika*	
muṉpaṉi	*mārkaḻi*	December	*Mārgaśīrṣa*	*hemanta*
	tai	January	*Pauṣa*	
piṉpaṉi	*māci*	February	*Māgha*	*siśira*
	paṅkuṉi	March	*Phālguna*	

Spring

The Spring is a pretty season with clear skies, the bright moon,[1] and the southern breeze (*dakṣiṇo mārutaḥ, malaya vāta* or *teṉṟal*)[2] which blows cool to allay the heat that might be felt.

Soon after the cold season[3] nature herself seems happy to feel the warmth of the sun and attires herself in gay and pleasing colours in the form of new shoots and flowers. Kālidāsa describes spring artistically:

> The gleaming red *aśoka* excels the paint that is applied
> to the *bimba*-like lip;
> The *kuravaka* with its dark, bright and red (colours)
> surpasses the paintings on the forehead;
> The *tilaka* blossoms, with the bees clinging to them
> like collyrium, have thoroughly grasped the art
> of adorning the forehead with the *tilaka* mark;
> Thus vernal beauty seems to hold up to ridicule
> the art of adorning the face as practised by women.[4]

Besides the trees mentioned in this verse, Sanskrit literature mentions the *palāśa, priyāla,*[5] *karṇikarā, navamallikā, kiṃśukā, cāru* and *kuṇḍa* flowers.[6] Tamil classical literature mentions the *iruppai, koṉṟai,*[7] *kuravam, pātiri,*[8] *murukku,*[9] *kōṅku,*[10] *vēmpu,*[11] *kaṭampu, cerunti, kāñci, ñāḻal* and *ilavam*[12] as trees that put forth fresh blossoms in this season. Because of this, the gardens and parks appear as if covered with scented flowers and Aśvaghoṣa refers to this season as *puṣpamāsa*[13] and Kālidāsa as *kusumamāsa,*[14] both meaning the month of flowers. Both literatures abound in descriptions of the mango tree with its tender, red shoots and the scented honey-filled flowers which attract the bees.[15] It is the favourite haunt of the cuckoo (*kokila, kuyil*) that lives on the pollen of flowers and honey. This bird is described in a Tamil poem as eating the pollen of the *murukku*[16] but its favourite is the mango blossom. Being intoxicated with the honey from the mango blossom, it calls for its mate, who, also pleased with the pollen and honey, answers its call.[17]

This season of youthful beauty is said to excite the passion and longing of love in all living creatures. Sanskrit literature, however, makes this season all-powerful. Of all the seasons, it is *vasanta* that Aśvaghoṣa describes in both his *kāvyas.* In the *Buddhacaritam* it is said to be the season that is beautiful. The prince, hearing of 'the forests with tender grass, with the trees resounding with the sound of the *kokilas* (cuckoos) and adorned with lotus ponds', all of which had been restrained in the cold season, wishes to go out.[18]

The various trees that bloom in this season are also described using feminine charm as comparison. One of the women assigned by his father to entice him to the pleasures of the body invites him:

> Come and listen to the intoxicated notes of the cuckoo
> that coos, while another coos as if consenting
> without care,

and adds that she wished his was the intoxication of the birds that the spring season produced in them and not that of a reflecting man.[19] Though in this *kāvya* the would-be Bodhisattva is pictured as being strong enough to withstand the assailance of the beautiful damsels and the influence of the spring season, in the *Saundaranandam*, the effect of this season on men with lesser self-control is depicted. Nanda though a Buddhist monk living in the *vihāra* is not a monk in his thoughts and desires. So at the sight of the lovely flowers of spring he thinks of his wife. The *aśoka* grove and the tender *priyaṅgu* creeper being dear to Sundarī remind him of her and seeing an *atimukta* creeper clinging to a mango tree wonders, 'When will Sundarī embrace me like this?'[20] These thoughts make his heart burn with the fire of passion.[21] On the whole, Sanskrit poems do not make self-control possible in this season. Bhāsa does not deal with this season except for a passing reference in the opening verse of the *Svapnavāsavadattam* which is necessitated by the elaborate device to introduce the names of the main characters of the drama including Vasantaka, the *vidūṣaka*.[22] In Kālidāsa's works, spring is a season of beauty and love. It is powerful enough to unsettle the firm, concentrating minds of the sages. This is the reason given for Viśvāmitra's transient passion for Menakā[23] and it is on this basis again that the God of Love sets out to conquer Śiva, the greatest of ascetics, by making Vasanta manifest itself before the proper time of year.[24] So it is no wonder that it strikes at the hearts of young men separated from their wives[25] or distracts the minds of youths given to passionate ways,[26] makes youthful maidens sorrowful[27] or even perturbs the minds of modest women from respectable homes.[28] For the animals, following the order of nature, it is the mating season. The bee becomes loving towards its mate and drinks honey from the same flower cup. The black antelope scratches with its horns the doe who closes her eyes experiencing the pleasant sensation of touch. The female elephant, out of great love, gives the male elephant the water held in her mouth. The *cakravāka* gives its beloved a lotus stalk half-eaten by him and the *kiṃpuruṣa,* a semi-divine being, kisses the face of the beloved.[29]

Tamil literature also accepts this season as one suited for the union of lovers and in the poems on separation *(pālai),* it only seems to heighten the poignancy of feeling. A lady separated from her lord, tells her friend:

He does not come.
But it has come,—the season
when the female cuckoo coos sweetly
and the water waves with fine black sand
forms curving lines,[30]

implying that the spring season when the water in the rivers begins to dry up and the cuckoos unite, has come. Another complains:

You say, 'My friend in distress!
Do not cry. He will return.'
Can I stop crying?
Even during the season
when the dark *kuyil* with shiny feathers
pecks at the mango blossoms
and is covered with the pollen
to look like a touchstone,
I have to stroke my unadorned hair.[31]

Yet another fears that there is no way in which she could hope to live any longer for the spring has come with the *kōṅku* putting forth fresh shoots and the *kuyil* calling its mate from the tall branches of the sweet mango tree. She adds:

This is indeed the spring of fresh joys
for those united to their consorts
who appreciate their great beauty.[32]

All these poems imply that the season of fresh flowers is one for personal adornment and the enjoyment of love. But women in separation miss all this. Even men who live far from home think of their loved ones during spring. One such man is afraid that the spring season would be most disturbing to his wife.

> In the days following the heavy downpour
> of rain that makes work possible
> on this big, broad earth,
> in spring when the fine river sand
> curves like the moving back
> of a striped serpent,
> each time the mating *kuyil* coos,
> on the mango tree that blooms in bunches,
> she will shed tears
> in solitude.[33]

Thus *iḷavēṉil* or *vasanta* is the season most conducive to love and reunion and the separation due to journeys or war made possible by the clear skies and fine weather is most painful.

The longer poems of the *Pattuppāṭṭu* and the Tamil epics show how the pleasures of love which are enjoyed in this season are further enhanced, especially by well-to-do people. They have open terraces above their houses (*veṉir paḷḷi*) from which they can enjoy the southern breeze and use sandal paste,[34] pearls[35] and an abundance of flowers[36] to allay the heat and produce a pleasant sensation conducive to love. All these objects, it must be noted, are from nature. The *Maṇimēkalai* refers to it as *irutu iḷavēṉil*,[37] using the word *irutu* (*ṛtu*) for season and describes it as the season to be spent with one's beloved, but out of doors—in the parks where there are fountains, bowers, lakes and marbled halls (*paḷikkaṟai*).[38]

This season is personified as a friend of Kāmaṉ (Tamil) or Kāmaḥ (Sanskrit), the god of love. The earlier Tamil anthologies hardly ever mention the god of love as an important factor or influence in the love between a man and a woman, though the word for love in those poems is *kāmam*. The *Paripāṭal* mentions that in the art galleries of Tirupparaṅkuṉṟam are paintings among which are found those of Kāmaṉ and his wife Ratī.[39] In this and other post-Caṅkam texts we see the gradual development of the Tamil concept regarding Cupid or Eros. The same text refers to him as 'the god with arrows made of fragrant flowers'.[40] The beauty of women bathing in the River Vaiyai is described as capable of causing pangs of love and the poet makes the youths say to one another:

> Look at their eyes!
> They are Kāmaṉ's armoury
> and his weapon (i.e. his bow).[41]

Another poem explains clearly what this armoury consists of.

> Their eyes resemble the
> five arrows of revered Kāmaṉ.
> Their fragrance attracts bees
> but have been sharpened on the rasp
> (to make them deadlier).[42]

Kalittokai poems too refer to this god and furnish further details regarding him and his insignia. For the first time in Tamil literature a flag with a fish emblem, variously named as a 'fish-banner' (*mīṉēṟṟukkoṭi*)[43] and a 'shark banner' (*cuṟāk koṭi*),[44] is ascribed to him. A festival held in his honour in spring is also mentioned (*kāmavēḷ viḻavu, villavaṉ viḻavu*), and this festival too is one that is joyful or enhances the sorrow of separation, depending on whether one is with his or her beloved or is separated.[45] A *tōḻi* tries to comfort her friend saying:

> Do not suffer with an afflicted heart.
> Your lover, thinking,
> 'In her loneliness without me
> in the season that aggravates it
> she will suffer
> during the festival of Kāmaṉ,'
> comes in haste,
> riding fast the frightful, firm chariot
> to be with you.[46]

A *marutam* poem shows a hero inviting his wife to sport on the banks of the River Vaiyai. He says:

> The dark *kuyil* on the flowering branches
> coos as if to say,

'Those who are united!
Do not separate.
Those long separated!
Unite.'
The men and women of Maturai
sport together in the park
filled with honeyed blossoms
celebrating spring's feast to Kāmaṉ.
Let us join them.[47]

The *Cilappatikāram* mentions March (*paṅkuṉi*) as the month when this festival of Kāmaṉ's bow (*neṭuvēḷ vilviḻā*) is celebrated.[48]

By the time the *kāviyam* (*kāvya*) *Cilappatikāram* was composed, the concept of the love god had developed in the Tamil country and so many names and features are comparable to those found in Sanskrit literature. Even in Sanskrit literature, the idea of the god of love is not very old, and hence we find some contradictions. The *Buddhacaritam* refers to him as Māra, the enemy of good *dharma* or order (*saddharmaripuḥ*). Though the world calls him 'Kāmadeva, the owner of various weapons, the flower-armed, the lord of the course of desire,' he is actually the enemy of salvation (*mokṣadviṣa*).[49] This perhaps is in keeping with the message that Aśvaghoṣa was trying to convey in his two *kāvyas*. This name Māraṉ is used in the Tamil epics, as well, but the *Cilappatikāram* uses it as one of the many names of Kāma (*Maṉṉaṉ Māraṉ*).[50] The *Maṇimēkalai,* however, uses this name in the special Buddhist meaning especially when praising Buddha as the hero who has overcome Māraṉ (*māraṉai vellum vīra*)[51] though the name Kāmaṉ is also used in this context (*kāmar kaṭanta vāman*).[52] He is also called *malark kaṇai maintaṉ,* the youth with flower arrows.[53] Another difference is in the role of Ratī. While all works refer to her as the wife and constant companion of Kāma, the *Buddhacaritam* assigns her the role somewhat similar to that of Menakā and the other *apsarās* of Indra's heaven. When the arrows fail to have the desired effect on Sarvārthasiddha, Kāma feels that the prince-sage is not worthy of them. Neither is he worthy of being tempted by Ratī.[54] Thus she seems to be the instrument for Kāma to arouse love or the erotic sentiment in those he wishes to bring under his sway.

Other classical works in Sanskrit portray him as a king, with the objects of nature, especially those of the spring season as his insignia. He has a bow made of *kiṃśukā* flowers with the bees for his bowstring[55] and five flowers (*aravindam* or lotus, *aśoka* or *sarasa indica, cūtam* or mango, *navamallikā* or jasmine and *nīlotphala* or *blue nelumbo*) as his arrows. Sometimes the brittle lotus-fibre is said to be his bowstring.[56] The *Ṛtusaṃhāram* pictures him as a warrior with the young mango blossoms for his sharp arrows and a row of bees as a resplendent bowstring.[57] In the *Abhijñānaśākuntalam*, the mango tree's pale, green but slightly pinkish flower is praised as the very essence of the life of spring,[58] while many other works refer to it as the favourite arrow of Madana or Kāma.[59] The mango shoots are the feathers attached to this arrow.[60] The moon is his friend[61] but it is Vasanta or Madhu who helps him without waiting to be asked.[62] Ratī, the personification of the feeling of love or the erotic sentiment, is his wife.[63] The cuckoo, well-versed in sweet talk, is his persuasive messenger[64] who proclaims the arrival of Cupid and urges all beings to unite in love. But the *Ṛtusaṃhāram* personifies this bird as his bard who sings his praises, the moon as his umbrella which is an insignia of royalty and the breeze from the Malaya mountains (i.e. from the south) as his rutty elephant.[65] His banner is the fish.[66] In the *Abhijñānaśākuntalam* we find mention of his festival. King Duṣyanta, grieving over his unjust repudiation of Śakuntalā, forbids the celebration of the *vasantotsava* which is held at the beginning of spring. The offering of the mango blossoms seems to have been customary in the worship of Kāma and the circumstances that lead to the forbidding of this festival shows that, as in Tamil literature, here too the festival is considered to be one that arouses poignant memories and intensifies sorrow for those separated from their beloveds.[67]

The *Cilappatikāram* contains a whole canto named after this season (*Vēṉiṟ kātai*) with references to the god of love in other cantos as well. Here he is personified as a king. The southern breeze (*teṉṟal*) is the messenger who comes with the news of the arrival of the king's friend, the pleasant spring (*iṉṉiḷa vēṉil*). The cuckoo (*kuyil*) who is the trumpet bearer for this fish-bannered king proclaims to his army (young women) to change into fitting attire[68] for the cold season is no more. The letter sent by Mātavi to her lover Kōvalaṉ when he walks out on her is based on this regalia of Kāmaṉ.

Pleasant spring who unites all beings
with their desired mates
is a young (inexperienced) king.
Moon who has appeared
on the crest of the evening
is not mature.
If those with their beloveds
stay away
or those separated
forget their loved ones,
it is not to be wondered,
were (Kāmaṉ) to take away dear life
with fragrant flower-arrows.[69]

The author of this epic, Iḷaṅkō, describes this love god as the king who rules over the Tamil country from the Vēnkaṭa hills to the seas of Kumari (Cape Comorin) with Maturai, Uṟaiyūr, Vañci and Pukār as his capitals.[70] But Kālidāsa claims that he rules the whole world including the gods and the demons with his bow which has only the gentle and brittle fibres of the lotus plant as its string and delicate flowers for arrows.[71] Thus he is shown as being all-powerful and transcending all boundaries. The relationship between the god of love and the spring season may be easily noticed in the following table (see p. 220).

Summer

The next season (*mutuvēṉil* or *grīṣma*) is the hottest season when the sun as red as fire, beats down mercilessly, drying up the crops in the fields,[72] the vegetation on the hillslopes[73] and the water in the lakes and rivers[74] and cracking up the soil.[75] A long summer can even cause the rocks to crack.[76] The large trees too, having shed their leaves, stand bare with only their empty branches.[77] Birds and beasts, due to the heat, and some fearing the sound of dry leaves,[78] go in search of water and shade which are most welcome but hard to come by. Oppressed by heat and thirst, the animals run after mirages.[79] The sun's rays, resembling fire in their colour and heat,[80] cause forest-fires which scorch the parched earth and burn up whatever vegetation is left. The dry trees and the bamboos as well as the strong gusts of summer wind (*kōṭai*

TABLE 2

Kāma and Spring

		Sanskrit	Tamil
Wife		Ratī	Rati
Friend/accomplice		*Vasanta/Madhu* Moon	*Iḷavēṉil* Moon
Messenger		cuckoo	southern breeze
Bard		cuckoo	-
Trumpet bearer		-	cuckoo
Weapons-	bow	*kiṃśuka* flowers	sugarcane
	bowstring	lotus fibres bees	
	arrows	lotus *aśoka* mango (*cūta*) *navamallikā* *nīlotphala*	lotus *acōku* mango *mullai* *nīlōtpalam*
	feathers on arrows	mango shoots	-
Elephant		southern breeze	evening
Emblem for flag		fish	fish
Umbrella		moon	-
Army		-	young women
Festival		beginning of spring	end of *muṉpaṉi* or March

in Tamil and *rūkṣapavanaḥ* in Sanskrit)[81] only help to feed and fan these fires which cause herds of cattle to tremble.[82] It is the strong, cruel summer caused by the anger of the sun (*kāy ciṉantirukiya kaṭuntiṟal vēṉil*).[83] Bhāsa describes these aspects of summer aptly in his play *Avimārakaṃ*. The prince, running away from the palace for fear of being caught by the king's men, travels aimlessly in the summer heat and cannot help observing that:

The world is caught in a harsh dry wind that howls
with fine sand ground into fire.
Trees lose in sweat their dried and brittle leaves
while the pulsing sun flows
as if its body had been turned to molten heat by forest-fire.
And this same baking sun
cracks the world open like a ripened fruit.[84]

The *Ṛtusaṃhāram* portrays how these hardships enforced by nature make the animals forget their natural enmity and fear for one another. The frog, unable to bear the heat rests under the raised hood of a snake, who scorched by the sun's heat and his own venom, is in no mood to kill.[85] The snakes themselves try to take shelter under a peacock's tail feather.[86] But the Tamil poems, though describing nature, deal actually with the *uripporuḷ* or emotion of the lovers, and show how even such hardships do not destroy the tender care and affection animals have for their mates. The deer that has gone astray mistaking a mirage for water, calls his doe with a disturbed heart and an anxious but weak voice.[87] The tiger waits for its prey to satisfy the hunger of the tigress who has recently been delivered of her cubs and is suffering for want of shade as well.[88] Such pictures of birds and animals that live in love and affection serve to console the heroine. The hero, seeing such loving sights and being reminded of her, would complete his mission and hasten back. A friend, trying to console the heroine, whose lover has gone away in search of wealth before marriage, says:

Were he to obtain the good Chola country,
rich in fields
yielding white padi,
he would not stay back.
He went, crossing the arid tracts
where summer prolongs
and the male bear,
large-pawed and open-mouthed,
lives happily on the tall slopes
with his black-furred cub
resembling a piece of darkness,
and his mate with drooping udders.[89]

In this poem, though the friend seems to describe the summer season when the mountain slope is parched and the bear that nurses its cub is without milk, the main aim is to portray the happy life of the bear with its family. This would remind him of his obligation to marry the woman he loves and raise a family. He would therefore not delay, but return soon.

Though it is the hero who is pictured as travelling in the summer heat, the pain of separation is equally acute for him, who is out in the parched arid tracts, and her, who lives in the comfortable house. Just as the heroine is pictured in Tamil poetry as being anxious for his safety and comfort, the hero also is shown to be thinking of her plight. A youth who has gone away in search of wealth thinks of his beloved who would suffer the pangs of separation and wonders:

> While I am alone
> in the wide, scorching forest
> studded with mountains and villages,
> she sheds tears, night and day.
> She suffers intensely
> like those wounded at Port Muciṟi
> when the Pandyas,
> with flags fixed to their chariots
> surrounded the port and killed many elephants.
> Would her tiny forehead
> losing its brightness and beauty
> like the cool moon with many rays,
> now resemble (in colour)
> the little flower of the sponge-gourd?[90]

He is afraid that pallor would spread on her lovelorn body and spoil the beauty of her face. Such poems are rare in the Sanskrit works under study. The *Avimārakam* is the only work that deals with this season and separation and it contains one verse in which the hero thinks of his beloved's tears and helplessness.

> Shamed by servants' gossip,
> frightened of the king's anger,
> now that she is closely guarded,
> without me her tears will drop

into the lonely night—
She will fall into unconsciousness.
And in those long nights
I can no longer help her.[91]

Here, the cause of her tears is not only the sorrow of separation but also the shame of gossip and fear of the father.

Similarly, the hero in both the literatures is shown as thinking of what he left behind and the harshness of the hot arid tracts. A hero in Tamil classical literature thinks of his lovely lady in her village which can be reached only after crossing many hills ruled over by kings or chieftains who do not follow *aṟam* (*dharma*) but punish their men for not killing the wayfarers even if they do not carry any wealth with them that is worth robbing. The description of such hills and the cruel acts of the chieftains is only used to show that the dangerous journey is worth the while for,

Her surm-lined eyes (are dark like)
the many-petalled tender flower (blue lotus).
Her sweet speech
is like the music from the good lute.
She would offer (me)
her *nalam*.[92]

The word *nalam* is one of those words that cannot be translated to bring out the wealth of meaning it conveys. It means beauty, love, goodness, joy and prosperity. Avimāraka too thinks of the beauty of the princess and the joys of love that they had shared before he had to leave the palace.

I have left her and all the richness
of her fresh and beautiful young love
that naturally increased as we grew familiar.
To continue to live now
shows ingratitude to love.[93]

But in this text, we find a sense of helplessness and surrender which is not to be found in the Tamil poems. The Tamil heroes are always shown to be more optimistic, with faith in their ability to overcome the dangers and to return as planned. This perhaps is due to the absence of any hindrance or danger from supernatural sources. We have to bear in mind that Avimāraka has no such obstacles to overcome for even the curse that he should live as a *caṇḍāla* is about to come to an end. In the Tamil poems, there is never any mention of the hero thinking of returning before accomplishing the task he sets out for or of fainting fits or the contemplation of suicide as in the *Avimārakam*.[94]

Though summer is most suitable for the portrayal of the poignant feelings of the lovers in separation, the love and passion roused by spring is no longer at its height, but neither is it completely extinguished. Both literatures mention various devices to allay the heat of the season and to create a delightful atmosphere conducive to love and the delights of love. Sanskrit literature mentions bowers and other shady places near rivers and fountains for habitation during the hot summer days[95] and balconies or terraces atop mansions for the enjoyment of the cool moonlight at night.[96] Pearls, sandal paste and flowers in abundance as well as thin garments are useful to allay the heat and produce a feeling of cool comfort.[97] Śakuntalā who is tormented simultaneously by the heat of love and that of summer is made to lie on a stone slab strewn with flowers, in a bower on the creeper-wreathed bank of the Mālinī. Around her arms are the tender lotus stalks serving as bracelets and her two friends fan her with lotus leaves.[98] The comfort of fans wet with a mixture of water and sandal paste is referred to in the *Ṛtusaṃhāram*.[99] Though most Tamil classical poems are too short to give details of the various means used to reduce the sensation of heat in summer, most of them contain references to water sports.[100] Such details are found in a negative manner in the longer poems of the *Pattuppāṭṭu*. The *Neṭunalvāṭai*, describing the sorrow of the queen during the cold rainy season (*kūtir*) because her husband is still at the war camp, mentions that the slab on which sandal is rubbed to a paste lies unused while the fan in its cover hangs on the wall, covered with cobwebs. The windows that admit the southern breeze into the retiring rooms in summer are locked securely. People do not drink the cool water from the pots.[101] Thus the sandal paste, the fan, the breeze and cool water are objects most useful in summer. The epic *Cilappatikāram* describes Mātavi as spending the summer in the company of Kōvalaṉ on the high balcony meant for the enjoyment of the cool rays of the moon.

These two works (*Neṭunalvāṭai* and *Cilappatikāram*) use the same words to describe the high balconies of the residence of the queen and Mātavi respectively.

> The summer apartments (*veṉiṟ paḷḷi*)
> on the upper floor
> touching the skies.[102]

The open terrace to enjoy the rays of the moon is described as

> *Nilavuppayaṉ koḷḷu neṭuveṇ muṟṟam*[103]
> *Nilavuppayaṉ koḷḷu neṭunilā muṟṟam.*[104]

Many other women unite with their beloved husbands or lovers. Their beds, cooled by the breeze from the south, are spread with the tender shoots and pollen-filled flowers of the lotus, the lovely blue lotus (*kuvaḷai*) *kaḻunīr* flowers (the red variety of *kuvaḷai*), green leaves, fragrant powders and strings of pearls. They give up the use of the smoke of aloewood (*akil*) and frankincense but use instead the sandal paste prepared by rubbing sandalwood on the grinding stone.[105] The Tamil epics also mention parks and gardens (*uyyāṉam*[106] or *uvavaṉam*)[107] frequented by lovers to enjoy the shade as well as the coolness of the fountains and pools erected there.[108]

The Rainy Season

A pleasant season comparable to spring is the rainy season. Tamil literature sings of two rainy seasons—*kār* and *kūtir*. *Kār* which is the beginning of the rainy season proper in the Tamil country corresponds to *varṣā* in Sanskrit. It has occasional showers and is very much like spring in its coolness, for the earth's heat is allayed by these showers which put an end to summer.[109] Earth rejoices and puts forth fresh shoots and flowers. The clouds move on making a pleasant sound (*manoharasvaraḥ, iṉkural*) satisfying the skylark (*cātakaḥ, vāṉampāṭi*) that feeds on raindrops.[110] According to the *Ṛtusaṃhāram* the shoots of grass, like cat's-eye gems, the green *kandali* leaves and the red cochineal insects (*indragopa*)—all of which appear with the onset of the rainy season—make the earth look like a beautiful damsel decked with pretty jewels other than white.[111] Similarly, a Tamil poem compares the earth adorned with the blue *kāyā* blooms, white *mullai* buds and the cochineal insects (*mūtāy*) to a piece of art created by an able artist.[112] Quite often the golden hued cassia (*koṉṟai*), the pink jasmine (*taḷavam*) and the water-lily (*neytal*) are also mentioned so that the forest looks as if decorated with flowers.[113] This is also the season when the peacocks that sing beautifully, spread their lovely feathers and dance with delight[114] and the deer eat tender shoots to their fill.[115]

At this time of the year, husbands who are away on business or war return to their waiting wives, realising fully well the grief and anxiety that they had undergone. In the *Meghadūtam*, the *yakṣa* seeing the cloud, not only longs for his wife's embrace, but also tells the cloud:

> When you ascend to the path of the wind
> the wives of men travelling away from home,
> cheered up through confidence (that they will return soon),
> will look intently at you,
> holding up the ends of their (dishevelled) locks.
> When you appear in the sky, girt for action,
> who but one like me whose life is dependant on another
> will neglect his wife afflicted with separation?[116]

The lonely wife of the traveller is depicted as being distressed and devoid of garlands, ornaments and cosmetics. The tears from her lotus-like eyes fall on her *bimba*-like lower lips.[117] Those whose husbands are with them, having heard the rumble of clouds, hurry to their bed chambers after having applied sandal paste and aloewood to their bodies and wearing chaplets of flowers in their hair.[118]

The *Cilappatikāram* also sings of this season as one most suited to the pleasures of bathing in the fresh waters, wearing various flowers that bloom in that season like the *mullai, kuvaḷai, neytal* and *mallikai* and spending the day in parks and gardens. At sunset, women wearing silk garments, flowers like *kuṭacam, tāḷi* and *kuṟiñci*, the paste of red sandal on their breasts, garlands of flowers and coral, spend their time with their lovers on beds also spread with flowers. Thus it is pictured as a time for love and union.[119] Though the season begins with the south-west monsoon (*kuṭak kāṟṟu*) it ends with the coming of the north-east monsoon (*vāṭai*).[120] The *Maṇimēkalai* does not treat *kār* as an important season, though it mentions that the *kaṭampu* blooms in this season.[121]

Apart from the rain cloud which itself is capable of tormenting those in love who are separated,[122] the flowers that bloom in the season and the love-making of the birds and animals arouse the longing of the waiting heroine at home. Kuraṅginī complains that the servants not knowing her frame of mind, constantly bring her flowers like *bakula, sarala, sarja, arjuna, kadamba, nīpa, nicula* and others 'which when the heavy rains come, send their perfume through the trees to intoxicate me.' The peacocks in the royal parks, 'strut about and flirt outrageously' with the peahens.[123] A heroine in a *Kuṟuntokai* poem tells her *tōḻi*:

> What is there to be said, my friend?
> Does the sound alone,
> of the rising cloud with lightning
> cause pain?
> The peacocks of the forest
> call their mates urgently.
> These two external happenings
> distress my foolish heart.[124]

A hero who has returned before the rainy season as promised, tells his beloved that he was afraid the mating of birds and animals, the flowers of trees and creepers and the sight of the fragrant thickets would sadden her further in his absence.[125] Avimāraka, whose separation though due to tear and his return is made possible by supernatural help, returns to find his beloved sad, with tears in her eyes and lost in thought for 'these are the rainy nights when lovers are together.'[126]

The *mullai* poems with *iruttal* or the patient waiting of the wife as the *uripporuḷ* deal with this return of the husband. By 'patient waiting' it is not meant that the heroines are calm and collected without tears or anxiety. There are tears and even complaints about the season and the hero's delay. But in the *mullai* poems the heroines do not abandon themselves to grief. Usually, there is an effort to control the grief, to trust the hero and to accept the separation as even necessary. For example, in the idyll *Mullaippāṭṭu* the heroine sheds tears for she misses her husband at the onset of the *kār* season. Yet, 'reflecting for long' (*nīṭu-niṉaintu*), she pushes back her bangles that have become too large for her emaciated forearms and though full of sighs, is confident that he would return as promised. This certainly is a trust not merely in his words but also in his ability to achieve his mission and this trust is not in vain for she hears the sound of his victorious return.[127] The poems that describe nature usually depict the animals that have been refreshed in the company of their mates. The wild cockerel scratches the wet earth for worms and invites the hen to eat it,[128] the deer embraces the modest doe and the male elephant is seen in the company of the female elephant.[129] A hero who has completed his mission successfully, thinks of his beloved wife at home. His home is close to the *mullai* region where the doe frisks about with its mate after being satiated with tender shoots and the bees with pretty wings hum about the *mullai* flowers. He feels that her eyes immersed in grief would shed tears and *pacalai* (pallor or paleness) would have spread over her lovely body. So he is anxious to return early to release the single braid of hair which is symbolic of her solitary state.[130] The same tears and the single braid of hair are also mentioned by the *yakṣa* when talking of his beloved in Alakā, though the pallor is not mentioned.[131] Another hero, also about to return, tries to imagine the state of his lonely wife. The rabbit, having eaten the luxuriant shoots of the common millet (*varaku*), retires among the bean-creepers. Then getting up, drinks water with its mate, from the small pool in their compound. He feels that his wife, residing there, would be more listless than himself,[132] probably because she sees the rabbits together. In the two poems mentioned above, the phrases, *ēṟu puṇar uvakai* and *iṉṟuyil* are used to describe the state of the doe and the rabbit respectively which are suggestive of physical union and they bring out subtly the ladies' longing and the desire of the heroes to satisfy that longing. One of the *mullai* poems depicts a hero who is anxious to return home before sunset so that his wife would be happy and he be rid of the discomforts of the war camp.[133] But those who have returned before the onset of *kār* are happy in their union with their beloveds. One such fortunate husband is able to say:

> In the pastoral region where bees hum
> intoxicated with the honey of choice flowers,

the elephant embraces its modest mate.
I am united with the modest maiden
wearing bright armlets.[134]

Another in the same situation, lets her know that he did think of her and longed to return to be with her during that season

O damsel!
This is the season I longed for.
That is the shrubland I remembered.
Sweet is youth spent together.
Sweeter is union with one's beloved.[135]

The Cold Season

While *kār* is only the beginning of rains in the South, the actual rainy season is *kūtir* (October-November), caused by the 'anger' or severity of *kār* (*kār katam paṭṭa*) and is characterised by thunder, lightning and heavy rainfall.[136] During this season, the clouds which have absorbed the water from the sea in the east move westwards and darken the sky like collyrium. Lightning, resembling copper vessels, brightens the earth. The clouds rain everywhere and when their duty is completed, they move southwards.[137] The heavy, continuous rain hides the sky and the rainwater covers the earth.[138] It is difficult to know day from night[139] and according to the *Neṭunalvāṭai,* the inhabitants of the palace know that it is sunset through the fragrance of the *piṭavu* buds which bloom at that hour of the day.[140] The *mucuṇṭai, pīr,*[141] *pakaṉṟai, īṅkai*[142] and the *kūtaḷam* put forth their blossoms.[143] Arecanuts are about to ripen, the paddy stalks grow heavy with ripening grain[144] and the sugarcane grows tall.[145] But the animals and birds as well as the hunters do not go out in the cold weather. Monkeys shiver and cows spurn their own calves in the rainy weather which makes even the mountains feel cold.[146] The pigeon, unable to search for food with its mate, remains in its hole, shifting its weight from one leg to the other.[147] The rivers flow with muddy water, unlike in spring or summer when the water is clear and blue.[148] The hunters, unable to go out in search of wild animals and finding the floor even within their homes chill, sleep on tiger skins.

Yet the heroine in the hilly district braves the cold weather to keep her tryst with the hero. The rain that prevents others from going out of the house provides her the secrecy but adds to the danger of the menfolk at home noticing her slip out of the house. The slippery mountain path and the darkness of the night enhance the danger and anxiety of the clandestine meetings. A heroine who goes out of the house to meet her lover in spite of the inconveniences is disappointed that he does not keep the tryst punctually. So she says to him:

Lord of the mountain!
On your hill in the rainy season (*kūtir*)
with sweet thunder and heavy rain drops,
the father of the bejewelled *kuṟava* maid
whose tresses smell of the honey of flowers,
is unable to find a suitable place
while hunting in the forest.
He sleeps at home at midnight
when all beings are asleep,
on the bed spread with tiger skins.
Sweeter than embracing repeatedly
throwing my bangled arms around you
so that my lovely young breasts are pressed
against your chest,
is my anxious lonely wait
at midnight
when the indiscriminate north wind
blows soft but cold.
I wait, leaning wearily
against the tree in the courtyard.[149]

The season is such that the father or men of the house do not go out but stay indoors. The rain and the cold breeze make it uncomfortable to stand outside the house. Yet the expectation of meeting her lover makes this waiting bearable and even pleasant. The description of the rainy season, however, has another purpose. It points out subtly to the hero the inconvenience of her waiting out in the rain while he himself comes only when he has no other work like hunting, to do. For those who do not have to wait in this manner, it would be much more comfortable with the windows shut and the fragrant heat and smoke of aloewood and the embrace of the lovers.[150]

In Sanskrit literature, the season that corresponds to *kūtir* in time is *śarat* or autumn. It is the time of the year when the clouds having shed their burden of vapour, appear white like silver, conch or lotus roots.[151] The sky is clear but appears like powdered collyrium[152] (*bhinnāñjana*) so that it shows the clear-rayed moon and the stars to advantage.[153] The *śaptacchada, bandhūka, mālatī* and the *śyāma* flower in this season while the ponds have lotuses (*padma and kumuda*) blooming.[154] This seems to be the season of harvest when the *śāli* corn and the *kalamā* rice are ripe.[155] This season does not seem to have much to excite passion or longing though the *Ṛtusaṃhāram* mentions the clear blue sky, the red pollen of *bandhūka* flowers and the earth covered with *kalamā* rice to create such longing in young men.[156] The only thing that may be considered an excitement of love peculiar to this season is the pair of swans that warble sweetly,[157] probably as a prelude to their love union.

Dewy Seasons

Hemanta is the coldest season in the north and in this respect corresponds to *kūtir*. But in the north, the cold is due to the fall of dew or snow[158] though it also seems to have some sunlight with soft rays.[159] The *lodhra* tree flowers, corn and rice ripen but the lotuses perish[160] and the *priyaṅgu* creeper becomes pale.[161] This season does not seem to be very different from the next one *śiśira* which is also described as being cold,[162] but having sunlight.[163] Even during *śiśira*, the fields are filled with clusters of well-grown rice and sugarcane.[164] During both these seasons the fields are filled with the music of the *krauñca* birds that excite passion.[165] Due to the cold, people do not use pearl necklaces or sandal paste.[166] Nor do they spend their time on the terraces that admit the moonlight and the cool breeze. Women give up the use of silk garments along with the use of jewels like bracelets, armlets, waistbands and anklets which get chilled in the cold weather.[167] Instead they make use of saffron paste,[168] the incense of black aloewood,[169] thick garments and the warmth of the embrace of their beloveds. They also keep to the inner apartments of their houses with the windows closed to keep away the cold wind.[170] Though nature does not seem attractive enough to induce *śṛṅgāra*, it is certainly capable of inducing passion or *rati*. Many verses in the *Ṛtusaṃhāram* deal with incidents relating to physical union and these bear ample testimony to the importance it gives to *rati*. There is said to be much sexual sport that keeps the women awake late into the nights and leave them exhausted and languid.[171]

In Tamil literature too, the period of dewfall is divided into two seasons, *mun̲pan̲i* and *pin̲pan̲i*, meaning the season of early dew and that of late dew. But very often these two seasons are referred to by the same term, *ar̲ciram*. The Tamil lexicon explains this word as one derived by the combination of *al* meaning night and the Sanskrit word *śiśira* meaning the dewy season.[172] This season of *ar̲ciram* begins when the clouds, having rained heavily, move southwards.[173] The water that had flooded the earth flows away, leaving the fine sand wet. The north wind blows, shaking the opening flowers of the sugarcane. The sun winks through the clouds, now devoid of water.[174] The *pakan̲r̲ai* blooms like the broad tip of the warrior's spear.[175] Separation becomes painful in this season when the cranes cry out because of the fall of the dew,[176] and those who are away try to return to their beloveds. One maid tells her friend:

> The *karuviḷai* blooms like eyes.
> The spreading *pīr* creeper
> blooms like gold among the dark bushes.
> He who longs to embrace your lovely shoulders
> will not forget this dewy season.[177]

Another friend tells her lady,

> O maiden with bright jewels!
> Even if your lover
> does not think of you in this season
> when the wind mixed with dew
> blows daily, chilling the wide earth,
> his wisdom
> which is the cause of his greatness
> will not let him forget your dark beauty.[178]

It is implied that he is intelligent enough to know that her dark beauty would be spoilt by the spreading of *pacalai* if he does not return to her before the dewy season sets in. Thus this season also seems to be one that arouses a longing for love and the company of the beloved.

Tiṇaimayakkam (A Combination of these Divisions)

There are, however, some instances in Caṅkam poetry where these divisions or *tiṇai* are not kept faithfully. Time, season and emotion being universal, are also used for regions other than thosę accepted by convention. Even the *Tolkāppiyam* accepts this as *tiṇai mayakkam*[179] meaning a mixing or confusion of these divisions. These are exceptions and not the rule but in these exceptions, land being the permanent and immovable element, is used to determine the division or *tiṇai* it should belong to.

One very common 'intermingling' is the treatment of clandestine love or *kaḷavu* in the *neytal* region. Though the coastal areas are said to be most suitable for the pining of the heroine, the sandy beaches, the parks along the shore and backwaters are also suitable places for the hero and heroine to meet secretly. Many *neytal* poems actually deal with this aspect of love.[180] The love of young people is sung in other regions as well. A *marutam* poem sounds very much like a *kuṟiñci* poem in the emotion depicted.

O chief of the agricultural region with sweet water!
This maiden with surm-lined eyes
like the water-lily,
and I
played in the morning when the sun was not hot,
with leafy garments
woven with water-lilies, lotuses and green leaves,
swaying on our hips.
Then approaching you, we laughed with you.
Is that the wrong we committed
for her sapphire-like complexion
to turn golden (with pallor),
so that her mother,
even after offering to the deity of their area,
toddy, garlands and a kid,
with upright horns and hanging ears,
not knowing the proper cure,
sheds tears?[181]

Only the description of the agricultural region and the term of address used for the hero show that this is love between a hero and a heroine from the *marutam* region. The pain of separation that pale the dark complexion of the lovelorn girl to look like gold, the anxiety of the ignorant mother and the effort of the *tōḻi* to get him to marry her are typical of the poems that use the montane districts as their background. Most of the poems in the *Mullaikkali*, again, do not deal with separation and the patient waiting of the wife but with love before marriage. The form of mate selection peculiar to that region, known as *ēṟukōḷ* is used to give this aspect of love a local colouring so that it looks natural and possible only in that region. A shepherdess who has fallen in love with the shepherd who accosted her while playing with her friends, relates the incident to her friend and asks for her help.

My friend,
having taken back the milking vessels,
I tied up the calves with their ropes
and brought them home.
Then, wearing the blue garment
with a border of flower-print
that mother gave,
I played together with the shepherd-lasses
in the garden
where the salvadora and jasmines grow.
A shepherd wearing a chaplet of *kuruntu* blooms
passed by.

He said: O beautiful, modest maiden adorned with jewels!
May I decorate your little house of sand?

I said: Why! You would live in a house built by others
thinking, 'I am lucky.'
Haven't you learnt anything (for yourself)?

He said: Beautiful maiden!
May I knot your flower-filled tresses
and adorn them further with garlands?

I said : Why! You seem capable of accepting flowers
offered by others.
You are not only a simpleton but worse!

He said: May I draw the *toyyil*
on your tender breasts sparsely spread with spots?

I said: You are indeed infatuated.
Leave me alone.
Friend!
When I disagreed with everything he said,
he left in distress.
If you could inform him
of the code of behaviour of shepherd-lasses
and inform my parents (of my feelings)
you could remove my malady.[182]

The background is definitely pastoral and the code of conduct fit for shepherdesses (*āyar makaḷir iyalpu*) is the social conventions like the form of mate selection and parental approval found in that community.

Infidelity of a husband, though prominently treated as a feature of *marutam* poetry, is not necessarily confined to cities or riverine plains. There are poems of the *kuṟiñci* region dealing with this aspect of love and using the flora and fauna of the hills to express the thoughts and feelings of the heroine whose husband has forsaken her.

The lord of the hilly country
where the white tusked boar
cares for the pretty-lined young
whose mother was killed by a tiger,
has forgotten (us).[183]

The reference to animals like the boar and the tiger and the hero being referred to as the lord of the hills clearly show that the geographical region is *kuṟiñci*, though the sentiment is the sulkiness of the forsaken wife. Just as in the *marutam* poems, the animals are used to show the irresponsible nature of the hero. Even the wild animals care for their young, while he the chief of that district does not. Another heroine, unable to bear the gossip regarding her husband and another woman, tells him:

In the fragrant park
filled with lovely blooms
swarming with bees,
you trysted yesterday with a woman
whose smile resembles a row of (*mullai*) buds.

So say the gossips.
The scandal is louder
than the sound of the dark cuckoo of the season,
living on the long branches of the *kurava* tree.[184]

Here too, sulkiness of the wronged wife is the prevalent emotion, but no land division is mentioned. We have reference only to the *kuyil* or cuckoo on the branches of the bottle flower (*webera corymbosa*). Since the cuckoo sings only during spring, the poem is classified as *pālai* according to the *mutal* and *karupporuḷ*.

The allocation of the time of day or *ciṟupoḻutu* is not strictly adhered to either. The meeting of lovers in the mountainous district does not always take place at *yāmam* or midnight. The lovers may meet for the first time during the day[185] and the subsequent meetings may be either during the day[186] or at night.[187] The terms *iravukkuṟi* or place for meeting at night and *pakaṟkuṟi* or place for meeting during the day are used by grammarians and commentators to denote this. A *tōḻi* tells a heroine how she and the hero discussed the problems of meeting stealthily and finally thought of elopement as the only solution.

"If (mother says)
'Guard the millet from parrots'
it is possible (to meet) during the day.
If you come at night
we fear injury to you.
What shall we do about our distressing malady?"
When I said thus,
the chieftain of the tall hills
thought of something and sighed.
Realising his intention
I said to him
'What you think is wise
but would also cause gossip.'[188]

In the *pālai* poems which are supposed to use the intense heat of the midday, we also find other cooler hours being used in the depiction of the sorrow of separated lovers. A hero, travelling through arid districts, thinks of his beloved, pale and emaciated, sitting with her fingers on her forehead and shedding tears, thinking of him in the evening (*mālai*).[189] Wayfarers, meeting a young couple on their way at sunset, advise the youth to rest for the night when the highway robbers are about and to continue their journey in the morning.[190] Since the young couple is shown to be travelling during elopement, and because elopement or *uṭaṉpōkku* deals with travel and the girl's separation from her family, this poem belongs to the *pālai* division of love poems. As such, the time of day should be noon and not evening. Some *pālai* poems deal with *kaṅkul* or night. A *tōḻi*, hearing of the imminent return of the hero is happy. She repeats the complaints of the heroine during the separation and adds that the only person who can remove this sorrow is coming. The heroine had complained that the north wind that blows through the flowers, the evening when the humming of the bees around the flowers sounds like the music of the lute and the moonlit night with the fragrance of the night lotuses afflict her.[191] Here too, the north wind or *vāṭai*, evening (*mālai*) and night (*kaṅkul*) are not actually in keeping with convention, but used nevertheless, to show the sorrow of the woman in separation and the various times of day and the objects of nature that intensify that sorrow. It is never forgotten that love and the pain of separation is ever present and cannot be obliterated or lessened by the different times of the day. A hero declares:

> Morning, noon, heart-rending evening,
> night when the village sleeps,
> dawn.
> If one (in separation) knows
> the difference between these,
> then that love is certainly false.[192]

As in the case of land divisions and time of day (*ciṟupoḻutu*) convention does not seem to have been adhered to strictly in the use of the seasons as well, for different seasons have sometimes been used to depict the same emotion. The season considered most suitable for clandestine love is *kūtir* or the rainy season. But a *tōḻi* desiring to put an end to such meetings with the celebration of their marriage, addresses the moon when the hero is within hearing distance.

White moon who shines long!
You are not helpful to his secret love.
He comes at night
passing through the forest
where the black rock
covered with withered flowers
from the black-stemmed *vēṅkai*
looks like a large tiger cub.[193]

In this poem, though the place of the meeting is the mountain slope as suggested by the tiger and the *vēṅkai* flowers, the time is night and the aspect of love is stealthy meeting, the brightness of the moon and the falling of *vēṅkai* flowers suggest that the rains have stopped and the warmer season (*vēṉil*) has set in. Besides, traditionally, the flowering *vēṅkai* is symbolic of the marriage season among the mountain dwellers and the fading of the flowers suggests that he should hurry with the necessary arrangements for the wedding. The rising of the moon, however, is considered one of the many obstacles to the secret meeting of the lovers at night.

An *Akanāṉūṟu* poem describes *kūtir* which is suitable for secret meetings on the mountain slope, as a background to the patient waiting of the wife, in the pastoral region. The heroine thinks of her husband still at the war camp and wonders if he would not think of his own plight and sorrow, even if he does not think of hers.

Like the cloudless sky adorned with stars
the luxuriant-leafed *mucuṇṭai* blooms brightly.
The cowherds, wearing in abundance
the thin-petalled gloriosa
that blooms in bent bunches
and the chaplets drenched by rain
return to the village
tending with forked staves
their cattle vexed by the rain during day.
The distant clouds colliding with one another,
produce loud thunder and heavy rain.
Beneficent waters rush through the streets
and *kūtir* has set in.[194]

The description of the rainy season is not in keeping with the emotion of *iruttal* or patient waiting of the wife who though anxious over his delay is worried that he may not be able to keep his word. The geographical situation of the poem is suggested by the herds of cows and those who tend them, while the emotion is evident from the heroine's words and the cause of the separation, war. Another heroine whose husband is also away at the war camp complains to her friend of her loneliness during the dewy season when the north wind blows incessantly.

> When the dark clouds have shed their rain
> with vibrating thunder,
> dewdrops as fine as smoke fill the flower cups.
> The *karuviḷai* blooms
> like tear-filled eyes of women
> separated from their lovers.
> The pretty shoots of the *īṅkai*
> with cotton-like flowers
> and spreading on thickets
> are wet as if dipped in oil
> and move gently like the two halves of a liver.
> The lovely *avarai* blooms in abundance.
> Ears of ripe paddy bend in the broad fields.
> Bees buzz around the branches.
> At midnight during such season of dew
> he still tarries in the camp
> of the ferocious king.[195]

The description of *aṟciram* or the season of dew is complete with the different flowers filled with dew and the ripening paddy bending with its weight. But the emotion is still *iruttal.*

The description of nature in its various seasons and geographical settings is important to Tamil classical poetry only as a background to human emotion which actually is the most important feature of the poem. Without this emotion or *urripporuḷ* there cannot be any *akam* or love poetry. As such the intermixture of the objects of nature, especially those that move or are movable and the time and season which are uniform throughout the country, are not the most important aspects in a poem. Sometimes this intermixture may even seem misleading. For instance a heroine asks:

It darkened as if (the clouds) were sleeping.
Lightning flashed as if winking.
They rumbled as if taking the water upwards,
thundered as if frightening the heart of the earth
and rained long and heavy.
Towards the end of the season
the white but not bright clouds
sway gently on tall mountains reaching the sky.
At dawn the shrubs are bright.
The deer with twisted horns
having drunk its fill of water
from the cool, fragrant pond
and eaten *harialli* grass,
rests happily with its beloved mate
in the shade of the flowering *piṭavu*
on the long sandy bank.
Cochineal insects as red as vermillion
crawl as if spread out beautifully
on the wet soil
from which the water has drained off.
If he has not come yet,
my friend with a pretty forehead!
then what is his condition?
Is this not the *kār* season
with thundering clouds
when he promised to return?[196]

In this poem there are references to high hills and shrubs that have grown well due to the rain. The deer with its mate and the cochineal insects remind one of the *mullai* region. But we have no definite description, like that of the cowherds with their cattle as in the poem that describes *kūtir* in the *mullai* district. In this poem, the *kār* season, though most suitable for portraying the patience of the wife waiting for her husband to return at the beginning of the appointed season, seems to have come to an end. The clouds are not heavy with rain any longer but white and light enough to sway in the breeze. The time of day portrayed is dawn when the shrubs washed and refreshed by the rain seem attractive and bright. The most important thing in the poem, however, is the anxiety of the heroine and not her patience. The rainy season by which time he is supposed to have returned is nearly over without his arrival. Her question 'Then what is his condition?' brings out the *uripporuḷ* which is *pālai* or separation with no sign of his imminent return. The description of *kār* which is about to end is the cause or justification for her anxiety.

Treatment of Nature

Thus the aspects of nature treated in both literatures are quite similar but there seems to be a great difference in the actual use and treatment of these aspects. The Caṅkam poems treat nature as a background with which the people are close and familiar as well as a means to an end in poetry, the end being the depiction of the emotion or *uripporuḷ*. In the Tamil epics and the Sanskrit *kāvyas* and dramas, it serves as a beautiful background and the description is so detailed and elaborate as to become an end in itself. For example, a description of water sports or bathing in the tanks, rivers, streams or sea is mentioned in both literatures and an analysis of some of these shows the kind of difference that exists in the use and description found in these works.

In the Caṅkam poems water sport is called *puṉalāṭṭu* in general and *aruviyāṭal* (bathing in streams, usually on hillslopes) or *kaṭalāṭal, kaṭalāṭṭu* (bathing in the sea). Often this bathing would seem to form the central theme of the poem. A *Kalittokai* poem begins, saying that, the heroine bathes in the fast but pleasing waters of a mountain stream. But this is merely an introduction to the actual theme of the poem—the *tōḻi* informing her mother of the heroine's love for the hero. The bathing in the river, whether true or imagined, is one of the most possible reasons or excuses a girl on the mountain slope could have for meeting the hero. Her slipping her footing and being carried away by the stream is a fitting incident for depicting the nobility of the hero and the accidental nature of their meeting.[197] In an *Aiṅkuṟunūṟu* poem, a hero who has returned home before the *kār* season sets in, exhorts his wife:

> The clouds with sounds of thunder
> shed plenty of rain.

> *Kār* season has begun
> in the lovely (region of) thickets.
> Let us sport in the pleasing fresh waters.
> So hurry,
> O maiden with long dark tresses.[198]

Here the eagerness of the husband to bathe and sport in the fresh waters is not an end in itself but a means of portraying the joy and satisfaction of a man who has returned with success and therefore is able to indulge in sport with his beloved. So the happiness of a man who has kept his word to return before the *kār* season and his love for his beloved whose waiting has not been in vain are more important in the poem. But these are suggested by the excited invitation to the wife to hurry. Similarly in another poem from the same anthology, the heroine says to the hero:

> We shall not be angry!
> So tell us not lies,
> O lord of the agricultural tracts!
> Your eyes are very red
> because you sported
> in the reddish water of the first rains
> and served as a float
> for the shoulders of beautiful women.[199]

The water sport during which the 'beautiful women' held on to his shoulders is not important by itself. It is important because of the hurt and jealousy it causes the wife with whom he did not sport in the fresh waters. Instead he had sported with the harlots. Hence *ūṭal* is the actual theme of the poem, though she says, 'We shall not be angry.'

A *Kalittokai* poem with the same aspect of love as its theme elaborates a little. The heroine, hearing the hero say that he is returning after bathing (*puṉalāṭi*) in the fresh waters of the Kāviri says:

> O yes.
> I heard you bathed in the water
> with cool, curly dark tresses
> as the fine sand; and

beautiful surm-lined eyes
as the *kayal* fish.
In the fragrant park
filled with cool, scented flowers
destroying your reserve (*nāṇ*)
you bathed
in the beautiful fresh waters
that came at noon,
with the *pāṇaṉ* as a float.[200]

In this poem, the number of lines used to convey the message that she knows all and there is no need to hide anything is more than the number in the previous poem. The length of a *Kalittokai* poem makes such details possible. But the intensity of feeling and subtlety is not comparable. The meaning is far more obvious than in the *Aiṅkuṟunūṟu* poem, though the art and imagination of the poet is not to be doubted. This feature is even more clear in the poems on the Vaiyai in the *Paripāṭal*. Such bathing in the fresh waters of the Vaiyai is the cause of *ūṭal* but often the message is hidden in a mass of description which does not have much bearing on this emotion. For example the sixth poem of the *Paripāṭal* is on the refusal of the hurt wife to allow the husband to come home (*vāyil maṟuttal*) which is merely a way of showing her anger and disapproval of his disloyalty. Of the 106 lines, the first 60 deal with the rain that causes fresh floods in the river, the description of the people and their preparations to bathe and sport in the waters, their mode of travel to the river banks, the crowds and the waters becoming muddy because of the crowds bathing there. The next 44 lines describe the anger of the hero's concubine because of his attraction to new women, his attempt to explain that he did not embrace anyone but merely tried to save the woman from drowning, the advice of the elderly women at the concubine's house not to be angry with him or else he might go off with the younger women, her relenting and their bathing together in the waters of the Vaiyai. The last two lines,

O Vaiyai, may your ability to produce such love
that swells in the hearts
of those who bathe in your waters
never decrease,[201]

suggest that she is still angry about what had happened. Though the whole poem is supposed to be what she herself said, the detailed description in the first 60 lines is not necessary to express her displeasure and annoyance.

In the epic *Cilappatikāram*, though a whole canto is named *Kaṭalāṭu kātai* (the Canto on Sea Bathing) it does not mention the actual bathing of Kōvalaṉ and Mātavi, but describes the preparations, their journey to the sea-shore and their tent in which the fateful Kāṉalvari songs are sung.[202] But while describing the city of Maturai, Iḷaṅkō sings of the various seasons. Of these *kār* is said to be the season when:

> Harlots, living in streets
> where the west wind causes flags to flutter,
> sport with their beloved, rich youths
> at the water front with tall *marutam* trees
> along the Vaiyai with fresh waters,
> in which are tiny islands of white sand
> spread with flowers.
> They sail boats tall as mansions
> and small wooden boats
> and swim holding to beautiful floats.[203]

This description does not in any way serve the main story or project the emotion of the youth, the harlot or the wife if he is married. But this description adds to the beauty and grandeur of the epic. A somewhat similar use of descriptions is found in the Sanskrit *kāvya* as well. In the *Raghuvaṃśam*, Kālidāsa describes how the very hot summer causes Kuśa to think of 'sport with young women in the water of the Sarayu which carries with it the flowers of the creepers on its banks and contains intoxicated swans anxious to swim in its waves.' Hence tents are pitched on its banks and crocodiles are dragged out with nets to make the river safer. Here too, many women are said to have rushed into the river—'hundreds of females of my inner apartment' according to the king himself. The sandal paste of their bodies spreads on the water and makes it look like the rise of twilight interspersed with clouds.[204] The description of their sport takes 20 stanzas though it is not essential to the main story. The only importance of this water sport is that it gives him the opportunity to meet

Kumudavatī and to marry her. This marriage is important for his son and heir, Atithi, is born of this marriage. As for emotion or love, there is nothing that this water sport seems to have caused, for Kuśa bathes not only with the women of his inner apartment but his wife as well,[205] and ends his sport by acquiring a new wife. Yet his own bathing in the river is described in four stanzas only. It is noticeable that the descriptions get longer as the poems get longer but the length of the descriptions tend to take away the purpose or use of nature. Nature in longer poems adds to the beauty and shows the poet's ability to describe ordinary scenes in an extraordinary manner.

Types of Descriptions

Apart from this difference in the use of nature, the actual description itself is quite different. The Caṅkam poems describe things in a concise and realistic manner. Using the same examples and verses as for the water sport we may see that the rainy season is described briefly in the first four lines of an *Aiṅkuṟunuṟu* poem.

> The clouds with sounds of thunder
> shed plenty of rain.
> *Kār* has begun
> in the lovely (region of) thickets.[206]

These lines give an exact idea of the season. There is usually thunder and rain caused by the rain clouds. This marks the beginning of the season and the thickets which are the main vegetation in the *mullai* districts become beautiful with fresh leaves from which the dust of summer has been washed away and the flowers begin to bloom. There is nothing that is out of the ordinary or fanciful in this description. It is realistic but suggestive. It suggests the joy of the husband who has returned in time to save his wife from the misery of separation which would be heightened by the sound of thunder and the flowers in the thickets. In the next poem (*Aink*, 80) the description of the water as 'reddish water' may not create a lovely picture or feeling as the phrase 'cool waters', 'fresh waters' or 'clear waters'; but being the water that rushes down after the first showers, it is bound to be red if it passes through reddish soil. Besides it brings out the impure relationship between the man and woman who bathed in the waters. In the *Kalittokai* poem there is already more imaginative description which involves a kind of personification and simile when the heroine talks of the hair as wavy lines of the sand, the eyes as fish and the *pāṇaṉ* as the float. The phrase 'beautiful fresh waters' is not true of a stream with water from fresh rain but is more sarcastic and useful to describe covertly, the harlot.

The *Paripāṭal*, however, is not very realistic in its description. The people of Maturai are said to have flocked to the river. It is so crowded that the not-so-strong cannot bathe, while the strong can. Because of their bathing, the water smells of toddy, scented pastes like sandal, fragrant oil and flowers. Hence the Brāhmaṇas leave the river because it is impure. Since it washes away faded or crushed flowers, garlands worn by men and women as well as the roots and fruits from the banks it had broken and cheap toddy drunk by lower class people, many others too think the waters impure and leave the waters of the river.[207] This description that concentrates on the impurities of the Vaiyai may be in keeping with the mood of the heroine who has heard of mistresses and harlots bathing there. But to describe the current as being strong enough to break banks and fell trees, and at the same time to say that people flock in large numbers is exaggerating either the force of the currents or the number of people who go to bathe in the water. Another poem from the same anthology describes how the sandal paste from the bodies of the bathers causes the sandy bank to be muddy and the water that drips from their clothes on the bank makes it seem as if *kār* has set in (i.e. wet with water as though it had rained).[208] This too is an example of exaggerated or fanciful description.

These descriptions are very much like those found in the epics. The *Raghuvaṃśam* refers to 'hundreds of females', even when the shore is specially prepared for the king and his women. The sandal paste spread over the water is said to unfold 'various colours',[209] which actually is possible only with oil. The beating of the water by these women is so loud and resonant that it sounds like tabours to their song and it is hailed with delight by peacocks on the slope of the bank, spreading their feathers.[210] This is so indirect and involved for the beating is like tabours and this though not explained, has to sound like thunder so as to excite the peacocks. These descriptions also portray women wearing various ornaments like armlets, waistbands, strings of pearls and chains while bathing,[211] which again is not realistic for people who are well-to-do and sophisticated wear different clothes to bathe in the waters. This, however, adds to the image of wealth and beauty.

Nature is also described in such a way as to depict certain ideas. This is seen clearly in the description of animals found in both literatures. A *tōḻi* in the *Aiṅkuṟunūṟu* tells the heroine that the hero has returned crossing the tracts where a wild dog (*ceṉṉāy*) united with its loving mate, refrains from killing a doe with its young.[212] The reason for this picture is to show that even wild animals in love are considerate to their prey or enemies and so it is only natural that the hero returns thinking of her. Another *ceṉṉāy* does not kill a piglet that passes by in the desert.[213] This description of the animals in the arid tract is said to be indicative of the disabling heat of summer and the dry regions. It could also be an assurance to the friends, to whom the heroine is sending the message, that the tracts she would have to traverse during elopement is not cruel but kind, especially to the young ones. Such descriptions are found in the *Ṛtusaṃhāram* verses that deal with *grīṣma*. The heat of summer makes the animals too weak to show their enmity to each other. They even try to find comfort in each others' shade.[214]

The epics, however, try to show such lack of enmity as being caused by rather abstract ideas like *dharma* and justice. In the *Cilappatikāram*, we are told that nature is kind because of the righteousness of the Pandya rule.

> In the hot forest
> the grabbing bear does not dig the bent anthill.
> The bright-striped tiger does not oppose the herd of deer.
> Snakes, deities that afflict, and crocodiles
> that search for food
> and thunder do not harm
> for it is the country of the just Pandyas.[215]

Here the animals are not directed by their own natural instincts but by the command of *dharma* followed by the ruler himself. This is contrary of nature, though such descriptions help to build up hope in the hearts of Kōvalaṉ and Kaṇṇaki and thereby enhance the tragic feeling when Kōvalaṉ dies unjustly. It also helps to show the power of fate.

Such changes in the normal or natural behaviour or occurrence is also described to show the influence of a higher being or an incident of higher importance. This is found more in the Sanskrit epics than in the Tamil ones. The *Buddhacaritam* describes the changes that occur in nature when the Bodhisattva is born.

When he was born, the earth
though fastened down by the monarch of mountains,
shook like a ship tossed by the wind,
and from a cloudless sky
there fell a shower full of lotuses and water-lilies
perfumed with sandal.
Pleasant breezes blew soft to the touch
dropping down heavenly garments.
The very sun, though still the same,
shone with augmented light
and fire gleamed, unstirred, with gentle lustre.
In the north-eastern part of the dwelling
a well of pure water appeared of its own accord.

The flowering trees too produce their blossoms at once.[216] These changes in nature are said to be caused by the birth of a great being. More or less the same idea is conveyed in the *Maṇimēkalai* when Buddha like a sun (*Putta ñāyiṟu*) appears.

The moon and the sun would shine without causing ills.
The everchanging stars will behave well.
The clouds shed rain and the broad earth prospers.
The embodied souls will find no sorrow.
The wind will blow properly.
The directions will prosper.
The water-filled sea will offer wealth.
The cows produce excess milk.
The birds having their fill,
will not leave their nests for food.
Beast and man will give up enmity.[217]

Other Sanskrit works also try to show the influence, especially of Śiva on nature. In the *tapovana*, though spring has manifested out of season and has affected the objects of nature like the trees and animals, Nandi still has a good command over the grove because of the power invested in him by Śiva.

> At his bidding the whole forest itself
> stood as if its movements were committed to a painting;
> the trees ceased waving about;
> the swarms of bees remained still;
> the birds withheld their music
> and the beasts stopped roaming.[218]

These are descriptions that are not true to nature but made to sound possible because of supernatural influence on the objects of nature.

Certain descriptions, though not personification in the strict sense, are used by epic poets to suggest a certain event that is to take place. These descriptions may be long or consist of a mere phrase but convey an idea of something that is to happen. When Kaṇṇaki enters the park on the outskirts of Maturai with Kōvalaṉ and Kavunti, she sees the river Vaiyai, various species of the lotus and the flag of the Pandyas. Ilaṅkō uses these to suggest that their entry into Maturai is fateful and would cause them sorrow. So he says,

> The truthful damsel called Vaiyai,
> as if aware of what is to happen to the maiden (Kaṇṇaki) ,
> covering herself with a shawl of pure flowers
> and hiding her tears,
> was praised by the women and him (Kōvalaṉ)
> as a river of flowers and not water.[219]

The *kuvaḷai, āmpal* and *kamalam* filled with honey shake in the breeze as if trembling and shedding tears for them. The flag of the Pandyas that has seen many a war flutters in the breeze as if to warn them by sign language not to enter the city.[220] These are normal sights near the river Vaiyai and the city wall but the tragedy that is to occur is hinted at. Similarly, Kālidāsa uses the breeze to foretell the fulfilment of the purpose of the journey undertaken by King Dilīpa and his queen. They desire a son to continue their line and enter the forest to meet their family sage and obtain advice on what rites could be performed to overcome this misfortune. On their way,

On account of the favourable wind
betokening the fulfilment of their wish,
they were untouched in their hair and the turban
by the dust raised up by (the hoofs of)
their horses.[221]

The blowing of the wind in a particular direction is a natural occurrence, but this is said to be a good sign that means their desire for an heir, will be more than fulfilled by the birth of the son Raghu, who would be a pride of the race.

REFERENCES

1. *Rtu*, 6:28; *Akam*, 259:9.
2. *Mala*, act 3. v. 4; *Akam*, 237: 4.
3. *Abhi*, act 3 v. 4; *Akam*, 259:8
4. *Mala*, act 3 v. 5.
5. *Kuma*, 3:29, 31.
6. *Rtu*, 6:5, 17, 19, 23.
7. *Akam*, 15:13-15.
8. *Ibid.*, 237: 16.
9. *Ibid.*, 229: 16.
10. *Ibid.*, 341: 1; *Aink*, 343.
11. *Kali*, 26: 1-5.
12. *Akam*, 259: 5-7.
13. *Saun*. 7:2.
14. *Rtu*, 6:27.
15. *Rtu*, 4: 1, 14, 15, 26; *Akam*, 355:1-5.
16. *Akam*, 229: 16-19.
17. *Ibid.*, 118:1-4.
18. *Budd*, 3:1.
19. *Ibid.*, 4:51, 52.
20. *Saun*, 7:1-8.
21. *Ibid.*, 7:12.
22. *Svap*, act 1 v. 1.
23. *Abhi*, act 1. p. 28.
24. *Kuma*, 3: 24.
25. *Rtu*, 6:20.
26. *Ibid.*, 6:23.
27. *Ibid.*, 6:16.
28. *Ibid.*, 6:21.
29. *Kuma*, 3:36-38.
30. *Aink*, 341.
31. *Kurun*, 192.
32. *Akam*, 341:12-13.

33. *Nar,* 157.
34. *Netu,* 51-52; *Cilap,* 8:18-20, 60-61.
35. *Cilap,* 8:19.
36. *Netu,* 53.
37. *Mani,* 11:40.
38. *Ibid.,* 19: 100-109.
39. *Pari,* 19:48.
40. *Ibid.,* 22:16.
41. *Ibid.,* 11: 123.
42. *Ibid.,* 10: 97-99.
43. *Kali,* 26:3.
44. *Ibid.,* 147: 42.
45. *Ibid.,* 27:14, 35:14.
46. *Ibid.,* 27:22-25.
47. *Ibid.,* 92:60-68.
48. *Cilap,* 14:111-12.
49. *Budd,* 13:1, 2.
50. *Cilap,* 8:6.
51. *Mani,* 11:61.
52. *Ibid.,* 5:77.
53. *Ibid.,* 19:100.
54. *Budd.,* 13:17.
55. *Rtu,* 6:28.
56. *Kuma,* 4:29.
57. *Rtu,* 6:1.
58. *Abhi,* act 4 vv. 3ff.
59. *Kuma,* 3:14.
60. *Ibid.,* 3: 27.
61. *Ibid.,* 3:13.
62. *Ibid.,* 3:21, 4:24.
63. *Ibid.,* 3:73.
64. *Ibid.,* 4:16.
65. *Rtu,* 6:28.
66. *Abhi,* act 3 v. 5.
67. *Abhi,* act 6 vv. 3ff.
68. *Cilap,* 8:5-13.
69. *Ibid.,* 5:56-63.
70. *Ibid.,* 8:1-6.
71. *Kuma,* 4:29.
72. *Akam,* 31:1-2.
73. *Ibid.,* 91:1-2.
74. *Rtu,* 1:17; *Akam,* 395:5-6.
75. *Akam,* 1:9-13.
76. *Ibid.,* 55:1, *Aink,* 322:1-2.
77. *Rtu,* 1:17; *Akam,* 31:5-6.
78. *Aink,* 325.
79. *Rtu,* 1:11; *Nar,* 84:4-5.
80. *Rtu,* 1:16; *Megh,* P. 53; *Aink,* 388:1; *Kali,* 11:6.

81. *Akam*, 101:14; *Aink*, 322:1; *Avim*, act 4, p. 85.
82. *Cilap*, 14:120-23.
83. *Perum*, 3.
84. *Avim*, act 4, v. 5.
85. *Rtu*, 1:20.
86. *Ibid.*, 1:16.
87. *Akam*, 395: 5.
88. *Nar*, 29:3-5.
89. *Akam*, 201:12-19.
90. *Ibid.*, 57:10-19.
91. *Avim.*, act 4 v. 2. p. 84.
92. *Akam*, 109.
93. *Avim*, act 4 v. 3. pp. 84-85.
94. *Ibid.*, act 4.
95. *Abhi*, act 3; *Rtu*, 1:2.
96. *Rtu*, 1: 21.
97. *Ibid.*, 1:2, 6.
98. *Abhi*, act 3.
99. *Rtu*, 1:8.
100. *Kurun*, 222; *Kali*, 39; *Akam*, 12, 166; *Nar*, 259.
101. *Netu*, 51-62.
102. *Netu*, 60-61; *Cilap*, 8:17-18.
103. *Netu*, 95.
104. *Cilap*, 4:31.
105. *Ibid.*, 4:31-44.
106. *Ibid.*,14:127.
107. *Mani*, 7:15, 21:13.
108. *Cilap*, 11:13-14; *Mani*, 19:100-106.
109. *Rtu*, 2:24; *Aink*, 452: 1, 484.
110. *Rtu*, 2:5; *Akam*, 374:9.
111. *Rtu*, 2:5, *Kali*, 40:20.
112. *Akam*, 134:2-6.
113. *Aink*, 412:1-3; *Megh*, P. 23.
114. *Rtu*, 2:6; *Akam*, 194:11-16.
115. *Rtu*, 2:8; *Akam*, 234:10.
116. *Megh*, P. 8.
117. *Rtu*, 2:12.
118. *Ibid.*, 2:21.
119. *Cilap*, 14:75-96.
120. *Ibid.*, 14:70, 96.
121. *Mani*, 28: 161.
122. *Avim*, act 5; *Kurun*, 314:1-2.
123. *Avim*, act 5. p. 102.
124. *Kurun*, 194.
125. *Aink*, 414.
126. *Avim*, act 5 v. 2.
127. *Mullaip*, 82-91.
128. *Kurun*, 21:8-12.

129. *Ibid.*, 319:1.
130. *Akam*, 234:10-18.
131. *Megh*, U. 30, 32.
132. *Akam*, 284.
133. *Ibid.*, 124:6-8.
134. *Aink*, 416.
135. *Ibid.*, 212.
136. *Akam*, 58:1-5.
137. *Ibid.*, 153:1-5.
138. *Ibid.*, 162:3-6; *Kurun*, 355:1-2.
139. *Nar*, 364:1-2.
140. *Netu*, 39-41.
141. *Ibid.*, 13-14.
142. *Aink*, 456.
143. *Nar*, 244:2.
144. *Netu*, 21-24.
145. *Akam*, 13:18-24.
146. *Ibid.*, 58:3-6; *Netu*, 9-12.
147. *Netu*, 45 and 48.
148. *Aink*, 11.
149. *Akam*, 58.
150. *Cilap*, 14: 97-101.
151. *Rtu*, 3:4.
152. *Ibid.*, 3:5.
153. *Ibid.*, 3:21.
154. *Ibid.*, 3:5, 13, 15, 18.
155. *Ibid.*, 3:5, 10.
156. *Ibid.*, 3:5.
157. *Ibid.*, 3:13.
158. *Ibid.*, 4:1, 18.
159. *Ibid.*, 4:14.
160. *Ibid.*, 4:1, 8, 18.
161. *Ibid.*, 4:10.
162. *Ibid.*, 5:16, 8.
163. *Ibid.*, 5:2.
164. *Ibid.*, 5:1.
165. *Ibid.*, 4:8, 5:1, 16.
166. *Ibid.*, 4:2.
167. *Ibid.*, 4:3, 4.
168. *Ibid.*, 4:5.
169. *Ibid.*, 4:5, 5:5.
170. *Ibid.*, 5:2.
171. *Ibid.*, 4:12-17, 5:6-12.
172. *Tamil Lexicon*, vol.1. p. 171.
173. *Nar*, 5:5-6.
174. *Ibid.*, 241:3-8.
175. *Ibid.*, 86:1-3.
176. *Aink*, 475:1-2.

177. *Ibid.*, 464.
178. *Ibid.*, 470.
179. *Tol. Porul*, 14.
180. *Aink*, 101-110, 191-200; *Akam*, 280; *Nar*, 149, 172.
181. *Akam*, 156:7-17; also *Aink*, 6, 7, 9, 10.
182. *Kali*, 111.
183. *Aink*, 265, also 240.
184. *Ibid.*, 369, also 370.
185. *Akam*, 48, 290; *Nar*, 102, 128; *Kali*, 59; *Kurinji*.
186. *Kurun*, 113, 114, 198; *Nar*, 187.
187. *Kurun*, 69, 121; *Nar*, 152, 251.
188. *Kurun*, 217.
189. *Akam*, 169; also *Kali*, 29; *Aink*, 339.
190. *Kurun*, 390.
191. *Kali*, 29:10-21.
192. *Kurun*, 32:1-3.
193. *Ibid.*, 47.
194. *Akam*, 264:1-10.
195. *Ibid.*, 294:1-12.
196. *Ibid.*, 139.
197. *Kali*, 39.
198. *Aink*, 411.
199. *Ibid.*, 80; also *Akam*, 6:6-11, 296:4-7,
200. *Kali*, 98:10-19.
201. *Pari*, 6:105-106.
202. *Cilap*, 6:111-74.
203. *Ibid.*, 14:70-75.
204. *Ragh*, 16:54-73.
205. *Ibid.*, 16:73.
206. *Aink*, 411.
207. *Pari*, 6: 40-51.
208. *Ibid.*, 12:97 and 98.
209. *Ragh*, 16:58.
210. *Ibid.*, 16:64.
211. *Ibid.*, 16:60, 62, 65; *Pari*, 6:14-16.
212. *Aink*, 354.
213. *Ibid.*, 397.
214. *Rtu*, 16, 18 etc.
215. *Cilap*, 13:4-9.
216. *Budd*, 1:40-42, 44.
217. *Mani*, 12:86-96.
218. *Kuma*, 3:42.
219. *Cilap*, 13:170-75.
220. *Ibid.*, 13:184-90.
221. *Ragh*, 1:42.

Chapter 11

Personification

Nature not only serves as a scenic background and the regulator of passion, but is also useful in the projection and expression of human emotions. Sometimes nature seems to be sympathetic while at other times, unsympathetic, depending on the emotions and experiences of the beholder or the character concerned. One, who is happy in his or her love, finds the beauties of nature ecstatic and the unhappy one sees cruel mockery in nature's beauty and change. Quite often there is a personification of natural objects endowed with human behaviour and emotions, especially love and passion.

Personification is the manner or figure of speech that attributes human characteristics and feelings to non-human organisms, like the flora and fauna, inanimate objects and sometimes to abstract objects. In this figure of speech, the personification may be complete or merely suggested, but the most important thing is to convey an idea or emotion with depth and feeling so that the reader or listener is able to form an idea of what is being said and to enjoy it. For example, in the *Kāṉalvari* of the epic *Cilappatikāram*, is a verse, sung to music by Mātavi.

> Oh honey-laden *neytal* flower!
> Unlike my eyes that shed tears at sunset
> which heightens pain (of separation),
> You are not immersed in sorrow, but do sleep.
> Do you in your dream, see,
> the heartless man approaching the maritime park?[1]

This is supposed to be the entreaty of a lovelorn maiden to the *neytal* or water lily. The whole plant is pictured as a person but more important are the flowers which usually serve as comparisons to beautiful eyes. The closing of their petals at sunset is imagined to be the closing of one's eyelids during sleep. So the maiden goes still further and asks if the *neytal* can see in its dream, her lover coming to the park in which they had met previously. Since it 'sleeps', it is obvious that the *neytal* is free from the type of sorrow that she herself experiences in the evenings when the sun sets. Such personifications are most useful in literature to enhance the emotion that is depicted. The contrast in the situation between the maiden and the flower, as well as the similarity between her eyes and the flowers are suggested. The sleepless tears of the girl are also contrasted with the *neytal,* whose eyes are filled, not with tears but honey. The *neytal* is also endowed with the human ability to dream, to recognise the girl's lover if it were to see him come to the park and finally to communicate this news to the maiden. All these are clearly human characteristics but attributed to the *neytal* by means of personification.

This personification need not always be used to enhance emotion only. It may merely be a part of a description of a particular scene. For instance, King Purūravas, with his companion, the *vidūṣaka,* notices the moon rising in the east. Attracted by the beauty of the sight, he says:

> Now that the darkness of the evening retires
> before the rays of the moon
> which was hidden behind the rising mount,
> the face of the east captivates my eyes
> as though her hair had been bound.[2]

The rising moon pushes away the darkness that covers the earth, but it starts from the east where it rises. Here, the very obvious personification is the eastern horizon as a beautiful lady. The darkness that has covered the area is likened to the loosened or untied tresses of a woman, which hides the beauty of her face. But now the receding of the darkness, leaving the east bright and beautiful, is like the tying up of her hair. It is tied away from the face so that the darkness that still lingers on is like the hair which is now dressed and the bright horizon is the face of the east. This personification may be further extended to make the Moon the Lord of the East and she like a woman in her husband's absence, has not taken the trouble to dress her hair, but looks so dismal and sad. With his arrival she dresses her hair and her face gains the brightness of joy and happy love. In this verse there is no particular emotion that is to be projected but creates the feeling of joy and hope. As a *śloka* this verse describes a natural scenery in concise, beautiful language that pleases the reader or the audience.

This manner of speech that endows nature with life and human emotions has been an important feature of Indian literature since the time of the *Vedas* when objects of nature like the Sun, Dawn, Earth, Sky and Rivers were not only personified but also deified. With a shift in the motif and the emotions in the literature of the various periods, the characteristics and feelings that are projected, changed, so that in the classical literature that deals with emotions and treats love as an important *rasa*, objects of nature are endowed with the relevant emotions of love and passion. In Tamil classical literature that deals chiefly with love and war, the objects of nature are endowed with the emotions relevant to these motifs.

Earth

The *Cilappatikāram* symbolises the earth as the wife or beloved of the sun. Sunrise is portrayed in true *kāvya* style, as an act of love and union between the Sun and the Earth. The Earth, with the sea as her garment, the hills as her breasts, the river as the string of pearls worn between them, and the clouds as her black tresses, had covered herself with a dark shawl. The Sun, rising in the eastern mount (*utayamāl varai*) spreads his rays and removes her shawl.[3] This relationship is better explained when at sunset, pallor (golden in hue) spreads over her, her flower-eyes shed tears of dew and her whole body trembles.[4]

This is by no means the first instance where the earth is personified as a woman in Tamil literature. The *Puṟanāṉūṟu* calls her 'the earth maiden' (*nilamakaḷ*) and personifies her as the wife of the king. Singing of the transient nature of wealth and power, a poet says that Earth, great and noble in many ways, has the sky for her face and the sun and moon for her eyes. She too sheds tears because when the able kings who protect her, die, she is not able to follow them but like the harlots (*vilainalap peṇṭir*) she is still around, with many people praising her greatness and beauty. Even though the final message of the poem is the transience of life, the personification is based on the relationship between the king and his country as well as the love and loyalty that exists in a human relationship of that nature.[5] The *Ciṟupāṇāṟṟuppaṭai* depicting summer when the volume of water in the rivers is reduced and flowers wither and fall in abundance, describes the vast earth as a maiden (*mānila maṭantai*). She has bamboos for her upper arms, the blue hills for her lovely breasts, the river as the string of pearls worn between them, the wavy lines of the sand on the river banks as her tresses let loose and the flowers which fall when the *kuyil* seeks honey in them as the flowers decorating her hair.[6] These two instances may have nothing that may be called sensuous or erotic, because the poems do not aim at depicting love. But the personification is significant especially in the latter poem, which being the longer of the two, describes the personification in greater detail as if it were a forerunner to the detailed description in the epics.

However, Bhāsa in his *Avimārakam* portrays her as keeping the lovers (*kāmuka jana*) indoors and sending out the brave of heart (*śūra*), while she herself prepares to meet night with a garland of stars.[7] The *Meghadūtam* personifies the earth, like the *Cilappatikāram*, as a woman with the mountains for her breasts. A single verse with a detailed description of the colours of a mountain is sufficient to suggest this personification. The Yakṣa tells the rain-bearing cloud that when it rests on Āmrakūṭa mountain the slopes of which are covered with mango trees laden with fruits, the mountain would 'look like the breast of the earth, dark in the centre and white in the rest of its expanse'.[8] In this verse, the detail is complete, while the personification is only suggested. In the *Raghuvaṃśam*, however, Kālidāsa, portraying the southern part of India as a woman ravished by Raghu during his *digvijaya*, says:

> Having enjoyed to his heart's content, the two mountains, Malaya and Durdura, both of which were covered with sandal on their summits, as if they were the two breasts of that region, he of irresistible valour, crosses the Sahya mountain left far by the sea, as if it were the hips (*nitambam*) of the earth, the woven garments of which had slipped off.[9]

This personification with the sandal trees on the slopes of the mountain to mean the sandal paste worn by women on their breasts and the sea that is usually referred to as the garment of the earth make the description apt and though the context of the verses is war and heroism the personification is erotic.

Cities

In Caṅkam literature cities and towns are used as comparisons to a woman's beauty for like a city that provides satisfaction to all the senses, a beautiful woman is a source of abundance and joy to the man who is married to or is about to marry her. Besides, cities are symbols of wealth and grandeur, especially if they are royal cities or great seaports. One of the oft-compared cities is Toṇṭi, a great seaport of the Cheras at that time. Women are said to be as pretty or as resourceful as Toṇṭi of the Chera king, 'the master of strong chariots',[10] or 'as the Toṇṭi of great abundance'.[11] Sometimes some specific qualities like coolness, or commodities like paddy obtained in abundance at such towns are mentioned as the specific reason for comparison, as in the lines:

as the cool Kuṭavāyil[12]
as Aḷḷūr of paddy wealth[13]

But in the epics of the later period this is reversed so that the cities are personified as women and sometimes related romantically with the king of the realm. The description of the city of Pukār at sunset pictures it as a well-endowed, well-adorned woman.

Pukār-maiden, excelling in wisdom
and like a flower-creeper,
with the sound of birds from the moat
filled with abundant water and adorned with variegated flowers
as clearly tinkling anklets for her feet;
The walls of the fort for her jingling, jewelled girdle;
The two bamboo posts at the entrance for her upper arms;
The two temples (of *Tarunilai* and *Vacciram*)
for her beautiful, youthful breasts;
The large, matchless palace built for the king
who wears *ātti* blooms
and lasting till the end of time
for her beautifully bright face;
wears
the full moon in the east
and the setting sun in the west

as silver and gold ornaments
to brighten further her praiseworthy face.[14]

This description which personifies the city of Pukār is not essential to the story or for the heightening of the emotion of love in the epic or canto. It conforms to the need for description in *kāvya* literature. Similarly in the *Meghadūtam*, the city of Alakā, nestled against the mountain Kailāśa is pictured as a woman on her lover's lap. The Yakṣa assures the cloud that he could not,

on seeing Alakā with her garment the Ganges
dropping from her, lying on its slopes
as if on the lap of a lover,[15]

fail to recognise his destination. This too is a mere description in *kāvya* style, but helps to show the Yakṣa's preoccupation with the sensuous and the erotic on account of his long exile from his beloved.

Rivers

Though rivers sometimes figure as a mere part of a personification, are often personified themselves as women and beloveds or wives of kings. In the *Meghadūtam*, though the first part (*pūrvamegha*) contains the descriptions of places between Rāmagiri and Alakā, there are descriptions that remind one constantly of the lovelorn Yakṣa longing intensely for union with his beloved. The cloud is personified as a *nāgarika* and the lightning as his wife.[16] But like other *nāgarikas* he also loves and enjoys the company of other women. Hence all the rivers on the way are described as women in love with him and in return being loved by him. The ancient Indian belief that clouds 'drink' water from rivers and seas is used to create a passionate relationship between the cloud and the River Vetravatī. Her quivering waves are the bent eyebrows and the cloud thus attracted and impassioned would taste the waters of the river as a lover his beloved's lips.[17] The River Nirvindhyā is another lady-love of the cloud with a row of birds for a girdle (*mekhalā*). She stumbles bewitchingly before him, showing her navel, the whirlpool, and the Yakṣa explains to the cloud that 'amorous gestures are the women's first avowal of love'.[18] Then, passing on, the cloud's good fortune of having the love and loyalty of the River Sindhu can be seen.

> O fortunate one,
> when you have crossed that, you yourself will have to find
> the way to banish the emaciation of Sindhu
> who indicates your good fortune by her lovelorn state
> having the thin stream of water for her single braid,
> and a pale complexion owing to the old (dry) leaves
> dropping from the trees growing on her banks.[19]

The river thus looks like a woman in separation or *virahiṇī*. The cloud also enters the heart of the River Gambhīrā, who being struck with love throws loving glances at him in the form of *saphara* fish and his firm mind is reduced to nought. The blue water is her garment that the cloud removes from her hips, the banks, and the cane (*vānīra*), like hands, try to hold on to the garment. The Yakṣa himself full of longing for love, seems to understand the difficulty of the cloud to part from her in such an erotic situation.[20]

The personification of rivers as women or beloveds is also found in Tamil literature. The shorter poems of the Caṅkam literature do not seem to have such descriptions, but the *Paripāṭal* with eight long poems on the Vaiyai contains such personifications. The river is likened to a maiden in love with the sea. Its flow from the hills to the sea is said to be like the journey of a young damsel from her parental home to that of her husband or lover, undertaken alone. This is considered disgraceful and the river is asked not to go on.[21] In the epic *Cilappatikāram*, the same river is represented as a virtuous wife of the Pandya king and is described in detail as a beautiful woman and the mother of his subjects.

> She has garments of variegated blossoms
> falling from trees (like the *kuravam, vakuḷam*
> *kōṅkam, vēṅkai, maravam, nākam, tilakam, marutam,*
> *cēṭal, cerunti*, tall *caṇpakam* and *pāṭalam*).
> Her broad high hip which is the curved river bank
> is encircled all round with a girdle of creepers,
> (*kuruku, taḷavam*, thick-stemmed *mucuṇṭai*,
> blossoming *atiral*, white *kūtāḷam, kuṭacam, vetiram*

luxuriant *pakanṟai, piṭavam* and *mayilai*),
joined together.
Flower-filled islets, formed by accumulation of sand,
opposite to each other and filled with flowering trees
are her bright and lovely, youthful breasts.
The *murukku* petals shed by the tree on her bank
are her red lips.
The *mullai* blooms washed down by the stream
are her teeth disclosed in a smile.
The black carps, jumping across and along (the river)
are her long, black eyes.
The black sand, never devoid of flowers
are her tresses.
Vaiyai, the truthful lady of the (Pandya) family,
with the great and noble virtue of protecting
and feeding the earth,
is ever on the tongues of poets.[22]

In the same epic, while the river Kāviri is depicted as the chaste wife of the Chola king and the mother of his subjects, the river Ganges and the river Kaṉṉi are said to be his mistresses.[23] The Kāviri, too, has the black carp (*karuṅkayal)* for her eyes and flowers falling from the trees as her pretty robes (*maṇippūvāṭai*). The Chola king is clearly called her husband (*kaṇavaṉ*).[24] The *Patikam* of the epic *Maṇimēkalai* gives not only the same status to the river but associates it with Tamil. She is the 'lady of the Chola line' and the 'damsel of cool Tamil' (*taṇṭamiḻp pāvai*) who does not swerve from her duty or honour even when the planets and stars swerve from their positions so that summer is prolonged.[25] Obviously her duty is that of a wife and mother, bountiful and benevolent, for later in the epic she is called 'the Kāviri damsel with unceasing waters'.[26] But erotic situations are not found in connection with this personification in Tamil for the context of this personification does not deal with the passionate dalliances of the king or his relationship with his mistresses. The connection between the rivers Vaiyai and Kāviri with the Pandya and Chola kings respectively is based on the bountiful nature of the life-giving rivers which feed the people of the two kingdoms as a mother would feed her children, their greatness, their loyalty to the king and their loving care towards the subjects to whom the king is a loving and protective father.

Flowers

Though both Tamil and Sanskrit literature mention numerous flowers, not all of them are personified in love poetry or drama. The most common is the lotus as the wife or beloved of the sun for it blooms at sunrise and closes its petals with the setting of the sun. In the *Meghadūtam* the Yakṣa warns the cloud not to stand between the sun and the lotus when he rises, for he is said to be coming back from his dalliances with some other women and as hurrying to dry the tears of his offended wife, i.e. the lotus with the morning dew.[27] Though this symbolism is not found in the shorter poems of the Caṅkam collections, it is found in the *Kalittokai*. A *Kalittokai* poem uses the same personification in more or less the same situation. An offended wife tells her husband that he might as well go back to the other woman who would miss him, while she would wait for him till he turned over a new leaf. While addressing him, she describes a pond in his country. The sun rose in the sky, spreading its rays and the lotus buds opened at the touch of his rays. But one lotus, hidden among leaves and untouched by the rays was dripping with dew and opened when the sun had risen a little higher up the sky. This lotus, though late, bloomed like the smiling face of a woman whose lover (or husband) had gone away, but realising his folly, had come back and falling at her feet, had asked for forgiveness.[28]

Quite often this personification is used without the sun so that a lotus flower is said to be the face of a pretty woman or vice versa. Though this too is not common in the Caṅkam collection, it is found frequently in the longer poems of the *Pattuppāṭṭu* and the *Kalittokai*. The *Maturaikkāñci* refers to women

with faces
like the bright-petalled, pollen-filled lotus
blooming in the sacred tank.[29]

The *Ciṟupāṇāṟṟuppaṭai* uses this in reverse, saying,

The divine, luxuriant lotus buds
resembling round, uplifting breasts
bloom like a face (of a woman).[30]

In the *Kalittokai*, a lotus that blooms next to a *pakaṉṟai* flower which looks like a silver cup is bright and this is likened to the face of a woman, brightened with liquor.[31] Of the two Tamil epics, only the *Maṇimēkalai* uses this as a simile. Sutamati, accompanying Maṇimēkalai to the park to pick flowers, points to her that the fragrant-flowered lotus is as beautiful as her (Maṇimēkalai's) face.[32]

This is not too common in the Sanskrit *kāvyas* under study. Aśvaghoṣa uses it to portray the handsome face of Sarvārthasiddha (*padmavaktra*)[33] though he also uses it for women's faces, for the face of Sundarī is also said to be like a lotus (*padmam iva*).[34] But the beauty of Pārvatī's face excels the beauty of the lotus[35] so that

> the fickle Goddess of Beauty could not enjoy
> the charm of the lotus while resorting to the moon
> or of the loveliness of the moon while resorting
> to the lotus.
> But when she approached the face of Umā
> she attained the pleasures peculiar to both.[36]

The reason is obvious for the lotus blooms during the day while the moon shines at night. So Lakṣmī is not able to enjoy the benefits of both except in the face of Pārvatī.

In Tamil classical literature the *neruñci* flower (*tribulus tenertris*) and the sun are used in a striking symbolism. Symbolism is the use of representation in which the object shown or mentioned, refers, by virtue of association to something *more* or something *else*. It may refer to another object or quality and connects the image or analogy and an idea or conception which the object evokes. The *neruñci* is a thorny plant with small leaves and golden flowers. These flowers are said to be always turning in the direction of the sun and fading when the sun sets. This symbolism is used to show how the happiness and thereby the beauty of the woman in love or the wife is dependant on her lover or husband. One heroine declares to her friend,

> My friend!
> The chief of the mountain,
> where the silver cascade flows
> like the rising moon above the sea,

is like the sun.
My plump, bamboo-like upper arms
are like the *neruñci*.[37]

In this poem, the chief of the mountain is symbolised as the sun and the plump, bamboo-like arms of the heroine as the *neruñci* flower. But these two are not the main ideas conveyed in this poem or analogy. The idea of the dependence of the *neruñci* flower on the sun and its fading when the sun is out of its sight which brings out its constancy that shuts off all other interests or subordinates them all, is used to convey the dependence of the heroine's happiness on her husband, her dedication of her whole life to him and the home which they have set up together. These concepts do not find mention in the poem but are meant by association with the relationship found between the two objects of nature—the *neruñci* flower and the sun.

Creepers

Some personifications of this type lead to certain symbolisms in the treatment of love and figure prominently in love literature. A very common personification is the creeper as a woman and the tree around which it entwines itself as a man. Most Indian literatures use this symbolism and the tree and creeper are said to be man and woman and vice versa. The sight of the tender creeper frail but beautiful, entwining itself around the tall, strong tree makes it possible for the two to be used together as a symbol of conjugal love. This symbol is most useful to create a certain atmosphere and to convey ideas in a compact and elegant manner. Śakuntalā and her friends are engaged in light banter while watering the plants in the hermitage. Among the plants watered is a *navamallikā* creeper, named Vanajyotsnā by Śakuntalā, which is wound round a mango tree that had grown nearby. Anasūyā calls it the self-elected bride of the mango tree while Śakuntalā admires the suitability of the season for the two to unite, for the creeper with fresh flowers is in her youth and the tree covered with soft, new sprouts shows its eagerness to enjoy such a union. Her appreciation of this pair makes Priyamvadā tease her saying that Śakuntalā herself is longing for such a union with a bridegroom.[38] Thus the scene with the tree and the creeper brings out Śakuntalā's youth and beauty and the fact that she is ready for marriage. While describing the effects of Vasanta or the spring sesason on the living beings in Śiva's *tapovana*, Kālidāsa does not fail to describe the trees and creepers, with the necessary details to show their manifestation of love.

> The trees, too, received close embraces from
> their creeper-wives' arms in the form of tender twigs,
> captivating with quivering lips in the form of
> young reddish sprouts and
> with breasts in the form of dense clusters of flowers.[39]

At times, this simile is reversed and a bride and bridegroom or any loving couple may be likened to a tree with an entwining creeper. Kālidāsa himself uses this simile in his *Raghuvaṃśam*. In his description of the wedding of Aja and Indumatī he says:

> That prince (Aja), taking the bride's hand in his own
> shown brighter
> As does a mango tree after having received with its
> foliage, the shoots of an *aśoka* creeper clinging to it, [40]

thereby reminding the readers of the *svayamvara* of Indumatī in which she has chosen him of her own free will. A poem in the *Aiṅkuṟunūṟu* also presents the same simile. The creepers entwined around the trees and waving in the breeze are compared to women dancing in the arms of their husbands.

> It is the spring of great beauty
> with the rare sight;
> women-like, swaying creepers
> dance,
> embracing the warrior-like oak trees.[41]

The *Paripāṭal* describes a woman dancing to the drum (*tuṭi*) beats made by her husband. She sways like a flowering creeper (*pūṅkoṭi*) and the swaying of her string of pearls, other ornaments and her clothes makes her resemble a bough filled with blossoms being shaken by the northern wind (*vāṭai*). The double simile here portrays the loveliness and the gentle movements of a woman.[42]

Apart from this complete symbolism, the Caṅkam poems treat the creeper alone as a symbol of beauty and tenderness. The *Akanāṉūṟu* depicting a heroine who is lonely and devoid of all jewels during separation, says that she moves about without the joy and beauty that is usually associated with her and looks like a creeper that has shed all its flowers (*pūvī koṭiyiṟ pulleṉap pōki*).[43] The *Kalittokai* also uses the same simile (*pūvīnta koṭi pōṉṟāḷ*).[44] But one who is happy in her love is 'like a creeper with dense bunches of flowers'.[45]

These similes and symbolism soon gave the name *koṭiyiyalār*[46] and *koṭiyiyal nallār*[47] to women so that Vaḷḷi, the beloved of Murukaṉ is called 'the Kuṟava creeper' (*kuṟappiṇāk koṭi*).[48] In the Tamil epics the term *koṭi* is used with various prefixes to mean a woman. Mātavi dancing at her maiden performance at Pukār is said to have expounded the art with grace and supple movements as if she were a gold-like flowering creeper,[49] and later when the emerald chain she wins as a royal gift is auctioned, it is made clear that the man who would pay 1,008 gold pieces (*kalañcu*) would be worthy of 'our creeper' (*naṅkoṭi*).[50] The routes to Maturai were believed to have been many and of them one was filled with wonder and extraordinary happenings like women described as *polaṅkoṭi* or gold creeper [51] and as *pūṅkoṭi* or flowering-creeper [52] appeared tempting the wayfarers to choose the wrong path. The *Maṇimēkalai,* though not in favour of love or the arts still uses the term *koṭi* freely for women, including its heroine Maṇimēkalai. A random look at one of the cantos would show how commonly this term is used. For example in the *Aṟavaṇarttoḻu Kātai* alone, which contains 121 lines, there are nine instances in which the word is used with prefixes to mean a woman, women or Maṇimēkalai herself.

iḷaṅkoṭi	—	young creeper (line 2)
pūṅkoṭi	—	flower-creeper (line 20)
pūṅkoṭi	—	flower-creeper (line 21)
maṭak koṭi	—	modest creeper (line 53)
maṭak koṭi	—	modest creeper (line 103)
pūṅkoṭi mātar	—	women like flower creepers (line 107)
iḷaṅkoṭi	—	young creeper (line 110)
maṭak koṭi	—	modest creeper (line 115)
iḷaṅkoṭi	—	young creeper (line 121)

This shows how the comparison or symbol which is so apt and beautiful came to stay and has ceased to be a simile or symbol but is now another term for a woman.

The aptness of this symbolism is brought out well in the *Avimārakam* and the *Kumārasaṃbhavam*. Kuraṅginī, overcome with love and fear at meeting Avimāraka stealthily is said to 'tremble like pale ivy in the breeze'.[53] Ratī in her lamentation over her husband's death, complains to Vasanta:

> Fate, sparing me while killing Kāman,
> has only done half the butchery.
> When the firm, supporting tree is broken by an elephant,
> the creeper (clinging to it) is bound to come down.[54]

The tree can very well thrive even if the creeper around it were destroyed and perhaps may have another creeper embracing it soon. It can also support more than one creeper at a time, but it is not possible for the creeper to exist once the tree or support is snatched away. In the *Raghuvaṃśam*, Aja wonders what turn of fate had changed the garland of flowers into the fire of lightning, for his wife Indumatī, who had been a creeper clinging to him had been struck while he himself has been left untouched.[55] But even here, he is shown only as lamenting her death, not daring to die with her for fear of scandal,[56] because the society expects him to go on doing his duties as a tree goes on even after the creeper is gone.

Birds

The fauna and avifauna also provide some symbols and similes. The most common symbol of connubial love and constancy mentioned in Sanskrit literature is the *cakravāka*. These birds are said to go about in pairs during the day and are unable to bear separation even for a while. They wail and cry even when the mate is hidden from the other by so much as a lotus leaf.[57] But these birds have to bid farewell to each other in the evening for they are doomed to separation at night,[58] when they call out to each other standing on the opposite sides of rivers, lakes or tanks. Thus the Yakṣa likens his lonely wife to the *cakravākī* without its mate,[59] while King Agnimitra compares himself to the *cakravāka*, Mālavikā, his beloved to its mate and Queen Dhāriṇī to the night that separates them.[60] Cankam literature does not seem to have any direct reference to this bird, but the description of the insepa-rability of the *makanril* suggests that it is the *cakravāka* with its Tamil name. The *makanril* is also an aquatic bird with short legs, always moving about in pairs. For it too, even a momentary separation caused by the intervention of a flower would seem as if it were a year. These birds are used to describe lovers who are always together and love that cannot bear separation.[61]

In both literatures, the curlews (Sanskrit *krauñca* and Tamil *anril*) are symbols of love whose sight and cries excite passion. The *Rāmāyaṇam,* the forerunner of Sanskrit *kāvya* poetry is said to have been born of the heart-rending cry of the *krauñca* whose mate had been struck down by the hunter. The *Ṛtusaṃhāram,* describing the fields in the cold season, mentions these birds stationed somewhere as being noisy but musical and exciting the feeling of love.[62] In Cankam literature, they are always described as being in the company of their mates or crying for the mate when separated.[63] Their slow, shrill but melodious cry that breaks the silence of the night enhances the sorrow of those separated from their dear ones.[64] One heroine, seeing the sun set with the usual accompaniments—the bats flying and the night owl screeching from the neem tree—wonders if she will also have to listen in loneliness to the voice of the *anril* from the palmyra tree.[65] This cry inflames the sense of longing in the hero as well as the heroine, for a poem shows the hero expressing his misery at night, espe-cially when the male *anril* calls its mate.[66] These birds are so well known for their constancy and their suffering when separated, that their mention is sufficient to convey the pain of separation. A friend of the heroine, seeing her suffer, decides to talk to the hero. Her actual intention is to make him realise the misery of the heroine so that he would marry her soon and put an end to this miserable condition of hers. But she does it subtly. She merely tells him,

> She,
> wasting the beauty
> of her lovely, dark complexion
> comparable to Kaḻumalar of Kuṭṭan
> with good chariots,
> is distressed with sleepless eyes.

You,
think of (returning to) your village
even at night
when the tiny, black female bird
not united with its mate,
pines with sorrow
in its nest woven with thorns
on the deity-dwelling tree.[67]

The *aṉṟil* is not mentioned by name. The mere description of the female bird as being tiny and black and pining for its mate is considered sufficient to bring out the pain and longing of the heroine in love, the friend's anxiety for her welfare and even to point out that perhaps he does not love her enough to be struck by the sad cry of the bird. The *Kuṟiñcippāṭṭu* and the *Maṇimēkalai* also describe the melodious call of the *aṉṟil* as one of the events at sunset[68] and the specific mention of this cry suggests that the night is a time for love and union except for those who are separated from their loved ones.

Bees

Just like the birds, the bees are also pictured as flying together. During spring and the onset of the rainy season, when the trees put forth their pretty flowers filled with pollen and honey, they go about happily sucking honey and this finds mention in both literatures. Though the love between the bee and its mate during these seasons is pictured in Tamil and Sanskrit literatures,[69] this relationship is not as important as its relationship to the flowers it visits in its round of honey-collection. Its habit of flitting from flower to flower to suck honey and forsaking it once the honey is taken, is used very cleverly in both literatures arising from a society that condones polygamy. The comparisons, however, are veiled as in an allegory and form 'suppressed similes'[70] or implied metaphors.[71] In such similitudes, the characters and details of the description of nature is in direct harmony and perfect balance with the idea or feeling to be conveyed by the speaker. For example in the *Abhijñānaśākuntalam*, Haṃsapadikā, the one-time favourite of King Duṣyanta, is hurt over his indifference towards her and his preference for Vasumatī, his Chief Queen. An open reproof would not be proper, considering their relative position in the palace; so she chooses to reprove him in a covert way by means of a simile. She merely sings a song addressing a bee.

> O Bee! How comes it that you, who eagerly long for fresh honey,
> having kissed the mango blossom in that way,
> should have forgotton it,
> now being satisfied with mere dwelling in the lotus?[72]

Duṣyanta understands it as an impassioned song meant to reprove him for it is he who is addressed as a bee. Haṃsapadikā in her youth is as exciting as the mango blossom, but like the mango blossom that is found only in the spring season, the passion that she arouses is also momentary, while the queen is like the lotus to which the bee always returns after its day's wanderings, though for 'mere dwelling'. She also points out the lack of passion in the attachment between the king and the queen. The much married king is aptly referred to as a bee and in the drama, this song prepares the audience for the repudiation of Śakuntalā. In Caṅkam literature too, a man who is always in search of fresh youth and variety in love is called a bee. One mistress, knowing the hero's weakness complains,

> Did the bee acquire
> the hero's wonderful quality?
> Or did he learn it from the bee?
> Unaware of this,
> the mother of his son (i.e. the heroine) blames me.[73]

In this poem, the quality of the bee is used to bring out the truth, that it is the insatiable passion of the hero that makes him stay away from his wife and not his mistress who has no permanent hold over him. Another wife, distressed over the behaviour of her husband, is consoled by her friend:

> O lady with thistle-like teeth!
> You have great beauty.
> It is he who is called
> not a man but a bee

that hums around fresh, fragrant flowers
of the pond
even at midnight.[74]

The *tōḻi* tries to tell her friend that if he is not loyal to her, it is not because she lacks beauty to please him. It is because he is one of those whose passion knows no satisfaction and therefore has to be tolerated if not excused.

The epics also use the bee as a symbol of infidelity and of those who need or desire novelty in their sexual affairs. Describing the various sections of Maturai, Iḷaṅkō mentions the street where *gaṇikās* live. It is a section of the city visited by various classes of people including youths who search for fresh flowers like the bees.[75] Citrāpati, the grandmother of Maṇimēkalai who cannot accept the idea of her daughter and grand-daughter becoming Buddhist nuns, tries her best to persuade them and later the Prince Utayakumaraṉ to make Maṇimēkalai give up the nun's garb. She is aware of Utayakumaraṉ's attraction for her and also of the fact that it will not make her the queen when he becomes king. Once, when talking to the prince about her, she refers to Maṇimēkalai as a desirable fragrant flower (*kāmar cevvik kaṭimalar*)[76] and adds that she has come to speak to him so that the bee, Utayakumaraṉ, may partake of the honey therein. This selfish flitting without any commitments seems to be the main idea in this symbolism, for Citrāpati, a *gaṇikā* herself, tells the prince:

We are not chaste women.
It is our way of life to take
the wealth of many for ourselves.
We are like the lute which does not die
with the musicians
but changes hands.
We are like the bees
that suck honey
and forsake withering flowers.[77]

Whether used for men or women, it seems to be the symbol of an unchaste, selfish person with regard to passion and sexual relationships.

Buffaloes

In Tamil literature, there are also certain animals that figure in such comparisons, the most frequently mentioned, being the buffalo of the agricultural tracts where harlotry is said to be more common. To an unaccustomed reader these similes and references may simply seem to fit into the description of nature or the natural wealth of the place that serves as a background to the poem. But there is always a definite idea involving the characters in the poem. For example, a *tōḻi* addressing a hero, describes his native place.

(You are)
Lord of the country
where the red-eyed buffalo
disliking its muddy shed,
breaking its strong leash at night
when the village sleeps,
removing the thorny fence (of the fields)
with its horns,
agitating the fish in the fields full of water,
bewildering the *vaḷḷai* creepers
that have pretty floral tubes,
eats the dew-filled lotus humming with bees.[78]

This could pass off as a description of the natural wealth and beauty of the fields owned by the hero, with fish, *vaḷḷai* creepers and lotuses. But each object mentioned in this description is brought in with the purpose of describing the behaviour of the hero himself. The hero leaves his own wife at night and with his desire, pushes aside all sense of decorum. Then he goes to that section of the town where harlots live. There, he sends away the harlot's mother and her friends and enjoys the company of the young woman to the accompaniment of music. The friend, instead of narrating such indelicate incidents in detail, takes refuge in the description of his country and the buffalo therein.

Uḷḷuṟai Uvamam

Such implications and suggestions are found in both literatures but have a definite purpose and convention in classical Tamil poetry that deals with love. Suggestion is generally termed *uḷḷuṟai* in classical literature, though Tolkāppiyar mentions five types of suggestion—*uṭaṉuṟai, uvaman, cuṭṭu, nakai* and *ciṟappu.*[79] Of these he explains only the first two as types that were still in use. The *uvaman* is generally called *uḷḷuṟai uvamam* (suppressed simile or implied metaphor) to differentiate it from other similes and metaphors.[80] In this simile which is used only in love poetry, words like *nēr, aṉṉa, kaṭuppa* etc. which show clearly that it is a simile or comparison are not to be found.

Neither does it mention the object which is clarified or illustrated by the comparison. For example, Nacciṉākkiṉiyar explains that in the simile coral-like lips or mouth (*pavaḷam pōlum vāy*)[81] if the coral alone is mentioned and the lips or mouth is not mentioned, it is *uḷḷuṟai uvamam* (implied metaphor or suppressed simile). On the other hand, if the word lip or mouth is mentioned, even without the word *pōlum,* it would not be an *uḷḷuṟai uvamam* but some other simile or metaphor. Thus coral-lips or coral-like lips do not make an *uḷḷuṟai uvamam* for the meaning is too evident and therefore not suitable for the particular purpose of conveying a meaning covertly. Yet in an *uḷḷuṟai uvamam* each object mentioned has a specific meaning and each object of nature mentioned should be from the *karupporuḷ* pertaining to the region concerned, though deities are never mentioned in such similes.[82] For example, in the poem above, each object of nature mentioned corresponds to a particular object or person involved in the extramarital affair of the hero.

buffalo	—	hero
leash	—	sense of shame or decorum *(nāṇam)*
muddy shed	—	house or normal place of residence
fence	—	*pāṇaṉ* and *viṟali*
horns	—	wealth
fields	—	suburbs or section of the town where harlots live
fish	—	friends of the harlot
vaḷḷai	—	harlot's mother
lotus at night	—	the harlot who does not accept him with love
humming of bees	—	music

This detailed implication is understood only in the right context and again only by the two or three characters who are directly involved with the situation. Thus when the *tōḻi* describes the countryside with the buffalo roaming at night, the infidel husband who is guilty of going out stealthily at night and his wife are aware of the implied meaning. To the others it would seem to be a suitable description of the *marutam* region.

This is a very important convention in the use of nature in Caṅkam literature and is most useful in the *marutam* poems where the disloyal husband is made to realise, ever so politely and delicately, his own folly and the hurt and anger of his wronged wife. This simile or metaphor is one that has to be felt and cannot be known through the literal meaning of the words used in the poem. Naccinārkkiniyar explains that it is an instrument for making one feel or realise the emotion of love and is something to be known or felt by the heart *(uḷḷattāl uyttuṇara)*,[83] thereby connecting the meaning 'which is inherent', 'resides in' (*uḷḷuṟu*) with the emotion of the heart. Hence this simile is not restricted to the *marutam* aspect of love alone, but to all aspects of love. The important feature, however, is that the objects of nature used to produce this feeling or convey the message must be chosen from the *karupporuḷ* of the region. A *tōḻi*, noticing the sorrow of her friend, decides to talk to the hero so as to put an end to her suffering. She addresses him as:

> O victorious chief of the mountain!
> on the flower-filled slopes
> the inhabitants of the villages
> wake to the sound of thunder
> caused by the strong wind and rain
> that seem to turn the mountain upside down.
> It mistakes the lovely gloriosa—
> blooming in bunches near the fragrant stream
> flowing by the broad rock
> surrounded by bamboo
> that prevents the morning sun (from shining there),—
> to be a snake with its rare gem
> drinking water.[84]

This seems to be a description of the natural beauty and abundance of the hero's mountain, but it actually conveys the problem she and the heroine face. The objects have been chosen carefully to seem natural enough but each has an equivalent idea or person pertaining to the clandestine love and convey a definite meaning.

broad rock	—	the heroine's house
lovely gloriosa	—	beautiful heroine
stream	—	her relatives
gloriosa looking like a snake	—	her clandestine love seeming to be improper
noise of thunder spreading over the mountain	—	gossip spreading there and reaching mother
people waking	—	mother guarding carefully and their own sleeplessness

The idea is that though their love is not wrong for it will be the cause and basis of their wedded life, others do not understand. So they tend to gossip. Hearing this, the mother tends to be watchful and this causes unhappiness to the heroine. The mother had been unaware of their love till she heard of it from the village gossips, just like the people on the village had slept through the heavy rain till they heard the thunder. The situation suggests that he marries her so that it would end gossip as well as the heroine's sorrow. All objects mentioned here—the rock, mountain stream, gloriosa, bamboo, snake with its gem, thunder and heavy rain—are *karupporuḷ* commonly found in the *kuṟiñci* region.

Similes of this type are also found in Sanskrit literature though they are not very common in the literature of this period. This is called *atiśyokti*[85] and the announcement from behind the curtain in the *Abhijñānaśākuntalam*, '*Cakravākavadhū* bid farewell to your mate for the night is approaching,'[86] is cited as an example. Here too, the sentence has a special implication only in the context. Otherwise it would merely be an announcement that nightfall is approaching. As in the *uḷḷuṟai uvamam,* in this *atiśyokti* too, we obtain exact equivalents in the implied meaning.

cakravākavadhū	—	Śakuntalā
its mate	—	Duṣyanta
night	—	Gautamī

The announcement asking the female bird to bid farewell is also pertinent to the context, for being the protected girl Śakuntalā is, it is she who should be indoors at the approach of darkness. Besides, of the two lovers, she is the one who would be more embarrassed if Gautamī were to see them together. The song of Haṃsapadikā found in the same play, is another example of this simile. As in the Tamil *uḷḷuṟai uvamam* this verse has equivalents for each of the objects mentioned and specific meaning for most of the words.

bee	—	Duṣyanta
mango blossom	—	Haṃsapadikā
lotus	—	Vasumatī
honey	—	beauty and youth for love or exciting passion
kissing	—	love-making
mere dwelling	—	the absence of love-making

The verses in Sanskrit literature, are free to choose the various objects of nature for they are not restricted by conventions regarding land or the *karupporuḷ,* as in Tamil.

Iṟaicci

The other type of suggestion found in Caṅkam literature is the *uṭaṉuṟai* or *iṟaicci.* This consists of the suggestion of an idea which is not evident in the words used but is suggested by the objects of nature mentioned in the poem. The idea suggested may be in keeping with the general meaning of the poem or it may be quite contrary to the words or description in the poem. For instance, when the heroine's friend tells the hero:

Lord of the slopes
rich in fruits growing
on the root of the jack tree
hedged by the small bamboo!
Be good to her.
Like the large fruit hanging
from the tiny branch on the hillslope
her love is great but
her life is frail.
Who would know this?[87],

the obvious meaning is that in spite of her physical frailty, her love is great. But the objects she has chosen to describe the hero's mountain and as comparison for her friend's love are such as to convey something more, besides the obvious meaning. He is said to be the lord of the mountain where the bamboo grows abundant forming a natural fence for the jack fruit trees. Besides, the species he knows well is the one that has fruits on its roots. Hence the danger of someone stealing the fruits or of their falling off and getting smashed is not there. The heroine's love on the other hand is compared to the large fruit that hangs from a tender branch. The comparison of her love with the large fruit and her life which suffers on account of this burden to the thin branch is very clear. There is, however, the added idea that her love, is also sweet like the ripe jack fruit, but he will have to claim her on time. Otherwise, there may be other proposals of marriage and the parents, not aware of their love, may agree to such a proposal and unable to face this, she would die. The mention of the fence for the fruit tree on his hill and not for the tree on the hillslope that is compared to her suggests, that perhaps he is not aware of this danger. Besides, the comparison to a ripe fruit suggests that she is not able to hold on to her life and that the bough might break due to the weight of the fruit i.e. she may die unable to bear the sorrow of her separation. All these ideas are conveyed in a short poem of five lines with the use of the flora from the mountain region itself—the two types of jack fruit, one which grows on roots and the other on branches, and the bamboo. But unlike the *uḷḷuṟai uvamam* it does not have exact equivalents for each object mentioned. Yet this kind of suggestion is important to convey the idea in a general manner which may or may not be contrary to the obvious meaning. For example, a *tōḻi* informs a hero:

The pond is near the village.
The rivulet, not far from the pond.
The park (nearby) is deserted
but for the white cranes looking for food.
We shall go there
to get sand for (washing) our hair.
The modest maiden would also come.[88]

While this would seem to be a mere statement of what they plan to do, there is the suggestion that the hero is welcome to meet his beloved, 'the modest maiden', there, for she too would go with them. The fact that the girls are going to the rivulet with a definite purpose suggests that they would in no way be a hindrance or nuisance to the lovers. The girls would be busy collecting the right type of sand. The park being deserted is not visited by others who might see them. The cranes being there shows that it is not visited by people and that even the cranes themselves would not be interested in what happens in the park for they are intent on looking for food. Thus the park near the rivulet is an ideal place for him to meet his lady. On the other hand, even when there is an apparent invitation to come to an appointed place, the objects of nature used in the descriptions in the poem would suggest the difficulty of the situation. Another *tōḻi* says to the hero:

> Lord of the high hills!
> The faded flowers fall
> covering the waters of the rushing forest stream
> in which are crocodile and
> whirlpool that beat against the rocks.
> The rutty elephant,
> gone astray from its herd,
> strikes and pulls fearfully at the torrents
> till cured of its frenzy.
> You cross such frightening waters fearlessly
> like a brave boar.
> Would others come here,
> passing such difficult and dangerous places?
> If you come to distress even once,
> my friend would not be alive the following day.
> Those who are familiar with safer paths,
> may slip too.
> We therefore suffer (fearing) your safety.
> Even if you come during the day
> to the bower of gloriosa
> in the dense clump of fruit-laden trees
> with honeycombs on high branches,
> next to our garden on the tall mountain slope,
> you would embrace the cool, gentle upper arms
> of my friend cherished by my mother.

They are like the portions between joints
of the bent bamboo that grows on the broad hill.[89]

The above poem contains what a *tōḻi* tells a hero who is in the habit of meeting the heroine at night. To do so, he swims through the crocodile-infested river which is dangerous enough even with its currents of water made stronger by the fresh rains on the mountain. Then he has to pass through forest paths to arrive at the appointed place. Though he is fearless and made bolder by his love, the heroine and her friend fear for his safety. So the friend asks him to come to the grove of gloriosa creepers during the day. This invitation seems to be the obvious meaning and the gloriosa bower sounds like a beautiful and romantic place for the meeting of lovers. But while describing the dangers that go with his nightly visits, she points out that such meetings cause them fear and anxiety and that the heroine would not live if she were to hear of any mishap to him. The grove described seems beautiful, safe and secret enough. But on closer examination it can be seen that it is really not safe or private enough. The trees with honeycombs would attract the mountain dwellers whose livelihood depends on the collection of honey. The groves with fruit-bearing trees would attract fruit gatherers. To make it worse, the bower is adjoining their courtyard and since the heroine had been brought up with tender care by the foster-mother, there is also the danger of the foster-mother coming out often to see if she is alright and noticing the two together. So the general suggestion is that meetings during the day are not possible without stirring up a scandal and the only choice left for him is to ask for her hand in marriage and to make arrangements for the wedding. This suggestion is certainly contrary to the words, 'You may unite with her even if you come during the day.'

Suggestions of this type, very common and important in Tamil classical poetry like the *uḷḷuṟai uvamam,* is not very common in the Sanskrit classical poetry under study though later it was developed to become one of the most important aspects of poetry in Sanskrit literature, with the name *dhvani. Dhvani,* meaning sound or echo, consists of suggestions other than or apart from what is obvious in the poem or verse, just like *uṭaṉuṟai* or *iṟaicci.* This *dhvani* is rarely used by authors before Kālidāsa for it became important and was propounded as a literary merit only

in the ninth century by Anandavardhana in his *Dhvanyāloka*. But it is found even in the verses of Aśvaghoṣa. While describing the plight of Nanda in the garden around his monastery during spring, he pictures the ex-king as being reminded of his beloved Sundarī. He is attracted by a mango tree, full of blossoms and swarming with humming bees. Then,

> Receiving from the mango tree a rain of tiny flowers
> like saffron powder, he was reminded of his wife
> and sighed deeply like a newly caught elephant in confinement.[90]

The context and the comparison of Nanda to a newly-caught elephant suggest the nature of his sorrow. It is spring, the season of love. The sight of the bees humming around mango blossoms is symbolic of the sexual union and the excitement of love. The sight of the flowers like saffron powder reminds him of the paste used to draw designs on the upper arms and breasts by the husband or lover as part of their love and union. These make him sigh deeply 'like an elephant that has been newly caught' and is held confined. This suggests that Nanda has been given to love and has never been separated from his wife as an elephant that roams the forest with its mate. He had been free and unrestricted in his love for Sundarī but being confined to the monastery unwillingly, is not able to indulge in such pleasures. He can only think of his wife and sigh just like the elephant that is not able to get out. Besides, the aim of the *kāvya* is to show that the life of a monk is better though devoid of the pleasures of love and that it merely takes the necessary practice to subdue one's senses; so the reference to a newly-caught elephant. After sometime the wildest elephants can be trained to do what those versed in elephant-lore want them to do. Here the Buddha who initiates him against his wishes is the one who catches and trains souls as one would catch and train elephants. In Indian religions, the free elephant is the symbol of a soul that has yet to be subdued by the mahout and Nanda, unaccustomed to the strict life of penance and celibacy has to be trained. As time passes by, he would not be a 'newly-caught' elephant. He would get used to the spiritual training and his sighs and restlessness will be subdued.

Another instance of *dhvani* or suggestion is found in the first act of the *Abhijñānaśākuntalam*. The king, attracted by the deer he is hunting, enters the hermitage of Kaṇva. There he sees Śakuntalā and though a much-married man, is attracted to her. He manages to speak to her and her friends who are quite surprised to see him, and find out some details regarding Śakuntalā's birth and her stay in the hermitage. Just then a warning and an appeal for help are heard from behind the scenes. They hear someone say that 'King Duṣyanta is diverting himself with the chase in the neighbourhood' and recite two verses, one of which says,

> An elephant, alarmed at the appearance
> of a chariot, enters the
> pious grove, scaring the herd of deer,
> with fetters formed by clinging of
> *vrarti* coils dragged along by his
> feet; having one of his tusks fixed in
> a tree trunk, struck by a cruel blow,
> a very interruption incarnate to our
> penance.[91]

In this verse, the obvious meaning is that there is danger from the elephant that has become agitated and they need someone who can subdue the elephant. The presence of Duṣyanta in the grove is fortunate and also there is the obvious suggestion that he is heroic enough to tame that elephant. But apart from this, the coming of Duṣyanta into the grove is also accidental. He meant to hunt and because he was following a deer, he happened to come into the hermitage, just like the elephant who had come because it did not mean to but because he happened to be frightened by the king's chariot. His coming had frightened the young and innocent girls, Śakuntalā, Priyamvadā and Anasūyā (like the elephant frightening the deer) who are so accustomed to the peace and quiet of the grove. The king does not arrive alone. He comes with his *vidūṣaka* and other officials who are interested in hunting and those who see to his personal needs and comforts. Though he brings them along, he is to find them restrictive and would rather be without them. So he sends the *vidūṣaka* who is a constant companion back to the palace, though with a legitimate reason. His retinue is restrictive like the *vrarati* coils dragged along by his feet that act as fetters to the elephant. In his madness the elephant had struck at a tree and got a tusk caught in a tree trunk. The king too, in his love and desire for Śakuntalā, is caught in passion and is not able to free himself to go away. Yet his commitment to Śakuntalā is not complete. He has his Chief Queen and other women in his harem. So he is caught partially like the elephant's single tusk, while the other is free. More than all this, his behaviour, like that of the elephant, is contrary to that of the hermits in the grove. He is to indulge in love in the penance grove and this is not in keeping with the spirit of the place, though his excuse for staying behind is to protect the hermits and their penance. This verse suggests a part of the story to come.

In the second act of the play, Duṣyanta is shown as being unwilling to indulge in his favourite pastime, hunting, because of his love. He is reluctant to aim an arrow at the deer for they remind him of his gazelle-eyed beloved. So he tells the general, who exhorts him to continue with the sport, that since he is now encamped near the hermitage, it would not be proper for him to do so. He adds,

> Let the buffaloes plunge into the waters of the tanks
> struck repeatedly with their horns;
> Let the deer herding together beneath the shade
> chew the cud;
> Let herds of boar, undisturbed,
> uproot the *mustā* grass in the pool;
> And let this bow take repose
> with a slackened string.[92]

This verse is usually accepted as an example of *svabhāvokti* or description of things as they are. Sanskrit *kāvyas* and dramas, no doubt, are known for their description of nature for its own sake. However, this verse does not describe something that is there but could be there if the king and his group did not hunt. It also suggests that the king is unwilling to hunt but would rather spend his time meeting Śakuntalā or at least thinking about her. The plunging of buffaloes in water, the chewing of cuds by deer with their families *(kula)* and the digging of *mustā* grass by boars certainly do not suggest mere rest, as mentioned in the last line of the verse. The rest is only for the bow. The king would indulge in more sensuous pleasures. The mention of all the animals in the plural suggests that he would not be alone himself.

Other Uses of this Simile

In Tamil poetry of the classical period, similes of this type also help to point out to the erring hero his duty to the family or to give advice, without having to blame him openly. A musician or *pāṇaṉ* is sent by his master to pacify the wife who is sulky over her husband's disloyalty to her. In his attempt to appease her, the musician tells her that his master is sweet and loving. She simply says:

> He is indeed sweeter than anyone
> and has great love.
> He is of the country where the male bird
> with its hoppety walk
> brings the odourless white flowers
> of the sweet sugarcane
> to prepare a nest for its pregnant mate.[93]

This of course is normal behaviour among birds. On closer examination we notice the actual situation in the master's house and his lack of a sense of duty or love. She very cleverly points out that she is with child and the hero, instead of being with her in her time of need, spends his time in the company of other women. His passion has no love or duty as its basis and is therefore inferior to that of the birds.

Interpretation

Many poems treat objects of nature as actual human beings and their normal acts are interpreted to suit the state of the lovers' minds. In the *Mālavikāgnimitram,* the lovelorn king enters the *pramadavana* in the company of the *vidūṣaka,* his constant companion and confidante in the affairs of heart. A cool breeze from the south blows there and rustles the leaves. The *vidūṣaka* explains that the garden itself beckons the king with the leaves for its fingers. To the king, spring itself seems friendly and concerned over his 'illness' caused by love. He says:

> By the sweet notes of the slightly intoxicated *kuil*

he seems to be compassionately enquiring
whether I can bear the torture of love;
while the southern breeze with its soft touch
with its incense of mango blossoms is like the palm
of Spring's hand, stroking my limbs.[94]

To Mālavikā, smitten by love, the *aśoka* with its own longing or *dohadā* seems to be inviting her to sit on the stone slab under its shade.[95] Descriptions of this kind are common in Tamil literature. One lady whose husband is away and is yet to return at the onset of the rainy season notices the white Arabian jasmine (*mullai*) buds that are comparable to pretty white teeth. She cries:

'Not heeding (your) youth,
he went desiring wealth.
He has not returned yet.
Why?'
Thus, O friend!
laughs the cool, fragrant *kār*
with the *mullai* buds brought forth by the rains
as its teeth.[96]

The voice of the cuckoo in spring is also interpreted variously. To one heroine it seems to say, 'Those who are united, do not part; those who are parted, unite.'[97] To another, suffering the pain of separation, the bird seems to coo so as to advise the men, who leave on long journeys for the sake of amassing wealth, 'O wise ones ! Do not go away for transient life (i.e. wealth).[98]

Even more poignant are the poems where nature is said to undergo or is treated as feeling the same emotions as the speakers themselves. A heroine asks:

Who caused you distress
O sea?
In the large harbour surrounded by parks
where the fish-eating storks
spread like a flock of goats with small heads
owned by Pūḻiyar,
I hear you even at midnight
when the waves toss
the white blooms of the screwpine.[99]

This poem does not mention a word about the heroine herself. To her, immersed in sorrow, even the sea seems to be suffering, for the dirge of the sea is like its wail of sorrow. The sea is never alone for in the large harbour are many white storks. Yet it is lonely and sad for they are interested only in catching fish for their food. This is merely a projection of the heroine's sorrow. She too is alone in her grief. The other inmates of the house are fast asleep, unaware of her clandestine love and the pain it causes during separation. Only she, being awake, wonders, if the sea which is also awake at that hour suffers like her because of love. In this poem the whole emotion is thrust on the sea and it is immaterial as to who is suffering, the hero or the heroine. The loneliness and the sleeplessness of a person in love becomes the most important thing in the poem.

Sometimes, the fauna and flora are used to enhance the feeling or to explain its intensity. A *tōḻi*, noticing the misery of her friend during separation, is happy when the husband returns. She wishes to let him know of her friend's sorrow. So she tells him of a sparrow and its family. The male sparrow had returned to its nest after having philandered with another female of its species. The hen sparrow, being hurt and angry, refuses him admission into the nest and lets him stand outside in the drizzle. But towards evening her heart softens towards him and calls him in.[100] She tries to show that evening is a time when love and affection increase and the female sparrow softens even towards its mate who has erred. How much more would the love of the heroine be towards him who had gone away on duty? All these may be attempts to read human behaviour in the movements and behaviour of nature, but are most useful in portraying the emotions and thoughts clearly with the right intensity.

Sympathetic Listeners

The objects of nature are also treated as being capable of listening sympathetically to the outbursts of those in love. Thus they are spoken to as if they are humans, capable of understanding all that is said. Tamil poetic convention refers to this generally as *kāma mikka kaḻi paṭar kiḷavi* or words spoken in distress due to excessive love. It is accepted that this situation of someone talking to birds, animals or other objects of nature is not something that takes place normally but only in literary tradition, in which a hero or heroine, due to intense love and longing expresses his or her feelings in this manner. Various objects of nature are addressed in such poems. In the Caṅkam poems, birds like the parrot (*kiḷi*),[101] the owl (*kūkai*),[102] the crow,[103] the *aṉṟil*[104] and the cockerel,[105] insects like the bee,[106] plants like the *vayalai*,[107] places like the pastoral region (*puṟavu*),[108] the river,[109] the sea,[110] rain,[111] the northwind (*vāṭai*),[112] the moon[113] and evening[114] are addressed by the various dramatic personae in love poetry. These apostrophes may further be divided as being meant for a particular character's benefit or as a means of expressing one's feelings. The speakers are usually the hero, the heroine, her friend or *tōḻi* and the foster-mother.

The hero may address an object of nature to express something that he is unable to convey to his beloved directly. For instance a hero in a *Kuṟuntokai* poem asks the bee:

> O bee with hidden wings!
> You spend your life selecting honey.
> So tell me truly without partiality.
> Of all the flowers you know,
> is there any that smells sweeter
> than the tresses of this maiden
> with peacock gait,
> close-set teeth
> and requitted, eternal love?[115]

The hero certainly does not expect a reply from the bee but has meant these words to be heard by his beloved. He wishes to let her know of his attraction for her and to convince her that this attraction is not momentary or transient passion but one that is the result of countless previous lives together. He has found in the bee a convenient excuse to voice his feelings.

Apostrophes in Ciṟaippuṟam

All utterances of the heroine and her friend that are classified as *ciṟaippuṟam* are also meant actually for the hero who is within hearing distance, though addressed to each other or to some object of nature. There are poems addressed to the millet grains (*tiṉai*),[116] the moon,[117] the rain[118] and birds like the parrot[119] and the owl. Of these, most of the poems are direct requests to the thing addressed to do something for them. For example, a *tōḻi* asks the owl not to screech at night when the heroine, unable to sleep, waits anxiously for the hero. She is afraid that its hoot might wake the others and thereby prevent the lovers from meeting as planned. The main aim of the *tōḻi* is to make the hero realise the heroine's plight and the difficulties involved in such clandestine meetings, so that he would think of marriage as the only solution.[120] Her apostrophe to the moon also has the same purpose. The brightness of its rays would be a hindrance to the secret meeting of the lovers. At times these poems may contain an actual message to the hero.

> Parrots with bent beaks
> who eat (millet) with your group!
> If you see under the *acōka* tree
> the hero with pretty garlands on his chest,
> holding his bent bow
> and wearing cool chaplets of flowers
> from the *kullai,* wild jasmine, *kūtaḷam,*
> water-lily and cleansing nut tree,
> could you please tell him something?
> After this maiden embraced him
> our unrighteous mother causes sorrow,
> thinking the deity (Murukaṉ) afflicts her.
> She does not permit us to guard the fields
> whose crops are wasted.
> Surely you know this.[121]

In this poem, though the parrot is asked to give a message, all that is said is meant for the hero who stands nearby. He would thereby know that the mother has noticed the changes in the heroine and does not permit her to leave the house. It would therefore be impossible for them to meet, and the only way to end her sorrow would be to marry her.

In Sanskrit literature, especially in the dramas, we have instances of characters listening to others conversing with one another but the situation is in no way comparable to the *ciṟaippuṟam* in Tamil literature. The overhearing in Sanskrit literature is more like eaves-dropping and is done unknown to the speakers. This is found in all of Kālidāsa's dramas and some of Bhāsa's. Padmāvatī, Vāsavadattā and their retinue overhear, though accidentally, the conversation between the *vidūṣaka* and Udayana in which the former asks the king which of the two queens is dearer to him.[122] In the *Abhijñānaśākuntalam* Duṣyanta overhears Śakuntalā, Anasūyā and Priyamvadā twice, once when they are watering the plants before meeting the king[123] and again when they are discussing Śakuntalā's 'condition' in the bower.[124] Urvaśī in her invisible form (*tiraskariṇī*) listens to the conversation between Purūravas and his *vidūṣaka,*[125] and Agnimitra overhears the conversation between Mālavikā and Bakulāvalikā.[126] This also helps the characters who are listening, to know the innermost thoughts of their beloveds, especially the heroines who would otherwise not voice their feelings. But, while in the *ciṟaippuṟam* the listener is the one who is unaware that the speakers know of his presence and that the words are actually meant for him to hear, in the Sanskrit dramas, it is the speaker or speakers who are not aware that their conversation is being overheard. Hence their words are more frank and less covert than in the *ciṟaippuṟam.*

Apostrophe

There are other apostrophes to objects of nature that are not meant for anyone else but for the thing or fauna addressed. These poems merely serve as a means of expressing the feelings and moods of the characters concerned. Here too, the object of nature is considered pleasant or unpleasant, friendly or unfriendly, welcome or unwelcome, depending on the situation and the mood or emotion produced by the situation. For example, the rainy season or *kār* is usually received with joy and its showers are considered sweet. But there are poems in the Caṅkam collection that portray thoughts and emotions that are different though the object spoken to is the same—the rainy season or *kār.* There are two poems in which the hero asks the clouds to rain heavily. In one he asks them to flash the lightning, thunder like the drums and shed large, cooling drops of rain for his heart knows the satisfaction of a mission well accomplished and is now united with the beloved.[127] In the other he says:

O cloud with a loud noise!
May you move about the mountain peaks
worshipped by all
as the support of the world.
You have favoured me by raining at night
with your sound

resembling the *paṭumalai* tune
from the well-tuned strings of the lute
and your thunder like the sound
of the paste-smeared head of a drum,
causing the various blooms of the slopes to fall.
I have enjoyed the sweet embrace
of the dark maiden
with long, curly tresses.[128]

In both these instances, rain is welcomed by the characters concerned for they are united with their beloveds. The emotions enhanced by the rain are pleasant for their love and longing find fulfilment in the company of their loved ones. But when there is no such fulfilment, the very same rain and the sound of clouds become painful and torturous. Hence a maiden waiting for her husband but finds that the rainy season is setting in, says to the cloud:

O dark cloud that causes the (*kār*) season!
Your coming here as if saying,
'Do you know his condition?'
does not resemble the behaviour
of noble people.
Your loud thunder may dull
the broad hoods of snakes in the rain,
but not soften his heart.
So your voice filled with thunder
is not sweet.[129]

The same sound, which the happy lover describes as resembling the music that emanates from the tuned strings of the lute and the sound of drums as if forming a background to their love and union, is here said to be harsh and cruel *(iṉṉātē)*. It can frighten or destroy snakes but not make the hero think of her and her plight at this time of the year so as to return. A *tōḻi* seeing her friend inconsolable, because of the beginning of the rainy season without any news of her husband's return, tries to console her. To do so, she too addresses the rain clouds.

He said,

the season of his return is *kār*
with heavy showers
when the small tender flowers of the *mullai* bloom,
spreading fragrance and honey
so that the cool bower is beautiful
like the spotted and lined face of an elephant.
Now, because you love her not,
you behave unnaturally
causing her distressed heart to tremble.
But I will not be cheated
like the ignorant group of peacocks
that burst into cries (of joy)
hearing your false thunder.
May you live long, O cloud![130]

Here the sound of the cloud is said to be the result of cruelty. It is accused of being unrighteous or not following the natural order for it is considered out of season simply because the sound of thunder is heard before the arrival of the hero. In all the above poems, the season is the beginning of *kār*, the background is the pastoral region and the object addressed is the cloud. Yet its sound is said to be sweet, unpleasant or cruel depending on the situation of the 'speaker' concerned. This difference is suggested in Purūravas' complaint about the rain cloud as well.

While all of a sudden, I have suffered separation
from my beloved,
and it is unbearably painful,
here the fresh clouds appear, making the days so genial
by mitigating their intense heat.[131]

The rain actually brings about a pleasant season which is a welcome change from the burning heat of summer. But it is cruel or unbearably painful to the lovers who are separated. Thus these apostrophes to the objects of nature are a means of depicting or expressing the feelings of the various characters, especially the hero and the heroine.

Apostrophe to One's Own Heart

Very much like these are the apostrophes to one's own heart

though the heart, strictly speaking, is not an object of nature. Though the content of the poem is very much like a soliloquy, there is a marked difference. In these poems that usually have the colophon, *neñcoṭu kiḷattal* meaning 'talking to the heart', the hero speaks to the heart as if it were a separate entity. Hence he might tell his heart not to go back to the heroine but accompany him.[132] These poems deal with separation in general but the contents can be as varied as possible. One hero tells his heart:

My heart!
You point to the broad, long path
to be traversed,
desirous of amassing wealth
in the form of ornaments.
Will your false words
that sound like truth now
remove my sorrow when the eyes
that clash with bent ear-rings
of the bejewelled maid
with loving sweet speech
and red lips like the petals
of the *murukku* blooms, prevent me
along the long distant tracts?[133]

Another hero tells his 'good heart' that if wealth can be obtained only through separation from his dark-eyed wife, then it should forget going away and think of staying back so that his wife, happy in her love, can carry out her wifely duties well.[134] These poems usually depict a conflict between reason or the need for wealth that makes a successful social life possible (*puṟam*) and his love for his wife who would suffer in loneliness and anxiety if he went away (*akam*). Though the *akam* element seems victorious, this happens only before a journey is undertaken. He is, however, bound to leave for distant lands later.

Once he has undertaken a journey, the most important thing is to complete his mission successfully. It does not mean that there are no more conflicts between his desire for wealth and his love for his wife. A hero advises his heart that it would certainly have been better to have stayed home with his beautiful wife but his heart did not allow him to remain there. It had goaded him to go in search of wealth. Now it wishes to go back but he will not.

You may not have known me then.
Now if you stop me from (pursuing) my efforts
won't you become
the laughing stock of others?[135]

Once the decision to go out and earn more wealth is taken, the victory in such conflicts seems to be for the decision he has made. Another tells his heart that there was no point in worrying over the separation after reaching the arid tracts.[136] On his return from such journeys, after obtaining the wealth he had gone in search of, his thoughts are full of his home and his wife. Then he tells his heart of his anticipation. A hero tells his heart that now he would go back to his tall, spacious house and embrace his wife with long dark tresses and a dark complexion.[137] These apostrophes, just like the others, bring out the thoughts, conflicts, hopes and fears of the hero. An *Aiṅkuṟunūṟu* poem, however, depicts the satisfaction of a lover who is able to think of his beloved and her lovable qualities on his way. He says:

My heart!
The qualities of the maiden you love
have come
crossing the forked paths
of the cruel desert
where the (wild) brown dog waits
in the cactus-filled arid tract
to prey on the boar
to satisfy the pregnancy-longing
of its sharp-toothed mate.[138]

Having seen the love and the sense of duty of the wild dog, he must have been reminded of his love for and the duty towards his wife, and felt consoled that his coming away was necessary like the dog waiting for its prey to feed its mate with the food that is not merely necessary but craved for. Hence his recollection of her good qualities is comforting and helps him to continue his journey with renewed vigour and eagerness.

While this is considered as a useful means of portraying the hero's emotion in Tamil poetry, Sanskrit literature does not seem to use this technique. The *Avimārakam,* however, contains a verse that is comparable to these in that the heart or mind (*manas*) is spoken of as if it were a separate entity or person. Separated from Kuraṅginī and traversing a desert region in summer, Avimāraka says:

Only my body could benefit
from the little luck left to me,
and barely escape from that palace.
My heart (*manas*) refuses to follow.
(Being) a prisoner of my beloved,
it will not even look at me.[139]

The situation in love and the geographical background in Tamil and Sanskrit are similar, though the reason for the separation is very different.

Requesting Favours

A different type of apostrophe or 'speaking to' is found when an object of nature is asked to do a favour for the character concerned. Usually, this favour is asked by the foster-mother, hero or the heroine. In Tamil poems that deal with elopement, the mother or foster-mother of the heroine who has left the house is depicted as being inconsolable. In her sorrow, the foster-mother who sometimes goes in search of the girl enquires from passers-by if they had seen her daughter. Some poems show her as asking objects of nature like the deer if it had seen her.[140] Another tempts the crow with rich food and asks it to caw so that her daughter would return as a guest to her house.[141] This type of favour is asked, depending on the nature of the object addressed and the mood of the speaker. For example, the moon being high up in the sky, is able to look about the whole world. So a heroine asks the moon:

O full moon with many rays
that seem like many portions of milk
in-between
and appearing on the nape of clouds!
You never stumble on bamboo ladders.
You are noble and righteous.
Since there is no (part of the) world

hidden from you,
won't you show me
where he hides from me?

Receiving no reply from the moon, she becomes angry and adds:

Because you do not speak truth
you fade gradually like my upper arms
that have lost their bangles.
Surely you are not capable (of showing).[142]

This is very similar to the requests made by Purūravas who is searching for Urvaśī. Seeing a group of swans *(rājahaṃsa)* he asks,

You king of aquatic birds!
Later you will go the Mānasa lake.
Let go the lotus stem, food for your journey.
You can pick it again.
First save me from despair by giving news
of my beloved;
for the good consider it worthier to render service
to the suppliants than to be concerned
with their own affairs.

Then he adds, 'Since he looks up, he seems to say that in his longing for the Mānasa, he had not noticed her.'[143] In both these instances, the intensity of the emotion of the dramatis personae concerned is depicted in the interpretation of the moon's natural silence and the swan's looking up once in a while during its search for lotus fibres.

Messengers and Messenger Poems

With this kind of a dialogue between nature and human characters, the next natural step is to treat them as messengers. Messages and messengers have been a fact of ancient life when even letters had to be brought by messengers. In literature that deals with love too, there is mention of human messengers like the *pāṇaṉ*, the *viṟali* and the *tōḻi* herself, at times, in Tamil literature and the *dūta* and the *dūtī* in Sanskrit literature. The classical Tamil literature makes use of the *pāṇaṉ* and passers-by as people who actually carry messages to those who are far away.[144] Fauna and avifauna like the parrots,[145] stork (*kuruku*),[146] the bee (*tumpi*)[147] and the crab (*alavan̲*)[148] are asked by the characters to take or bring back messages for them. At times they are chided as being hardhearted and cruel for not doing so. All these poems are sung as if by the heroine. Except for the poem that asks the parrot feeding on the millet crop to let the hero know that she had been appointed to guard the millet field, so that he would know of the possibility of meeting her during the day, all other poems convey a message of sorrow and anxiety during separation. In the Sanskrit literature of the period under study, the only but the most popular ever messenger is the cloud or *megha* in the *Meghadūtam.*

All objects chosen as messengers are those commonly found in the region which becomes the background of the poem. In the above poem, the heroine appointed to guard the millet field and the treatment of love before marriage show that it belongs to the hilly region. Parrots are common there, especially at the time when the grains in the field are ripening and have therefore to be guarded from them and other birds that feed on the grains. In the coastal region, the storks that fly about looking for fish and the crab are found all over the beach. The bee of course is the commonest insect found wherever there are flowers. Kālidāsa's cloud, though not a sentient being like the birds, crabs and insects, still moves and is found anywhere. The added advantage is that during the rainy season in North India, it moves with the monsoon winds from the south-west to the north-east where Alakā is situated on Mount Kailāsa in the Himalayas.

The person wishing to send the message asks the chosen messenger with respect and consideration to do the favour. The heroine in the *Nar̲r̲iṇai* poem, before asking the parrot to take the message, says:

> O green parrot with a red beak
> who pecks off ears of grain!
> Do not be afraid.
> Having satisfied your need for food,
> do me a favour.
> I beg you with joint palms.[149]

Another heroine asks a stork, that comes from the hero's district to catch fish in her district but returns to its own abode after having eaten its fill, if it is grateful enough to think of the benefit he derives from her district and to do a favour in return by giving her lover a message from her.[150] One heroine tries to arouse a sense of pity in the heart of a crab which she wishes to send with her message. She says:

> The coastal park will not speak.
> The backwater will not tell him.
> Neither will the *puṉṉai*
> with fragrant flowers on which bees hum.
> I have no one but you,
> O crab!
> Only you can tell him,
> the lord of the harbour where
> the bees
> mistaking the fragrant petals of the *neytal*
> blooming like eyes
> in the dark backwater
> to be nectar,
> suck honey (in abundance)
> and are unable to fly.[151]

The Yakṣa, of course, seeing a cloud clinging to a peak and overcome with love and concern for his beloved wishes to send her tidings of his own welfare (*svakuśalam*). So he makes an offering of *kuṭaja* flowers and welcomes the cloud with affectionate words (*prītipramukhavacanam svāgatam*). After praising its lineage, its connection to Indra and its ability to take any shape it pleases, he also gives his reason for asking the cloud to do him that favour.

> A request made to one distinguished by virtue,
> though fruitless, is better
> than to one who is base,
> though sure of success.[152]

He adds, as if to flatter and win its pity with his own helplessness and dejection; 'O cloud! You are the refuge of the afflicted.'[153]

When sending a message, the person to whom it is sent and the place where he or she is to be found are important. Hence the poems that request objects of nature to be messengers normally describe the place where the recipient of the message is. In the *Naṟṟiṇai* poem, the maiden merely tells the parrot:

> If you go to your relatives
> on the many-branched jack tree
> on his slopes,
> please tell the chieftain of the hill.[154]

Here, there is no need for a detailed description of the hero, his country or the path to be taken by the parrot to reach his hill. It is where the parrot would go and there can be only one chieftain for those slopes. Because of his position, he would be well known to the residents on those slopes. In the *Akanāṉūṟu* poem above (fn. 151), the heroine describes to the crab the harbour and adds that he is the lord of that harbour. Being a crab that runs around that seashore, it is expected to know the place. In the case of the Yakṣa, he meets a cloud that knows neither him nor his beloved. It may be travelling north-eastwards annually but there had been no need for it to look for any particular place or person. So he describes the path to be taken by the cloud to reach Alakā, then the city of Alakā itself, the garden surrounding his house, his house itself and then his wife, emaciated with the grief of long separation. Only then does he give the actual message.

The message is meant to be the most important part of these poems, for it conveys the emotion or sentiment of the whole poem. Except for the heroine who sends word that:

> The modest daughter
> of the forester of this hill
> guards the millet,[155]

all other Caṅkam heroines seem to send a general message conveying their sorrow at being separated from their loved ones.

> Many a time at midnight
> when the small seagull rested wearily
> with its loving mate
> on the low branches of the screwpine
> dreaming of white prawns
> in the forbidding shark-infested area,

she removed your sorrow.
Can she overcome her own sorrow?[156]

This is the message the crab is supposed to take to the chieftain of a harbour. The message of the Yakṣa is somewhat different. He has been separated by a curse and is not involved in any duty or activity that would help in bettering himself or his finances. He is away from home, devoid of his supernatural powers and is not to return home though it is the season when all lovers and husbands return. So there is bound to be greater anxiety and the Yakṣa therefore sends her not only a message that carries news of his sorrow at being separated, but also news of his well-being, an avowal of his love and also words of comfort. He also relates to the cloud an incident that is known only to him and his wife so that she would be sure that the cloud is speaking the truth.[157] It is this proof which shows that the messenger is genuinely from the husband and the poem itself is to be regarded as having been modelled on Rāma's message to Sītā carried by Hanumān. But for this, the rest of the *Meghadūtam* and its spirit seem to be very similar to the Caṅkam poems that ask objects of nature to carry messages of love. In spite of the influence the *Rāmāyaṇa* might have had on Kālidāsa and his composition of this lyric, he has been hailed as the first poet to make this innovation and he himself gives his reason for asking the cloud to bear the message, because it was a new idea as far as Sanskrit literature was concerned.

In Tamil poetry, this device is so common that the whole format is changed at times. One heroine blames the bee as being cruel and pitiless for not having informed the heartless hero of her plight which she is supposed to have related to it and asks it:

You are cruel, O bee!
(yet) may you live long!
I may die (though)
I have told you of my sorrow.
Is your mind also black
besides your body, O Pitiless One?[158]

Apart from being an interesting poetic device, these objects are useful in the portrayal of the innermost feelings of the speakers. In the *Meghadūtam*, the Yakṣa unburdens his feelings frankly and even relates some intimate incidents to the cloud. This would not have been possible if he were to speak to a human being. In the Tamil poems, the heroines are in no position to discuss their love with anyone; let alone send a message, for, it is still in a clandestine stage and not known to anyone, perhaps not even to her closest friend, the only person with whom she may talk about it. So natural objects like the parrot, crab, bee and the like are used as listeners to such passionate messages and outpourings.

Substitute

One other important use of nature is as a substitute for the lover or beloved. Anything that has been connected to or still has some connection with the hero or heroine, or has some resemblance to the loved one is considered dear and valuable. It is believed that it helps a great deal in overcoming the pain of separation.

When a *tōḻi* wonders how her friend would bear the separation of the hero who is going away to amass wealth so that he can marry, the heroine tells her:

> Look at my forehead, my friend.
> Is it not as before?
> I merely looked at the hill
> in his country.
> It had rained heavily on the slopes
> causing the black monkey and its young
> to shiver with cold
> in the forest where
> flocks of peacocks cry (for joy).[159]

This suggestion is that the heroine had found it difficult to be separated even for a few hours. In spite of the short duration of their separation pallor had spread on her bright forehead. But after looking at the hill, though from a distance, her heart feels better and the pallor or *pacalai* disappears making the forehead as bright as before. The sight of the hill gives her satisfaction nearly as great as when seeing him in person. Another heroine explains that she has lived through her separation in spite of the cold season (*aṟciram*) with the north wind *(vāṭai)*, the evenings (*mālai*) that intensify sorrow and her mother's suspicion, because she was able to see his high mountains where clouds rest.[160] Like the hill, other things from the hill also become a source of comfort to the maiden in love. One girl who is secretly in love with a youth is able to bear her loneliness with forbearance till her marriage to the youth is arranged. Seeing this, her *tōḻi* commends her on her strength and ability to contain her emotions. By way of explanation she relates what happened earlier.

> Listen, dear friend!
> The highest heaven itself
> would be a reward too small for mother.
> One morning, I fetched the gloriosa tuber
> washed down by the fragrant stream
> fed by the rain on his hill.
> I kissed the tender leaves repeatedly
> so that they withered.
> Then I planted it at home.
> She breathed not a word.[161]

The gloriosa plant that grew from the tuber and the care that she showered on it helped her face her loneliness. The fondling of the tuber and kissing it show that her calm is not one of indifference or due to a lack of passion. In Tamil poetry, such solace and consolation seem necessary only in the section that deals with clandestine love, for after marriage, the home provides the necessary comfort.

In Sanskrit literature, however, this is found in the *Meghadūtam* where the lover is separated by circumstances beyond his control. The Yakṣa , sent far away from Alakā by Kubera's curse is in no position to see anything in Alakā or the mount on which it stands. So he embraces the breeze that blows southwards from the Himalayas, in the hope that it would have touched his beloved's body.[162]

REFERENCES

1. *Cilap.* 7, v. 33.
2. *Vikr.* act 3 v. 6.
3. *Cilap,* 5:1-6.
4. *Ibid.,* 4:5-6.
5. *Puram,* 365.
6. *Ciru,* 1-6.

7. *Avim,* act 2 v. 13.
8. *Megh,* P. 18.
9. *Ragh,* 4:51-52.
10. *Akam,* 60:7.
11. *Ibid.,* 10:13.
12. *Ibid.,* 44:18.
13. *Ibid.,* 46:14.
14. *Mani,* 5:109-22.
15. *Megh,* P. 66.
16. *Megh,* U. 55.
17. *Megh,* P. 25.
18. *Ibid.,* 29.
19. *Ibid.,* 29.
20. *Ibid.,* 43, 44.
21. *Pari,* 11:40-44.
22. *Cilap,* 13:151-70.
23. *Ibid.,* 7:v. 2, 3, 4.
24. *Ibid.,* 7:v. 2, 3, 4.
25. *Mani, Patikam* 22-25.
26. *Ibid.,* 3:55.
27. *Megh,* P. 41.
28. *Kali,* 71:1-9.
29. *Matu,* 70-72.
30. *Ciru,* 72-73.
31. *Kali,* 73:3-5.
32. *Mani,* 4:15-16.
33. *Budd,* 4:36.
34. *Saun,* 4:21.
35. *Kuma,* 7:16.
36. *Ibid.,* 1:43.
37. *Kurun,* 315; also *Akam,* 336:18.
38. *Abhi,* act 1, pp. 21-23.
39. *Kuma,* 3:39.
40. *Ragh,* 7:21.
41. *Aink,* 400:1-3.
42. *Pari,* 21:59-63.
43. *Akam,* 19:16.
44. *Kali,* 132:18.
45. *Ibid.,* 62:4-5 also 92:1.
46. *Pari,* 20:94.
47. *Kali,* 88:1.
48. *Pari,* 19:95.
49. *Cilap,* 3:157.
50. *Ibid.,* 3:166.
51. *Ibid.,* 11:109.
52. *Ibid.,* 11:121.
53. *Avim,* act 3 v. 19.
54. *Kuma,* 4:31.

55. *Ragh*, 8:47.
56. *Ibid.*, 8:72.
57. *Abhi*, act 4 v. 15; *Vikr.* act 4 v. 20.
58. *Abhi*, act 3 vv. 23ff.
59. *Megh*, P. 23.
60. *Mala*, act 5 v. 9.
61. *Aink*, 381; *Kurun*, 57; *Pari*, 8:44.
62. *Rtu*, 4:18, 5:1.
63. *Nar*, 152, 338; *Akam*, 50.
64. *Kurun*, 160, 177.
65. *Nar*, 218; also *Mani*, 260.
66. *Nar*, 152.
67. *Akam*, 270:7-15.
68. *Kurinji*, 219; *Mani*, 5:126-27.
69. *Akam*, 4:10-12; *Kuma*. 3:36; *Svap*. act 4 v. 3.
70. M. Varadarajan, *The Treatment of Nature in Sangam Literature*, Madras, 1957, p. 63.
71. T.P. Meenakshisundaram, Tolkappiyar's Literary Theory in *Proceedings of the First International Conference Seminar of Tamil Studies*, vol. II, Kuala Lumpur, 1969, p. 6.
72. *Abhi*, act 5 v. 1.
73. *Aink*, 90.
74. *Nar*, 290:6-9.
75. *Cilap*, 14:162-63.
76. *Mani*, 18:59-60.
77. *Ibid.*, 18:15-20. 109.
78. *Akam*, 46.
79. *Tol. Porul*, 238.
80. *Ibid.*, 49.
81. Naccinarkiniyar, *Tolkāppiyam: Poruḷatikāram*, Madras, 1963, p. 114.
82. *Tol. Porul*, 50, 51.
83. Naccinarkiniyar, *Tolkāppiyam: Poruḷatikāram*, p. 110.
84. *Kali*, 45:1-7.
85. Daniel H. H. Ingalls, *Sanskrit Poetry*, Harvard University Press, 1968, p. 2.
86. *Abhi*, act 3. p. 88.
87. *Kurun*, 18.
88. *Ibid.*, 113.
89. *Akam*, 18.
90. *Saun*, 7:3 and 4.
91. *Abhi*, act 1 v. 33.
92. *Ibid.*, act 2 v. 6.
93. *Kurun*, 85.
94. *Mala*, act 3 v. 4. p. 55.
95. *Ibid.*, act 3 p. 60.
96. *Kurun*, 126.
97. *Kali*, 92.
98. *Nar*, 243.
99. *Kurun*, 163.

100. *Nar*, 181: 1-8.
101. *Ibid.*, 376.
102. *Ibid.*, 83.
103. *Aink*, 391.
104. *Kali*, 129.
105. *Kurun*, 107.
106. *Ibid.*, 2.
107. *Akam*, 383.
108. *Aink*, 420.
109. *Akam*, 389.
110. *Kurun*, 163; *Kali*, 129.
111. *Kurun*, 158, 270; *Nar*, 139, 235; *Akam*, 188.
112. *Kurun*, 235; *Nar*, 193; *Akam*, 125, 163.
113. *Kurun*, 47; *Nar*, 196.
114. *Aink*, 183.
115. *Kurun*, 2.
116. *Nar*, 251.
117. *Kurun*, 47.
118. *Akam*, 188.
119. *Nar*, 376.
120. *Ibid.*, 83.
121. *Nar*, 376:4-12.
122. *TTP*, pp. 53-56.
123. *Abhi*, act 1. pp. 16-22.
124. *Ibid.*, act 3. pp. 70-74.
125. *Vikr*, act 3. pp. 80-92.
126. *Mala*, act 3 and 4. pp. 70-78.
127. *Kurun*, 270.
128. *Nar*, 139.
129. *Ibid.*, 238.
130. *Ibid.*, 248.
131. *Vikr*, act 4 v. 3.
132. *Akam*, 21:9.
133. *Ibid.*, 3:11-18.
134. *Ibid.*, 51:8-14.
135. *Ibid.*, 33:18-20.
136. *Ibid.*, 79.
137. *Ibid.*, 93.
138. *Aink*, 323.
139. *Avim*, act 4 v. 1.
140. *Akam*, 7.
141. *Aink*, 391.
142. *Nar*, 196.
143. *Vikr*, act 4 v. 15.
144. *Aink*, 384, 385, 478, 479.
145. *Nar*, 102.
146. *Ibid.*, 54, 70.
147. *Ibid.*, 277; *Kurun*, 392.

148. *Akam*, 170.
149. *Nar*, 102:1-4.
150. *Ibid.*, 70:1-6.
151. *Akam*, 170:1-8.
152. *Megh*, p. 6.
153. *Ibid.*, 7.
154. *Nar*, 102:5-7.
155. *Ibid.*, 102:7-9.
156. *Akam*, 170:8-14.
157. *Megh*, U. 51.
158. *Nar*, 277:1-4.
159. *Kurun*, 249.
160. *Akam*, 278:10-24.
161. *Kurun*, 361.
162. *Megh*, U. 47.

Conclusion

A study of the characters found in the treatment of love in Tamil and Sanskrit classical literature shows that in spite of the fundamental difference in the basis of social stratification, the idea that heroes and heroines are to be from the upper strata of society is common to both. Though love is accepted as a universal emotion that can rise in the heart of a prince or a peasant, the manner of expression and the conventions involved, suggest a certain level of culture, sense of propriety and sophistication. The kind of love depicted in these literatures presupposes a certain amount of leisure and freedom which is rarely, if ever, enjoyed by the others. Besides, the few poems in the *Kalittokai* which depict the love between those who do not belong to this section of society, show clearly the difference in the knowledge and practice of conventions regarding love. The language lacks finesse for while the heroines in Sanskrit and Tamil usually refer to the hero with such respect and hardly speak freely in his presence, the women in these poems are depicted as conversing directly with the men and using terms like *ellā* and *nāṇili* to address the hero.*

There is also noticeable, a considerable amount of mutual influence between these literatures, in the stratification and use of these characters. The Tamil poems that had, in the Caṅkam period, mentioned heroes as chieftains of the respective land divisions only (as *veṟpaṉ, nāṭaṉ, cērppaṉ,* and *ūraṉ*) though with a number of dependants like the charioteer (*pākaṉ*) and the musician (*pāṇaṉ*), use their caste divisions in the two epics. It is most clear in the *Cilappatikāram* where Kōvalaṉ is mentioned as the son of a rich trader. This may suggest the development of city life in South India which enabled people to amass wealth through overland or maritime trade, but certainly does not follow the

---

* *Kali*, 113:11, 116:17.

tradition of classifying a hero from the city as *ūraṉ*, especially when his behaviour is in keeping which the chieftains or heroes depicted in the *marutam* poems. The comfortable life of Kōvalaṉ and his penchant for music and dance depict him more as a *nāgaraka*, the central character of Sanskrit classical literature. In the *Maṇimēkalai* too, Utayakumaraṉ's royal position is never forgotten. Besides, the convention of anonymous heroes and heroines, which is considered important in love poetry, has given way to the heroes being named and a number of personal details furnished. This is inevitable when the very form and length of Tamil poems are changed so that lyric poetry gradually developed into narrative epic poetry.

In Sanskrit literature, however, there is a different kind of change, with the composition of lyric poetry. The finest specimen of such poetry in Sanskrit is the *Meghadūtam* which contains a number of characteristics found in the Caṅkam poems. It has as its hero a *yakṣa* and this term denotes a class of semi-divine beings just as terms like *kuṟavaṉ* or *iṭaiyaṉ* in Tamil refer to a class of people. There is no name mentioned and no personal details given except that he is in the service of his king Kubera and is exiled for a year. His original place of residence to which he would return is Alakā. Except for such contextual information, which for the Tamil poems are found usually in the colophons, we have nothing to form a story. Like Caṅkam poems, it is a monologue expressing his sorrow and his message to his beloved who is not mentioned by name. We are not even told if they are married but the descriptions and the season suggest a situation very similar to the *mullai* poems in Tamil. Though the cause of separation is different in the *Meghadūtam*, the idea that the rainy season is the time of year when lovers or husbands who are away from home return to their beloveds is the underlying concept that enhances the pathos of the *yakṣa* who cannot return home like the others. Even the *yakṣī* is pictured as waiting for him like the *mullai* heroines, chaste in thought and deed, but sad and desolate because the rainy season would pass without the union that it should normally bring for parted lovers. The *Ṛtusaṃhāram*, though of a descriptive nature, also mentions no names. The verses are supposed to be what a lover or hero tells his beloved and this is suggested by terms of address like 'beloved' (*priye*) and 'lady with beautiful thighs' (*varoru*). Such general names for the listener and no name at all for the speaker gives no indication as to who the speaker or listener is or to their social or marital status. The description, depicting a strata of society that can afford to indulge in the pleasures of the wealthy, suggests that they too belong to the section of society from which heroes and heroines are usually chosen.

Among the other characters, the *tōḻi* or the heroine's friend is the most important from the point of view of the heroine's love affair. But in the Sanskrit dramas, the *vidūṣaka* is more important, though in the epics, both these characters are not important. Only the *Buddhacaritam* uses a friend of brāhmaṇa lineage. In the Caṅkam poems, the mother or the foster-mother is often mentioned and is important but in the Tamil and Sanskrit epics as well as in the dramas the mother is not an important character. Another important factor is the position of 'the other woman'. In Tamil literature, she is invariably called *parattai* and the highest position she can achieve is that of a *kāmakkiḻatti* (mistress or kept woman) but she never attains the position of wife or *talaivi*. In Sanskrit literature, the heroine is not necessarily the wife or would-be-wife of the hero. In fact she can be an 'other woman' or even a *gaṇikā* who later becomes a co-wife (e.g. Mālavikā, Śakuntalā, Vasantasenā, Urvaśī). In Tamil literature, we see a gradual change in the position awarded to the other woman, for the *Cilappatikāram* treats with dignity, though not as a heroine in the strict sense, Mātavi who is a *gaṇikā* and the epic *Maṇimēkalai* has for its heroine a *gaṇikā* who had become a Buddhist nun. Both these characters are made to condemn verbally or actually go against the social code. Mātavi becomes a Buddhist nun and being ashamed of her caste, refers to her daughter Maṇimēkalai as the daughter of Kaṇṇaki. To make sure that the evil of prostitution is not perpetuated in her family, she initiates Maṇimēkalai into the Buddhist faith and makes her also a nun. In the earliest Tamil literature no other woman in the hero's life is given the kind of importance and respect as the *talaivi* who is invariably the heroine.

Both literatures use nature as a setting for human emotion and the various seasons or time of day make it possible for the poets to choose the softer and sterner aspects of nature to suit the emotion depicted, to contrast her with the moods of the hero or heroine in love or merely to express the emotion with more depth.

Yet there is difference in the manner in which nature is used. In Caṅkam poetry, nature is treated as two of the aspects (*mutal poruḷ* and *karupporuḷ)* of love poetry, the third being love (*uripporuḷ*). In these poems, nature is described in minute detail, and the picture painted is always simple but true and realistic. It is never out of the ordinary for it is used with a specific purpose, and descriptions are not important for their own sake. In the Tamil *kāvyas* and Sanskrit literature under study, descriptions are important and the length of the works make lengthy descriptions possible and even necessary. These descriptions are often fanciful involving personifications and many details, but not always realistic or true. The most important use of nature is for suggestion of some idea or feeling and it is most important not only as the exposition of poetic art but also as a means of conveying or implying something, especially when it is not too decent, with art and finesse as in *uḷḷuṟai, iṟaicci, atiśyokti* and *dhvani*. The study of the literature of this period shows that the technique of suggestion was originally found in Tamil literature with specific conventions regarding its use. It entered Sanskrit literature sometime before Kālidāsa for we have very clear examples of the use of *atiśyokti* and *dhvani* in his works. It was only centuries later that it came to be developed as an aspect of Sanskrit poetics. On the other hand, Tamil literature began to use nature and descriptions of nature as an adornment (*alaṁkāra*) for poetry without always necessarily implying something. Some idylls from the *Pattuppāṭṭu* and both the epics abound in such descriptions which are pleasing and pretty but not altogether necessary for the narrative or depiction of an emotion or character. The *Cilappatikāram* is the finest example of the use of such descriptions, and the graces of a *kāvya* together with the conventions of earlier Tamil literature. The two Tamil epics do not use the conventions regarding the use of nature like land divisions, seasons or time of day. In the *Cilappatikāram* land divisions become part of the descriptions of life among various communities the hero and heroine meet on their journey and the seasons form part of the description of the life of the harlots in Maturai. They are not important in the depiction of Kōvalaṉ's or Kaṇṇaki's feelings. The epics begin to mention the evening and the spring season in particular as time and season that enhance love and aggravate the feeling of loneliness in those who are separated. The moon which does not play an important role as an exciter of passion in Tamil literature takes a prominent place, together with evening or sunset. The *Maṇimēkalai* uses the form and descriptions of a *kāvya* to expound religious teachings, especially Buddhist ideas, and in this aspect is comparable to the *kāvyas* of Aśvaghoṣa.

Bibliography*

Aggarwal, H.R. *A Short History of Sanskrit Literature*, Delhi, 1963.

Amarasimha. *Amarakośa*, with the commentary of Ācārya Kṛṣṇamitra, Ed. by Satya Deva Mishra, Varanasi, 1972.

Apte, M.V. The Flora in Kālidāsa's Literature, *Annals of the Bhandarkar Oriental Research Institute*, Vol. 32, 1952, pp. 76-84.

Arunachalam, P. *Cilappatikārac Cintaṉai* (T), Madras, 1971.

———. Puṟanāṉūṟṟup Pāṭalkaḷil Akam, *Pulamai*, Vol. 1, No. 3, Madras, 1977, pp. 82-94.

———. *Tolkāppiyar* (T), Madras, 1975.

Ashar, J.M. *Kumārasaṃbhavam*, I-IV of Kālidāsa , Bhavnagar, 1950.

Aśvaghoṣa. *Buddhacaritam*, Ed. by Edward B. Cowell (The Buddha-carita or Life of Buddha by Asvaghosha), Amsterdam, 1970.

———. *Saundara-nandam Kavyam*, Calcutta, 1910.

Belvalkai, S.K. (Ed.) *The Abhijñānaśākuntalam of Kālidāsa*, New Delhi, 1965.

Bhandare, L.S. *Imagery of Kālidāsa*, Bombay, 1968.

Bhat, G.K. The Problem of the Mahābhārata Plays of Bhāsa, *Annals of the Bhandarkar Oriental Research Institute*, Vol. 35, 1954, pp. 73-83.

———. *Tragedy and Sanskrit Drama*, Bombay, 1974.

Bhattacharya, Asoke Kumar. A Comparative Study of Bhāsa and Kālidāsa, *Indian Culture*, Vol. VI, No. 1, 1939, pp. 83-93.

Bhattacharya, Biswanath. *Sanskrit Drama and Dramaturgy*, Varanasi, 1974.

*An asterisk before the name of the book indicates that of the various editions or translations of the same book given, that particular edition or translation was followed for reference.

Biese, Alfred. *The Development of the Feeling for Nature*, New York, Originally published London, 1905.

Bowra, C.M. *The Greek Experience*, London, 1961.

Brahmam, K.S.N. The Date of Kalidasa, *Sri Venkateswara University Oriental Journal*, Tirupati, Vol. 1, 1958, pp. 75-88.

Cami, P. L. *Caṅka Ilakkiyattil Ceṭi Koṭi Viḷakkam* (T), Madras, 1967.

Campasivam, C. *Tamil̲ Ilakkiyattil Neytal Tiṇai* (T), Madurai, 1964.

Chelvanayagam, V. *Tamil̲ Ilakkiya Varalāṟu* (T), Jaffna, 1965 (4th Edn.).

———. Tradition in Early Tamil Poetry, *Proceedings of the Second International Conference Seminar of Tamil Studies 1968*, Vol. II, Madras, 1971, pp. 3-8.

Comacuntaranar, P. V. *Paripāṭal* (in 2 vols.), Madras, 1957.

Cowell, Edward, B. *The Buddha-Carita* or Life of Buddha by Asvaghosha, Amsterdam, 1970.

Das, Abhinna Chandra. (Tr.) *Ṛtusaṃhāra of Kālidāsa*, Varanasi, 1958.

Dasgupta, S.N. (Ed.) *A History of Sanskrit Literature: Classical Period*, Vol. I, Calcutta, 1962.

De, S.K. *Ancient Indian Erotics and Erotic Literature*, Calcutta, 1959.

———. Some Commentators on the Meghaduta, *Annals of Oriental Research, University of Madras*, Vol. 13, Pt. 1, 1957, pp. 49-64.

*Devadhar, C.R. (Ed.) *Dramas of Kālidāsa*, Delhi, 1966.

Dhandayudham, R. *Caṅka Ilakkiyam* (T), 2 Vols., Madras, 1978.

Dikshitar, V.R. Ramachandra (Tr.) *The Śilappadikāram*, Madras, (O.U.P.) 1939.

Dikshit, Ratnamayidevi. *Women in Sanskrit Dramas*, Delhi, 1964.

Dimock (Jr.), Edward C. (Ed.) *The Literatures of India. An Introduction*, Chicago and London, 1974.

Dorairangaswamy, M.A. A Note on KurinjippaaTTu (Kuṟiñcippāṭṭu) *Proceedings of the Second International Conference Seminar of Tamil Studies 1968*, Vol. II, Madras, 1971, pp. 9-18.

Emeneau, M.B. Kālidāsa's Śakuntalā and the Mahābhārata, *Journal of the American Oriental Society*, Vol. 82, No. 1, 1962, pp. 41-44.

Franklin & Eleanor Edgerton. *The Cloud Messenger,* The University of Michigan Press, 1964.

Gajendragadkar, A.B. *The Abhijñānaśākuntala of Kālidāsa,* Surat, (6th Edn.) - no date

Ghose, Aurobindo. *Ḳālidāsa,* Pondicherry, (First Pub.), 1929.

———. *Kālidāsa,* (Second Series), Pondicherry, 1954.

*Ghosh, Manomohan. *The Nāṭyaśāstra,* 2 vols., Calcutta, Vol. 1, 1950. Vol. 2, 1961.

Gnanasambanthan, A.S. *Akamum Puṟamum,* (Akam) (T), Madras, 1956.

Goldstucker, Theodore. *Sanskrit and Culture,* Calcutta, 1955.

Gonda, J. *Aspects of Early Viṣṇuism,* Delhi, 1969.

Gupta, Shankar Sen. (Ed.) *Tree Symbol Worship in India,* Calcutta, 1965.

Hart, George L. III. Common Elements Between Early Tamil and Indo-Aryan Literature, *Proceedings of the Second Conference Seminar of Tamil Studies 1968,* Vol. II, Madras, 1971, pp. 168-70.

———. *Poets of the Tamil Anthologies,* Princeton, New Jersey, 1979.

———. The Monsoon in Ancient Tamil and Indo-Aryan Poetry, *Proceedings of the Second Conference Seminar of Tamil Studies, 1968,* Vol. II, Madras, 1971, pp. 162-67.

———. *The Poems of Ancient Tamil: Their Milieu and Their Sanskrit Counter-parts,* University of California Press, 1975.

———. *The Relation Between Tamil and Classical Sanskrit Literature,* Wiesbaden, 1976.

———. Women and the Sacred in Ancient Tamilnad, *The Journal of Asian Studies,* Vol. 93, No. 2, 1973, pp. 233-50.

Hatto, Arthur T. (Ed.) *Eos, An Enquiry into the Theme of Lover's Meetings and Partings at Dawn in Poetry,* London, The Hague, Paris, 1965.

Herford, C.H. *Shakespeare's Treatment of Love and Marriage and other Essays,* London, 1921.

Ilakkuvanar. *Tolkāppiya Ārāycci* (T), Pudukkottai, 1961.

*Ilampuranar (Com.) *Tolkāppiyam: Poruḷatikāram* (T), Madras, 2nd Edn., 1956.

Indra. *The Status of Women in Ancient India,* Banaras, 1955.

Ingalls, Daniel H.H. (Tr.) *Sanskrit Poetry* (from Vidyakara's 'Treasury'), Harvard University Press, 1968.

———. Words for Beauty in Classical Sanskrit Poetry, *Indological Studies in Honour of W. Norman Brown*, New Haven, Connecticut 1962, pp. 87-107.

Jash, Pranabananda. Ancient Indian Spring Festival, *Vishveshvaranand Indological Journal*, Panjab University, Vol. 10, 1972, pp. 102-11.

Jesudasan, C. and H. *A History of Tamil Literature*, Calcutta, 1961.

Jhala, G.C. *Kālidāsa—A Study*, Bombay, 1949.

*Johnston, E.H. *The Saundarananda of Aśvaghoṣa*, Motilal Banarsidass, First Edn., 1928, Reprinted, Delhi, 1975.

Kailasapathy, K. *Ilakkiyamum Tiṟaṉāyvum* (T), Jaffna, 1972.

———. *Oppiyal Ilakkiyam* (T), Madras, 1969.

———. *Tamil Heroic Poetry*, Oxford, 1968.

Kale, M.R. *The Abhijñānaśākuntalam of Kālidāsa*, Bombay, 1957.

*———. *The Kumārasaṃbhava of Kālidāsa*, Motilal Banarsidass, 1967 (6th Edn.).

*———. *The Meghadūta of Kālidāsa*, Motilal Banarsidass, 1969 (7th Edn.)

*———. *The Ṛtusamhāra of Kālidāsa*, Motilal Banarsidass, 1967 (2nd Edn.).

———. *Svapnavāsavadatta of Bhāsa*, Bombay, 5th Edn., 1961.

———. *The Vikramorvaśīyam of Kālidāsa*, Bombay, 1932.

Kane, P. V. *History of Sanskrit Poetics*, Delhi, 1971 (4th Edn.).

Karamarkar, R.D. *Kālidāsa*, Dharwar, 1960.

Keith, A.B. *A History of Sanskrit Literature*, London, 1920.

———. *Sanskrit Drama*, London, 1942.

Kesavan, M.S. Ilakkiyaṅkaḷil Akapporuḷ (T), *Sri Venkateswara University Oriental Journal*, Tirupati, Vol. 1, 1958, pp. 1-12.

Kulshreshtha, R.B. Svapnavāsavadatta: A Study in Mythological Symbolism, *Vishveshvaranand Indological Journal*, Panjab University, Vol. 8, 1970, pp. 109-15.

———. Svapnavāsavadatta—A Study in the Subconscious, *Vishveshvaranand Indological Journal*, Panjab University, Vol. 5, 1968, pp. 63-70.

Kunbae, Bak. *Avimāraka and Bālacarita*, Delhi, 1968.

Kunhan Raja, C. Notes on Kālidāsa, *Annals of Oriental Research*, University of Madras, Vol. 6, Pt. 1, 1941-42, pp. 1-32.

———. Studies in Kālidāsa, *Annals of Oriental Research*, University of Madras, Vol. 5, Pt. 2, 1941, pp. 17-40.

———. *Survey of Sanskrit Literature*, Bombay, 1962.

———. The Hero in the Mālavikāgnimitra, *Annals of the Bhandarkar Oriental Research Institute*, Vol. 23, 1942, pp. 369-78.

Kunjunni Raja, K. *Indian Theories of Meaning*, Madras, 1963.

Lienhard, Siegfried. Akapporul and Sanskrit Muktaka Poetry, *Proceedings of the Third International Conference Seminar of Tamil Studies Paris 1970*, Pondicherry, 1973, pp. 111-18.

———. Pālai Poems in Sanskrit and Prākrit, *Nilakanda Shastri Felicitation Volume*, Madras, 1971, pp. 416-22.

Macdonell, A.A. *A History of Sanskrit Literature*, Delhi, 1972.

Mahadevan, K. *Oppilakkiya Nōkkil Caṅka Kālam* (T), Madurai, 1975.

Mainkar, T.G. *Kālidāsa: His Art and Thoughts*, Poona, 1962.

Malaviya, Debi Prasad. *Nalopākhyāna*, Allahabad, 1958.

Manickam, V.Sp. *The Tamil Concept of Love*, Madras, 1962.

———. *Tamiḻk Kātal* (T), Madras, 1962.

*Masson, J. (Tr.) *Avimāraka*, Delhi, 1970.

Meenakshisundaram, T.P. *A History of Tamil Literature*, Annamalainagar, 1965.

———. *Collected Papers*, Annamalainagar, 1961.

———. *Mullaippāṭṭu*, Bombay, 1958.

———. Tolkappiyar's Literary Theory, *Proceedings of the First International Conference Seminar of Tamil Studies*, Kuala Lumpur, 1969, Vol. II, pp. 3-9.

———. *Vaḷḷuvar Kaṇṭa Nāṭum Kāmamum* (T), Madras, 2nd Edn., 1957.

Mirashi, Vasudev Vishnu & Navlekar, Narayan Raghunath, *Kālidāsa: Date, Life and Works*, Bombay, 1969.

Mirashi, V.V. *Studies in Indology*, Vol. IV, Varanasi, 1966.

Misra, Vidya Niwas. The Mango-Blossom Imagery in Kālidāsa, *Journal of the American Oriental Society*, Vol. 82, No. 1, 1962, pp. 68-69.

Monier-Williams, Monier (Tr.) *Sakoontala or the Lost Ring*, London, 1898 (8th Edn.)

Muller, F. Max (Ed.) *Sacred Books of the East*, Vol. 2, 1896.

———. *Sacred Books of the East*, Vol. 12, O.U.P., 1882, Reprinted 1963.

———. *Sacred Books of the East*, Vol. 25, O.U.P. 1886, Reprinted 1967.

———. *Sacred Books of the East*, Vol. 26, O.U.P., 1885, Reprinted 1963.

*———. *The Sacred Books of the East*, Vol. 49, Pt. I, O.U.P., 1891, Impression of 1927.

Muthukumaran, Pon. Raghuvaṃsam, *Ganeshaiyer Souvenir*, Īḻakēcarip Ponniah Ninaivu Veḷiyīṭṭu Maṉṟam, Jaffna, 1960, pp. 316-21.

*Nacciṉārkiṉiyar (Com). *Kalittokai*, Madras, 1967.

———. *Tolkāppiyam Poruḷatikāram*, (Akattiṇaiyiyal and Puṟattiṇaiyiyal), Madras, Reprint of 2nd Edn., 1963.

Nacciyappan, C.N. *Kōvalaṉ Mātavipāl Maṉamiḷantatu Ēṉ?* Karaikkudi, 1961.

Nadarajah D. *Women in Tamil Society: Classical Period*, Kuala Lumpur, 1969.

*Nandargikar, Gopal Raghunath. *The Raghuvaṃśa of Kālidāsa*, Motilal Banarsidass, 1971 (4th Edn.).

*Narayanacami Iyer, A. *Naṟṟiṇai*, Madras, 1956.

Naravane, V.S. *The Elephant and the Lotus*, Bombay, 1965.

Nathan, Leonard, (Tr.) *The Transport of Love: The Meghadūta of Kalidasa*, University of California, Berkeley, 1976.

Parimelalakar (Com.) *Tirukkuṟaḷ*, Madras, 1956.

Periakaruppan, RM. *Caṅka Ilakkiya Oppīṭu: Ilakkiyak Koḷkaikaḷ* (T), Madurai, 1975.

Pillay, K.K. Aryan Influence in Tamilakam during the Sangam Epoch, *Proceedings of the First International Conference Seminar of Tamil Studies*, Vol. I, Kuala Lumpur, 1968, pp. 271-79.

Pillai, S.K. (Publisher). *The Ancient Tamils as depicted in Tholkappiyam Poruladiharam*, Pt. I, Madras, 1934.

Pisharoti, K.R. Sex-Life in Ancient India: Some Thoughts, *Annals of the Bhandarkar Oriental Research Institute*, Vol. 23, 1942, pp. 336-41.

Princeton Encyclopaedea of Poetry and Poetics, Princeton, 1974.

Pusalker, A.D. *Bhāsa—A Study*, Delhi, 1940, 2nd Edn., 1968.

Radhakrishnan, R. and Others (Ed.) *Paralkaḷ—3* (T), Muttu Patippakam, Madurai, 1978.

Raghavan, V. *Love in the Poems and Plays of Kālidāsa*, Bangalore, 1955.

———. Raghuvaṃśa, XII 21, *Annals of Oriental Research*, University of Madras, Vol. 13, 1957, Centenary Volume, pp. 82-85.

———. *Sanskrit Literature*, Delhi, 1961.

———. Women Characters in Kālidāsa's Dramas, *Annals of Oriental Research*, University of Madras, Vol. IV, Pt. 2, 1939-40, pp. 1-32.

Raghavan, V. and Nagendra (Ed.) *An Introduction to Indian Poetics*, Madras, 1970.

Raghunathan, N. *Six Long Poems from Sangam Tamil*, Madras, 1978.

Rajagopalan, N.V. Influence of Tholkaapiyam and Akapporull in Sanskrit Poetics, *Proceedings of the Second International Conference Seminar of Tamil Studies*, Madras, 1968, Vol. II, pp. 171-78.

Rajamanikkam, M. Caṅka-kālattiṟ kātal (T), *Ganeshaiyer Souvenir*, Īḷakēcarip Ponniah Niṉaivu Veḷiyīṭṭu Maṉṟam, Jaffna, 1960, pp. 163-67.

———. *Pattuppāṭṭu Ārāycci* (T), Madras, 1971.

———. *Kāla Ārāycci* (T), Madras, 1957.

———. *Tamiḻ Moḻi-Ilakkiya Varalāṟu* (T), Madras, 1971, (3rd Edn.).

———. The Date of Tholkaappiyam, *Annals of Oriental Research*, University of Madras, Vol. 19, Pt. 2, 1964, pp. 1-17.

Ramakrishnan, S. *Iḷaṅkōviṉ Pāttirap Paṭaippu* (T), Madurai, 1964.

Ray, Kumudaranjan. *Bhasa's Charudattam*, Calcutta, ?

Reddiar, N. Subbu. Highlights of Tamil Cultural Influence Abroad in the Classical Period, *Sri Venkateswara University Oriental Journal*, Tirupati, Vol. 8, 1965, pp. 73-80.

Roychowdhury, Krishna Chandra. Kālidāsa's Imagery in Meghadūta, *Indian Literature*, Volume 19, No. 1, New Delhi, 1976, pp. 92-118.

Ruben, Walter. *Kālidāsa*, Berlin, 1957.

Ryder, Arthur, W. *Kālidāsa*, Translations of Shakuntala and other works, London.

Sabnis, S.A. *Kālidāsa: His Style and His Times*, Bombay, 1966.

Sambamoorthy, Lalita. 'A Study of Imagery Relating to Colours in the Anthology of Kuṟuntokai—Classical Period', University of Malaya, Kuala Lumpur (Unpublished thesis).

———. The Psychological Symbolism of Paalai in Kutunhthokai (Kuṟuntokai), *Proceedings of the Second Conference Seminar of Tamil Studies 1968*, Madras, Vol. II, pp. 25-33.

Samy, P. L. *Caṅka Ilakkiyattil Vilaṅkiṉa Viḷakkam* (T), Madras,

1970.

Sanjeevi, N. Geography—A Prime Factor in Ancient Tamil Poetry, *Annals of Oriental Research*, University of Madras, Vol. 22, Pt. 2, pp. 1-6, 1969.

Santhanam, K. (Ed.) *An Anthology of Indian Literatures*, Bombay, 1969.

Saradaranjan Ray. *Kālidāsa's Abhijñāna-Śākuntalam*, Calcutta, 1953.

Sarma, Dimbeswar. *An Interpretative Study of Kālidāsa*, Calcutta, 1968.

Sastri, K.S. Ramaswami. *Kālidāsa: His Period, Personality and Poetry*, Srirangam, 1933.

Sastri, Sankara Rama, C. *Mālavikāgnimitra of Kālidāsa*, Madras, 1944.

Sastri, Vyakaranacarya Satyavrat. *Essays on Indology*, Delhi, 1963.

Seenivasan, A. *Kuriñci* (T), Madurai, 1977.

———. *Mullai* (T), Madurai, 1977.

Sehgal, S.R. *Kālidāsa's Kumārasaṃbhavam*, Delhi, 1966.

Selvanayagam, S. The Regional Concept in Geography and the Classification of Land in the Ancient Tamil Country, *Proceedings of the Second International Conference Seminar of Tamil Studies*, Madras, 1968, Vol. II, pp. 219-25.

Sethu Pillai, R.P. Neyhtal or the Coastal Region, *Annals of Oriental Research*, University of Madras, Vol. 16, Pt. 1, 1961, pp. 1-3.

Shairp, J.C. *Poetic Interpretation of Nature*, New York, 1877.

Sharma, D. Dutt. Supernatural Element in Kālidāsa, *Sri Venkateswara University Oriental Journal*, Tirupati, Vol. 9, 1966, pp. 83-91.

Sharma, P. P. The Principle of Suggestion in Sanskrit Poetics, *Indian Literature*, Vol. 19, No. 1, New Delhi, 1976, pp. 114-19.

Shastri, Surendra Nath. *The Laws and Practice of Sanskrit Drama*, Vol. I, Varanasi, 1961.

Singaravelanar, S. Nallaranum Narriṇaiyum (T), *Ganeshaiyer Souvenir*, Īḷakēcarip Ponniah Niṉaivu Veḷiyīṭṭu Maṉram, Jaffna, 1960, pp. 122-34.

Sivaraja Pillai, K.N. *The Chronology of the Early Tamils*, Madras, 1932.

Sivathamby, K. Economic Activities and Conduct-code Ascribed to Mullai Tiṇai, *Proceedings of the First International Conference Seminar of Tamil Studies,* Vol. I, Kuala Lumpur, 1968, pp. 320-31.

Sockalingam, T.A. Iḷaṅkō Pukuttiya Putumai (T) *Proceedings of the First International Conference Seminar of Tamil Studies 1968,* Madras, 1971, Vol. III, pp. 81-85.

Somasundaram Pillai, J.M. *A History of Tamil Literature,* with texts and translations, Annamalainagar, 1968.

Soutar, George. *Nature in Greek Poetry,* London, 1939.

Stein, Burton (Ed.) *Essays on South India,* Honolulu, 1975.

Stobart, J.C. *The Glory that was Greece,* London, 1933.

Subbu Reddiar, N. *Kavitaiyaṉupavam* (T), Madras, 1961.

Subramaniya Acariyar, V.S. *Cilappatikāra Ārāycci* (T), Madras, 1947.

Subramaniam, V.I. The Dating of Sangam Literature, *Proceedings of the Third International Conference Seminar of Tamil Studies,* Paris, 1970, Pondicherry, 1973, pp. 75-80.

Subramanian, N. The Avifauna of the Tamil Country, *Tamil Culture,* Vol. XII, No. 4, Madras, 1966, pp. 259-68 and supplement pp. 1-16.

Sundaramoorthy, G. *Early Literary Theories in Tamil,* (in comparison with Sanskrit theories), Madurai, 1974.

Surya Kanta Sastri. *Kālidāsa's Vision of Kumārasaṃbhava,* Delhi, 1963.

Suryakanta (Ed.) *The Kumārasaṃbhava of Kālidāsa,* New Delhi, 1962.

*Swaminathaiyar, V. (Ed.) *Aiṅkuṟunūṟu,* Madras, 5th Edn., 1957.

*———. *Cilappatikāram,* Madras, 1960.

*———. *Kuṟuntokai,* Madras, 1962.

*———. *Maṇimēkalai,* Madras, 5th Edn., 1956.

*———. *Paripāṭal,* Madras, 1956.

*———. *Pattuppāṭṭu,* Madras, 5th Edn., 1956.

*———. *Puṟanāṉūṟu,* Madras, 5th Edn., 1956.

Tambimuttu, T. *India Love Poems,* New York, 1954.

Tamil Lexicon, Madras, 1924-34.

Taranibaskar, Mrs. Cilampil Irucuṭar (T), *Proceedings of the First International Conference Seminar of Tamil Studies 1968,* Madras, 1971, Vol. III, pp. 86-94.

Thaninayagam, X.S. Caṅka Ilakkiyattiṉ Ciṟappu (T), *Ganeshaiyer Souvenir,* Īḻakēcarip Ponniah Niṉaivu Veḷiyīṭṭu Maṉṟam, to Mullai Tiṇai, *Proceedings of the First International Conference Seminar of Tamil Studies*, Vol. I, Kuala Lumpur, 1968, pp. 320-31.

Sockalingam, T.A. Iḷaṅkō Pukuttiya Putumai (T) *Proceedings of the First International Conference Seminar of Tamil Studies 1968*, Madras, 1971, Vol. III, pp. 81-85.

Somasundaram Pillai, J.M. *A History of Tamil Literature*, with texts and translations, Annamalainagar, 1968.

Soutar, George. *Nature in Greek Poetry*, London, 1939.

Stein, Burton (Ed.) *Essays on South India*, Honolulu, 1975.

Stobart, J.C. *The Glory that was Greece*, London, 1933.

Subbu Reddiar, N. *Kavitaiyaṉupavam* (T), Madras, 1961.

Subramaniya Acariyar, V.S. *Cilappatikāra Ārāycci* (T), Madras, 1947.

Subramaniam, V.I. The Dating of Sangam Literature, *Proceedings of the Third International Conference Seminar of Tamil Studies*, Paris, 1970, Pondicherry, 1973, pp. 75-80.

Subramanian, N. The Avifauna of the Tamil Country, *Tamil Culture*, Vol. XII, No. 4, Madras, 1966, pp. 259-68 and supplement pp. 1-16.

Sundaramoorthy, G. *Early Literary Theories in Tamil*, (in comparison with Sanskrit theories), Madurai, 1974.

Surya Kanta Sastri. *Kālidāsa's Vision of Kumārasaṃbhava*, Delhi, 1963.

Suryakanta (Ed.) *The Kumārasaṃbhava of Kālidāsa*, New Delhi, 1962.

*Swaminathaiyar, V. (Ed.) *Aiṅkuṟunūṟu*, Madras, 5th Edn., 1957.

*———. *Cilappatikāram*, Madras, 1960.

*———. *Kuṟuntokai*, Madras, 1962.

*———. *Maṇimēkalai*, Madras, 5th Edn., 1956.

*———. *Paripāṭal*, Madras, 1956.

*———. *Pattuppāṭṭu*, Madras, 5th Edn., 1956.

*———. *Puṟanāṉūṟu*, Madras, 5th Edn., 1956.

Tambimuttu, T. *India Love Poems*, New York, 1954.

Tamil Lexicon, Madras, 1924-34.

Taranibaskar, Mrs. Cilampil Irucuṭar (T), *Proceedings of the First International Conference Seminar of Tamil Studies 1968*, Madras, 1971, Vol. III, pp. 86-94.

Thaninayagam, X.S. Caṅka Ilakkiyattiṉ Ciṟappu (T), *Ganeshaiyer Souvenir*, Īḻakēcarip Ponniah Niṉaivu Veḷiyīṭṭu Maṉṟam,

Vyas, S.N. *India in the Rāmāyaṇa Age*, Delhi, 1967.

Warder, A.K. *Indian Kāvya Literature*, Vol. 1, Delhi, 1972.

Weber, Robert Bruce. *Love in the Secular Poems of Christian Hofmann von Hofmannswaldau*, Ph.D. thesis, New York University, 1970, Published on demand by University Microfilms Inc., Ann Arbor, Michigan, U.S.A.

Wells, Henry, W. (Ed.). *Six Sanskrit Plays* London (Printed in India), 1964.

Wilson, H.H. (Tr.) *Kumarasambhavam or The Birth of War God*, Varanasi, 1966.

Winternitz, M. *History of Indian Literature*, 3 Vols., New Delhi, I & II, 1972, Vol. III, 1st Edn. 1963.

*Woolner, A.C. & Sarup, Lakshman (Tr.). *Thirteen Trivandrum Plays Attributed to Bhasa*, Vol. I & II, O.U.P. London, 1930, 1931.

Zvelebil, Kamil Veith. Tamil Literature, *A History of Indian Literature*, edited by Jan Gonda, Vol. X, 1. Otto Harrassowitz, Wiesbaden, 1974.

———. *The Smile of Murugan on Tamil Literature of South India*, Leiden, 1973.

Index